SACRED SPACE

SACRED SPACE

The Quest for Transcendence in Science Fiction
Film and Television

Douglas E. Cowan

BAYLOR UNIVERSITY PRESS

© 2010 by Baylor University Press
Waco, Texas 76798

Cover Design by Nicole Weaver, Zeal Design

Library of Congress Cataloging-in-Publication Data

Cowan, Douglas E.
  Sacred space : the quest for transcendence in science fiction film and television / by Douglas E. Cowan.
      p. cm.
  Includes bibliographical references and index.
  ISBN 978-1-60258-238-5 (alk. paper)
  1. Science fiction films--History and criticism. 2. Science fiction television programs--History and criticism. 3. Religion in motion pictures. I. Title.
  PN1995.9.S26C68 2010
  791.43'615--dc22

                              2009039507

Printed in the United States of America on acid-free paper.

For Joie,
with whom the Prophets walk . . .

CONTENTS

PREFACE

For as long as I can remember, I have had a love affair with science fiction. At first, Verne and Wells; later, Heinlein, Clarke, Asimov, Pohl, Bradbury, Sprague de Camp, Dick, Silverberg, and Leiber—these and more were the literary companions of my childhood. Despite its imposing heft and impossibly small print, I devoured Frank Herbert's *Dune* (1965) when I first came across it in my elementary school library. Then, with the naïveté of a sixth grader, I wrote to Herbert to express my admiration for the book. To my surprise, the great man answered and I still have his brief letter, thanking me for my interest in his work and encouraging me in my own. It hangs framed on my office wall. Although I was terrified by the salt-sucking monster in the *Star Trek* pilot, "The Man Trap," I was hooked on starships, phasers, transporters, aliens, and everything that went along with them. More than four decades later, I still am.

As a sociologist of religion and popular culture, I am fascinated by the ways in which different cultural products both inform and are informed by our deepest questions about life, the universe, and everything—what many people call "religion," others "the sacred," and still others "the quest for transcendence." There are often significant differences, however, between the various ways in which these concerns are portrayed in science fiction and the concept of religion in the genre itself. Clearly, some have used science fiction to promote a particular religious or antireligious agenda, or to illustrate a specific religious point of view. C. S. Lewis' famous space trilogy—*Out of the Silent*

Planet (1938), *Perelandra* (1943), and *That Hideous Strength* (1945)—uses science fiction to explore an explicitly Christian worldview. It is not inconceivable that L. Ron Hubbard either mined his science fiction for at least some of the material that became Dianetics and Scientology, or reflected them in his pulp sci-fi writings. That there would be no relationship between the two is unlikely. On the other hand, science fiction has often been used to explore what some writers consider the dangers inherent in devout (read: fanatical) religious belief and practice. Walter M. Miller's classic novel, *A Canticle for Leibowitz* (1959), for example, foreshadows the kind of postapocalyptic religion that shades into the atomic bomb–worship we find in Ted Post's 1970 film, *Beneath the Planet of the Apes*. Those who worship the bomb die by the bomb. Published more than a generation apart, and by writers who could not be more dissimilar, Robert Heinlein's short story, "If this goes on . . . " ([1940] 1953), and Margaret Atwood's novel, *The Handmaid's Tale* (1985), both envision a dystopic future in which fundamentalist religion has given rise to corrupt theocracies.

Often it appears as though religious sensibilities are presented as little more than straw characters in science fiction—useful for demonstrating the futility or puerility of religious belief, but little more. Belief in this god or that is worthwhile only until, for example, the stalwart crew of the *Enterprise*—the Prime Directive notwithstanding—arrive with the gift of enlightened rationalism. For many critics, the issues are no more complex than this. Religion in science fiction is there to be recognized, acknowledged as retrogressive, and dismissed as the cultural vestige of a less sophisticated age.

Sacred Space suggests otherwise. However it is understood, the quest for transcendence plays a significant role in science fiction cinema and television, and will continue to do so. Because they operate under such different production constraints than books—a forty-minute episode or a hundred-minute movie, for example, rather than a thousand-page novel—television shows and movies frequently raise more questions than they answer. Rather than resolve the issues with which those who produce and consume them are concerned, they reflect and refract them. In doing so, film and television participate in the ongoing cultural conversations by which those issues are configured, contextualized, and contested. Critics who dismiss or deride the religious elements in science fiction often do so on the basis of a very narrow definition of "religion," a superficial understanding that limits their critique in terms of both the breadth of religious experience and the depth of religious commitment. The reality is that the human quest for transcendence takes an astonishing variety of forms and shows little sign of diminishing in importance anytime soon. Failing to appreciate these rather fundamental realities inevitably limits our ability to understand what happens not only onscreen, but offscreen as well.

As always, there are more people to thank than can reasonably be accommodated in a brief preface, but let me mention three. First, my thanks to Casey Blaine, my first editor at Baylor University Press. Her confidence in both this book and its predecessor, *Sacred Terror*, was a constant source of encouragement. Second, I want to thank John Morehead, my friend and co-conspirator in all things horror and sci-fi, for his ongoing support. If anything, he has been more excited about these projects than I have, and if you read only one blog regularly, read his: http://www.theofantastique.com. Finally, there is my wife, Joie, who patiently read every draft—which alone should merit her a place in the stars.

Part I

SCIENCE FICTION
AND THE QUEST FOR TRANSCENDENCE

1

THE BRIGHTNESS AGAINST
THE BLACK

OUTTAKE: *CONTACT*

```
                    ELLIE
    So beautiful . . . So beautiful . . . So
    beautiful . . .
```

As establishing shots go, it is a reverse zoom to end all reverse zooms. From a stark, black screen and a brief title credit, Robert Zemeckis' *Contact* snaps open with a satellite view looking down at the southeastern United States, a cacophony of advertising, rock music, and indiscriminate noise blaring from a dozen different radio stations. Almost immediately, though, the camera begins to move away, the North American continent receding and the sun appearing over Earth's rapidly diminishing horizon. The radio traffic shifts as well, changing quickly from AM to shortwave to comm chatter from NASA's flight control center in Houston. The farther we get from our "pale blue dot" (Sagan, 1994), the further back in time are the radio signals we encounter. For the next two minutes and fifty-five seconds, the camera retreats, assuming something of a God's-eye view, widening our field of vision, challenging our sense of perspective, and shattering our illusions of centrality in the universe.

Passing through the asteroid belt that clutters the seemingly vast distance between Mars and Jupiter, the radio signals break up as the primordial detritus of our solar system's creation—thousands of objects ranging in size from a grain of dust to a minor planet—interrupt the line of sight between Earth and our swiftly receding point of view. Through the intermittent contact, though, we hear the unmistakable voice of Richard Nixon insisting to anyone who will listen, "I'm not a crook." We pass Jupiter and a radio announcer tells a stunned America that Robert Kennedy has been shot. As the gas giant contracts against the brightness and the black, Martin Luther King Jr. exults, "Thank God, we are free at last!" and a moment of horror later we learn that a sniper has fired at John F. Kennedy Jr. We leave the solar system to the words of another president, Franklin Delano Roosevelt, decrying the Japanese attack on Pearl Harbor as "a day that will live in infamy." From this point, indistinct and gradually diminishing radio noise is broken only occasionally by an understandable word.

But the journey is not over.

As we pass infant stars emerging newborn from the immense gas columns of the Eagle Nebula—"magnificent" is far too pale a word for these—silence reigns. Nearly seven thousand light years from Earth and so large it would take light itself almost ten years to travel them from top to bottom, even the towering pillars of this stellar nursery shrink until they too are but an indistinguishable speck in a tiny section on the outer edge of one unremarkable galactic arm. God's camera speeds up, pulling away faster now. The Milky Way disappears into a darkness alive with light as our field of vision widens to include billions of other galaxies swirling and eddying in the vast ocean of the universe. As these myriad points of light collect and collapse into a kind of psychedelic starstorm, a young girl's voice says tentatively, "CQ, this is W9GFO. CQ, this is W9GFO here, come back."

Much later in the film, the young girl has grown into a woman, a scientist who no longer wonders if there is a radio transmitter powerful enough to reach her long-deceased parents, but whose quest for transcendence is now driven by SETI, the search for extraterrestrial intelligence. Sitting in the New Mexico desert beneath orderly rows of radio telescope dishes, listening for an artificial rhythm in the constant wash of interstellar static, astronomer Dr. Ellie Arroway (Jodie Foster) is the first to realize that contact has finally been made. From the immensity of space, a radio signal has found the infinitesimal speck on which we live. Offering greetings—after a fashion—its complex, tightly compressed transmission yields instructions for building The Machine, a gigantic vessel with only one purpose: first contact with an extraterrestrial lifeform.

The monumental expense of construction has been shouldered by a multinational consortium whose members have also assumed responsibility for selecting Earth's first representative to the stars. Sitting at one of the final interviews, in a room designed explicitly to highlight the importance of the assembly but which also calls to mind the trials of others who dared to think outside the bounds of conventional wisdom, Ellie faces a question that has haunted visionaries from Copernicus to Galileo to Giordano Bruno.

PALMER JOSS

Do you believe in God, Dr. Arroway?

ELLIE

As a scientist, I, uh, rely on empirical
evidence, and in this matter I don't believe
there's data either way.

CHAIRWOMAN PATEL

So your answer would be that you don't
believe in God?

ELLIE

I just--I--I don't understand the relevance
of the question.

BRITISH COMMITTEE MEMBER

Dr. Arroway, 99 percent of the world's
population believes in a supreme being in one
form or another. I believe that makes the
question more than relevant.

These scenes present us with two vastly different visions of transcendence—one limited by a terracentric conception of deity, the other open to the wonder of distance—yet each demarcated by the question, "Do you believe in God, Dr. Arroway?" Which "God" is this, though? In whose deity is she expected to believe, especially when a significant portion of those who believe "in a supreme being in one form or another" do so in ways often mutually exclusive of all others? Or is this an example of astronomer Carl Sagan's basic critique of human religious understanding?

Toward the end of his first Gifford Lecture in 1985, Sagan—who both wrote the novel on which *Contact* is based (1985) and prior to his death in 1996 was intimately involved in the film's production—remarked that "a general problem with much of Western theology in my view is that the God portrayed is too small. It is a god of a tiny world and not a god of a galaxy, much less of a universe" (2006, 30). Note that Sagan does not say that Western religion is too small—though he may well have thought that too, since our practice is inevitably bound by our beliefs. Theology, though, describes our thinking about God, our notions of deity or divinity, our conceptions of the relationship between humanity and what some have called the sacred (Durkheim, [1912] 1995; Eliade, 1958; Otto, [1923] 1950), others the "unseen order" (James, [1902] 1999, 61)—and how that relationship is negotiated and managed. It expresses how we understand the nature and limits of transcendence, and, by implication, how we envision the forms our various quests for transcendence may take. In view of the universe shown to us at the beginning of *Contact*, it is our theological imagination, our pretension to understanding, that Sagan considers too limited, not the possibility of a relationship with something far greater, far grander than ourselves. For him, we simply think too small; our concerns with transcendence are too narrow, too qualified, too provincial—a topic to which we will return throughout this book.

When Ellie finally does make the initial journey in The Machine, we are allowed a glimpse of the transcendence she experiences. Falling through what Sagan's novel calls an artificially created "naked singularity" (1985, 329), a massive distortion in the curvature of space-time that occurs without the presence of a black hole (Hawking, 1988, 46; Wolf, 1988, 142–43), the dodecahedral walls of The Machine's occupant pod become transparent, revealing to her the wonders of a galaxy that have, until now, been limited to background static, pulsars and quasars, the complex mathematics she has used to interpret them—and hope.

"Some celestial event," the astonished scientist almost weeps, her eyes wide and brimming with tears. "No words to describe it . . . poetry. They should have sent a poet." As the universe unfolds before her, she becomes giddy with wonder at what she is witnessing. "So beautiful . . . so beautiful," she repeats, over and over.

Is this an experience of transcendence, of moving beyond the limits of perception, of understanding, of the empirical data that have grounded her search for so long? Although William James' model of the "mystical state" has been criticized in the century and more since he presented it in his 1902 Gifford Lectures, Ellie's journey in The Machine pod epitomizes the hallmarks he maintained identify such a state. An experience many religious traditions equate with the notion of transcendence, for James the mystical state is characterized by ineffability, noesis, transiency, and passivity ([1902] 1999, 413–68; cf. Sison, 2005). Ellie herself identifies the first marker: the inability to communicate the experience to others. Here, the scientist, the rationalist charged with redescribing the intricacies of experiment, data, and interpretation, has no words for what confronts her. She can only stare in awe and fascination. How could she possibly tell anyone who has not seen what she is seeing? How could they possibly hope to understand? Second, mystical states are noetic, marked by "insight into depths of truth unplumbed by the discursive intellect. They are illuminations, revelations, full of significance and importance, all inarticulate though they remain" (James, [1902] 1999, 414–15). While a lesser actor might easily have let such a moment slip into the nether space between sentimentality and slapstick, Foster's understated tour de force in this brief sequence makes it one of the most powerful in the film. We are left with no doubt that, though she may not understand entirely what is happening, her experience embodies revelation.

According to James, transiency is the third characteristic of the mystical state; that is, it "cannot be sustained for long" ([1902] 1999, 415). Although he places the outer limits at "half an hour, or at most an hour or two" (James, [1902] 1999, 415), Ellie's headset records eighteen hours of what turns out in the end to be static, but which Zemeckis clearly means to indicate the experiential length of her extraordinary journey. The paradox, however, is that all the terrestrial observers, both human and mechanical, the thousands of people and dozens of cameras monitoring The Machine, saw the occupant pod fall from its gantry straight through into a catch-net a few hundred feet below. "Nothing happened," insists the skeptical national security advisor, Michael Kitz (James Woods). In his novel, Sagan points out that "near a singularity, causality would be violated, effects could precede causes, time could flow backward" (1985, 329). In this state, perception, reality, and the relationship between them lose whatever meaning they may once have had—especially in terms of theological metanarratives that are so often reduced to platitudes like "God loves you and has a plan for your life." Every notion of what we think we understand simply melts away.

Finally, there is passivity. While we can prepare ourselves for a mystical state, once it begins we are no longer in command. We can build The Machine, but once we turn it on it takes us where and how it will, and those in control of the journey determine when it will end. We can sit in meditation, calm our mind, focus on our mantra or our breath, but the mystical experience that marks the "overcoming of the usual barriers between the individual and the Absolute" (James, [1902] 1999, 457) is not ultimately under our sway; we cannot step in and out of it at will. "Mystical states," concludes James, and which I interpret as one species of transcendent experience, "are never merely interruptive. Some memory of their content always remains and a profound sense of their importance" ([1902] 1999, 416).

Called before a "Special Executive Inquiry" to explain what many are charging either as fraud on her part or as a hugely expensive joke perpetrated by the film's *éminence grise*, industrialist S. R. Hadden (John Hurt), Ellie maintains the reality, the validity, the profound sense of importance imparted by her experience in a scene that mirrors—and reverses—her earlier testimony to The Machine Consortium.

COMMITTEE MEMBER

Dr. Arroway, you come to us with no evidence, no record, no artifacts, only a story that to put it mildly strains credibility. Over half a trillion dollars was spent, dozens of lives were lost. Are you really going to sit there and tell us we should just take this all on <u>faith</u>?

ELLIE

Is it possible that it didn't happen? Yes. As a scientist, I must concede that, I must volunteer that.

KITZ

Wait a minute, let me get this straight. You admit that you have absolutely no physical evidence to back up your story?

ELLIE

Yes.

KITZ

You admit that you may very well have hallucinated this whole thing?

ELLIE

Yes.

KITZ (louder)

You admit that if you were in our position you would respond with exactly the same degree of incredulity and skepticism?

ELLIE

Yes.

KITZ (shouting)

Then why don't you just withdraw your testimony and concede that this journey to the center of the galaxy in fact <u>never</u> <u>took</u> <u>place</u>!

ELLIE

Because I can't.

Days prior to its release, the *New York Times'* Hollywood reporter Bernard Weinraub wondered whether Zemeckis was demanding too much of his audience, asking them to think seriously about questions that "are generally not the sort raised by Hollywood movies these days" (1997, H9). On the one hand, Weinraub is probably correct. Relatively few films deal with these kind of questions in so open and forthright a manner. On the other hand, while it may not be raised as explicitly as in *Contact*, the question of human exceptionalism is implicit in every extraterrestrial contact film ever made. From *2001: A Space Odyssey* (the sublime) to *Plan 9 from Outer Space* (the ridiculous), from *Star Wars* (which has no "Earth" in it) to *The War of the Worlds* (in which Earth is the prize coveted by "intellects vast and cool and unsympathetic"), whether we are alone in the universe either drives the plot overtly or logically underpins the narrative in every case. Indeed, *Contact* was competing in theaters with Barry Sonnenfeld's *Men in Black*, a science fiction action-comedy about a secret government agency "protecting the earth from the scum of the universe" and starring the eminently bankable Will Smith and Tommy Lee Jones. Depending on our expectations, however, depending how neatly and clearly divided are the boxes into which we have placed issues of religion and science, faith and rationality, the questions raised will seem either profound or petty nonsense.

Not surprisingly, *Contact* opened to mixed reviews. *Variety's* Todd McCarthy dubbed it "a serious and sober piece of speculative fiction" (1997, 43), while the *Hollywood Reporter's* Duane Byrge thought it "a disappointingly earthbound production" (1997). Calling the film "technologically dazzling but intellectually strained and emotionally chilly," *New York Times* critic Stephen Holden somewhat simplistically equated Ellie's Machine journey with a trip to heaven (1997, C3). That is, when Ellie finally meets those who sent the radio signal, she does so in a visionary experience compounded of her own memories—principally her deceased father and a childhood drawing of a Pensacola beach, both clearly designed to ease the inevitable shock of first contact. Though it may not have been his choice, Holden's review was headlined, "Which Route Upward, On a Wing or a Prayer?"—a characterization that arguably misunderstands the implications of the film in the most fundamental way possible and refuses to engage seriously the questions Sagan and Zemeckis pose to their audience. Writing for the *Chicago Sun-Times*, however, Roger Ebert concluded that "movies like *Contact* help explain why movies like *Independence Day* leave me feeling empty and unsatisfied. When I look up at the sky through a telescope, when I follow the landing of the research vehicle on Mars, when I read about cosmology, I brush against transcendence" (1997, 29).

APPROACHING THE EVENT HORIZON
SCIENCE FICTION AND THE QUEST FOR TRANSCENDENCE

Sacred Space explores some of the ways that science fiction cinema and television have both challenged and reinforced the limits of belief, redefining the quest for transcendence, which is, put simply, the search for something beyond ourselves, the belief that outside the boundaries of everyday living something greater exists. For some, the quest for transcendence is our trust in a purpose larger than the faint echo registered by a single life, and the possibility of transcendence a conviction that invests our lives with meaning and value. For others, it is something else: the *beyond* that hovers on the other side of the horizon, the edge of the map marked *hic sunt draconis* (here be dragons), the "second star to the right" that guides our imaginations into the unknown. As both academic and popular commentators have noted, science fiction is *the* genre of possibility, a principal cultural canvas on which writers, artists, and filmmakers have sketched their visions of transcendent potential.

In this brief introduction I cannot hope to distill the voluminous literature debating various understandings of the transcendent, but some prefatory comments will help dress the set for the discussions that follow. While few theologians have had trouble pronouncing on the nature of transcendence—indeed, as many would argue, this is their primary function—as an analytic category transcendence has proved more difficult for those who are less confessionally inclined. As sociologist William Garrett points out, three modes of engagement have marked social science attempts to deal responsibly with the transcendent: scientific reductionism, symbolic functionalism, and phenomenological numinalism (1974).

Scientific reductionists simply reject the transcendent as a useful investigative category, some on the grounds that they do not believe it can be measured empirically, others because they have decided a priori that it does not exist. Both groups, however, ignore the reality of the transcendent in terms of its social effect, its quite measurable ability to influence human thought and behavior. Whether it exists or not, whether it is objectively verifiable or not, both the concept of and the quest for transcendence exist as indisputable social facts, and, as Émile Durkheim, one of the more systematic critics of scientific reductionism, argued, "the first and most basic rule is *to consider social facts as things*" ([1895] 1982, 60; emphasis in original). Symbolic functionalists, including Durkheim, recognize that human notions of the transcendent are powerful motivators at both the individual and social levels. They bind constituencies together in times of stress and upheaval; rituals intended to mark the transcendence of different life boundaries structure and reinforce cultural hierarchies; the mythistories in which the quest for transcendence is often embedded establish the group in larger contexts of meaning and significance. Without positing the reality of the transcendent, or evaluating the validity of one vision of transcendence over another, these critics ask what effect such visions have, what function they serve in particular societies, how they change over time, and, most importantly, why. Addressing theistic rather than scientific reductionists, for example, sociologist Robert Bellah illustrates the symbolic functionalist position clearly. "Arguments based on metaphysical proofs or revelation are not very compelling today," he writes at the height of North American scholarship's love affair with the theory of secularization. "It is not so much the substance of what is claimed to be transcendent as it is the *function of the claim itself* that is of interest now" (Bellah, 1969, 85; emphasis in original).

Still, though, many functionalists take the reality of the transcendent no more seriously than their scientistic colleagues. It is a mask that other forces wear, a sign pointing to something else, "camouflage for more basic psychic or social realities" (Garrett, 1974, 170–71). Garrett's third category, phenomenological numinalism, approaches the problem of transcendence certain that "the non-empirical component of religion contains analytical characteristics which are neither contingent on nor reducible to other empirical causes" (1974, 173–74). They may not be measurable in and of themselves, they may be known only in their effects, but their reality should not be dismissed for lack of direct empirical evidence. Among human beings and the societies they create, things are not necessarily cut and dried. If nothing else, ambiguity reigns, and the "absence of evidence is not evidence of absence" (Sagan, 1996, 213)—an argument used as often in astronomy and physics as in theology and metaphysics. All of these approaches, however, both in Garrett's sources and in his own analysis, are based on a rough equivalence between the transcendent and the supernatural, another problematic concept for social science. If the latter is not accepted or cannot be demonstrated, the former loses any analytic or explanatory power it may have. Fortunately, these are not the only terms in which we can conceptualize the issue.

Put broadly, three different domains shape our understanding of transcendence: (a) the problem of human limitations, both physical and technological; (b) the reality of sociocultural hierarchies and the rites of passage that facilitate personal development and group cohesion; and (c) theological conceptions of the relationship between humanity and the unseen order, however those are ritualized, systematized, or mediated perceptually.

First, there is the quest for transcendence of human limitations. To run faster or jump higher, whether through intense training and dedication or with the help of steroids and synthetic growth hormones, are among the most obvious examples. The four-minute mile, world-record free diving, reaching the summit of Everest solo and without bottled oxygen—these and other so-called barriers to physical and mental strength and endurance populate lists epitomized by the *Guinness Book of World Records*; they constitute the legends of human performance and set new goals for human potential. The history of aeronautics is a record of human technological advancement and the quest for transcendence in the face of popular derision and putative technological limits. Many of those who thrilled to reports of the Wright brothers' flight at Kitty Hawk in 1903 watched in wonder with their own grandchildren as Neil Armstrong set foot on the moon in 1969. Less than one lifespan from powered flight to Tranquility Base. While Jules Verne's fictional voyage "From the Earth to the Moon" was the product of a nine-hundred-foot cannon and two hundred tons of gun-cotton ([1865] 1967), by 1968 Stanley Kubrick's cinematic vision had transformed spaceflight into a delicate ballet of momentum, rotation, and deceleration—all set to a Strauss waltz. Human biotechnological development was also harnessed by popular entertainment media. From 1974 to 1978, for example, millions of viewers tuned in weekly to ABC and heard Richard Anderson's famous opening narration for *The Six Million Dollar Man*: "Gentlemen, we can rebuild him. We have the technology." In 2004 the six million dollar man, Steve Austin (Lee Majors), along with his spin-off counterpart, *The Bionic Woman* (Jamie Sommers, played by Lindsay Wagner), were named to *TV Guide*'s "25 Greatest Sci-fi Legends." Whenever a boundary has presented itself—there is a depth below which our submarines cannot descend, a height our aircraft cannot reach, a speed our powered machines cannot exceed and a distance they cannot cross—human ingenuity, tenacity, avarice, courage, foolhardiness, and dumb luck have combined in various measures to transcend what some regard as fixed limits, others merely as challenges.

Social boundaries mark the second domain of transcendence. Whether they are considered immutable or permeable, whether they have been established by divine fiat or determined by relative consensus, whether they are based on gender, race, class, education, religion, or any one of a number of biosocial characteristics we use to construct the boundaries between "us" and "them," limits frame the order of group life and establish the parameters of meaning and identity within that order. In every society some boundaries may be crossed while others may not. Some require transcendence, others invite it, while still others forbid it. Some boundaries permit a return to one's former state; others mark an entirely new way of being. Some indicate passages that are predominantly social—graduation as the completion of one's formal education or apprenticeship; tests that determine fitness for responsibilities such as childcare or driving; promotion through the ranks of the military or within one's profession. Others are intended to connect participants within and across different orders of meaning, the seen and the unseen. Age, for example, and the physical changes that accompany the stages of development constitute one of the most common sets of interlinked boundaries guiding the generational advance of human societies. In the life of a Jewish boy or girl, the bar mitzvah or bat mitzvah is such a moment of transcendence. Participants in these ceremonies become responsible to the law of God as adults, and in many congregations, orthodox, conservative, and reform, they now count in the *minyan*, the number of observant Jews required to establish a quorum for communal prayer and worship. Once the boundary is passed, these young men and women cannot return to their previous state, but have begun the process of integration into a new state, a new realm of boundaries and potential transcendences. Not dissimilarly, Roman Catholic children around the world prepare diligently to make their First Communion, learning the history and symbology of the church, entering into their first official act of confession (now known as a sacrament of reconciliation), and taking the eucharistic elements as full members of a religious community that counts nearly one in every six people on the planet. Both of these not only signal the attainment of a certain physical age, but are meant to signify a qualitative difference in a child's relationship with God. Unlike a graduation or a driver's test, these boundaries form something of a Rubicon in the life of the individual and the community.

Rituals and rites of passage structure both the transcendence and the reinforcement of social boundaries, connecting the participants to all who have preceded them and presaging all who will proceed in generations to come (cf. Turner, 1969; van Gennep, [1908] 1960). They make immanent the framework of transcendence within which meaning is located. Both science fiction cinema and television have explored these areas extensively. During "Amok Time," for example, one of the most famous episodes in the original *Star Trek* series, Mr. Spock (Leonard Nimoy) is overtaken by *pon farr*, a traumatic regress from the dictates of logic into the unpredictability of emotion, a change that determines when a Vulcan is ready to mate. In the postapocalyptic society portrayed in *Logan's Run*, the ecological limits of a population condemned to live in domed cities demands that those who reach the age of thirty participate in the rite of "Carousel"—ritual suicide in the service of population control. In *The Empire Strikes Back*, while training under the impish Jedi master, Yoda, Luke Skywalker (Mark Hamill) must face rites of passage drawn almost directly from the archetypal hero's quest (Campbell, 1968; Gordon, 1995); he must transcend the limits of who he thinks he is in order to realize the possibilities of who he will become.

In the *Stargate* universe, which I explore more deeply in chapter 6, the principal threat is the Goa'uld, a parasitic race that takes other species as hosts, dominating them and convincing less advanced cultures to worship them as gods. To enforce their rule and reinforce the perception of their divinity, they use the Jaffa, a warrior people, as both a standing army and as temporary hosts for larval Goa'uld. Teal'c (Christopher Judge) is a Jaffa who renounces the Goa'uld as gods and vows to set his people free from their tyranny. Exploring the ramifications of this conflict, the episode "Bloodlines" illustrates the often complex nature of boundaries and transcendence, the ambivalent relationship between the seen and the unseen orders. Teal'c returns to his homeworld to prevent his son, Rya'c (Neil Denis), from receiving his first infant Goa'uld. Because Teal'c is considered a traitor, a *shol'vah*, his wife has had to beg the priests to perform the implantation ritual. Teal'c interrupts the ceremony, kills one of the priests, and takes Rya'c. On the one hand, he has interfered in the most important moment of transcendence in a young Jaffa's life, the moment when he or she begins to carry the infant form of their god. He has attacked at the most fundamental level the unseen order in which Rya'c and his mother still very much believe. On the other hand, he has seen the Goa'uld for what they are—parasites who feed on the fear of those they take over—and he would rather die himself than see his son so enslaved. In this case, the loss of one transcendence points the way to another, but neither comes without cost or risk.

For hundreds of millions of people, arguably most of those who cluster under the "sacred canopies" of the current world monotheisms, "transcendence" is a supernatural category. Like the relationship between the Jaffa and the Goa'uld, it is inextricably linked to belief in a transcendent God, a deity utterly unlike humanity—*totaliter aliter*, to use Karl Barth's phrase—something wholly other on which we wholly depend. It has nothing to do with our potential for progress and everything to do with the fixed limits of our ontology and the limitless nature of divine largesse. In this sense, transcendence is one half of a binary opposition. There is immanence (that which exists as part of us and which constitutes us) and there is transcendence (that which exists apart from us and in which we may not take part except in the most unusual, and usually fleeting, circumstances). God is transcendent; we are immanent. God is the Creator; we are the creation. God is radically absolute; we are radically contingent. Of course, in classical Christian theology, God's transcendence becomes immanent in the Christ, the one who, according to many streams of Christian belief, allows us a part in divinity, a place in God's kingdom. Not unlike a Hindu avatar, for Christian believers Christ has excerpted infinity and eternity, rendering them finite and temporal. None of this, however, changes the fundamental difference between humanity and divinity.

For hundreds of millions of Buddhists, Hindus, Sikhs, and Jains, however, transcendence does not mark such an immutable boundary, but suggests instead a far more permeable membrane. Indeed, because concepts of reincarnation anchor the cosmologies of these traditions in one way or another, the notion of "boundary" loses some of its power. Millions more, many of whom are either directly affiliated or loosely associated with what is popularly known as the "New Age" (cf. Ferguson, 1980; Hanegraaff, 1996; Heelas, 1996), similarly challenge the monotheistic dichotomy, insisting that the ontological dualism imposed by the concept of *totaliter aliter* is primitive and destructive, regressively reinforcing limitations that threaten to keep humanity forever locked in an evolutionary adolescence.

Transpersonal theorists such as Stanislav Grof, for example, who for decades has used psychedelics and a technique he calls "holotropic breathwork" to explore alternate forms of reality, believe that consciousness exists "transpersonally," independent of its individual embodiment (cf. Grof, 1985, 1988; Grof and Bennett, 1993). Although we have bodies, although we manifest our consciousness corporeally, this is not the limit of consciousness—only the perception of a limit imposed by scientific reductionism. Rather, transcendence is the potential that "transpersonal consciousness" can breach the boundaries of time and space as these have been established by material existence and reinforced through social and cultural frameworks that will not allow for the possibility of a world (or worlds) beyond those boundaries. Calling on Jung's seminal work on the "collective unconscious," Grof and his colleagues argue that we participate in a much wider and deeper universe, and that we have the ability to participate with far greater intentionality and far keener awareness of our place in that universe, than most of us imagine. For Grof, evidence for the transpersonal, or the transcendent experience of the transpersonal, is found among other places in embryonic and fetal memories (Grof and Bennett, 1993, 114–18). For psychiatrist and researcher Ian Stevenson, on the other hand, though he is far more cautious in presenting his conclusions than Grof, phenomena such as xenoglossy (speaking in language one does not know and could not have learned), near-death experience, and reincarnation at least suggest that our understanding of the limits of human consciousness, both in terms of ability and durability, are equally limited (cf. Cook, Greyson, and Stevenson, 1998; Stevenson, 1966, 1974, 1975, 1984). Both, however, highlight the possibility that, as geneticist J. B. S. Haldane suspected (in a remark that is often attributed to astrophysicist Sir Arthur Eddington), "the Universe is not only queerer than we suppose, but queerer than we *can* suppose" (1928, 298).

If transpersonalism is predicated on the existence of non-ordinary states of consciousness to which we have access and which we can use to transcend the limitations of the physical brain, transhumanism posits that we can do the same for the physical body. We can transcend the limitations of the meat-bot. Of course, we have been doing this for some time, though at relatively primitive levels by transhumanist standards: iron lungs, pacemakers and artificial hearts, portable oxygen systems, dialysis, and now cosmetic surgery. In all these cases, when the organic components deteriorate or fail, technology allows for life to continue. Even the ubiquity of corrective eyewear focuses attention on our willingness to address our disabilities technologically. In broad terms, for there are a number of varieties, transhumanism proposes to take this process out of the reactive realm of medical intervention and into the proactive domain of life enhancement and progressive immortality through cybernetics and other forms of organo-technological hybridity, nanotechnology, and "uploading"—releasing dependence on the physical body entirely and transferring the entirety of one's consciousness into a computer. In these instances, Haldane's observations in the early twentieth century appear amazingly prescient: for many people, science fiction is becoming science possible (cf. Bainbridge, 2005; Bostrom, 2005; Brooke, 2005; Young, 2006).

Religious consciousness and the social relationships with the unseen order to which it adverts often instantiate a chain of connected and coordinated boundary events, a structured series of negotiations around the place and relative permeability of restrictions and limitations. It could be argued, albeit from a limited theistic perspective such as that criticized by Carl Sagan, that science (or the scientific imagination that expresses itself in science fiction) destabilizes belief in the possibility of transcendence, that it short-circuits whatever quest for transcendence religious consciousness implies. I suppose that would be the case if we limited ourselves to the rather restrictive dichotomy that God is transcendent and we are immanent—and ne'er the twain shall meet. But, fundamentalist Christians notwithstanding (although even they will have their say on the issue in chapter 3), the emergence, development, and polymorphic evolution of human religious belief and behavior, the myriad ways in which human societies have conceptualized the unseen order and negotiated their relationship with it, are exercises in the transcendence and conservation of boundaries, processes that have often been dogmatically inscribed and ritually embodied.

Put differently, what happens to our sense of transcendence, our belief that there is something beyond ourselves, when that belief no longer offers adequate explanation for the problems of everyday life? What happens to the gods when we realize that thunderstorms are the result of unstable atmospheric conditions seeking a return to equilibrium—not the anger of the gods for whatever petty transgression we have attached to the storm? In climatology and meteorology, in atmospheric science and geophysics, the veil of the unseen order is stripped away. We see the unseen, or at least we see with vastly different eyes. What happens when the revelation of transcendence is revealed as little more than the redaction of immanents? God did not write the Bible, human beings did—and the vastly conflicting visions of transcendence reflected in those redactions demonstrate, if nothing else, the shifting boundaries along which we line up our competing understandings of the unseen order. It is not that transcendence disappears so much as it relocates. The boundaries that constitute the current limits of the quest are reset. Transcendence, then, is not a function of immanence, but of boundaries, and in every boundary lies the of hope of passing beyond.

THE ENGINES OF MEANING
STORYTELLING, MYTHMAKING, AND THE SOCIAL CONSTRUCTION
OF HOPE

We have gone through many stages of development in our brief history as a species, and we have called ourselves many things. Among others, we are *Homo erectus*, the ones who walk upright—though the famous "Dawn of Man" sequence in *2001: A Space Odyssey* suggests that this ability emerged when our Australopithecine ancestors learned that using a club on two feet is infinitely more effective than on four. Our bipedal stance is a product of our will to wage war. We are *Homo sapiens*, the ones who think—though for thousands of years many of us have arrogantly (and perhaps naïvely) believed that we are the only ones who do so. We are *Homo faber*, the ones who use tools, the ones who can translate the abstraction of an idea into a concrete reality—though the things we choose to imagine and create do raise questions about how far from the "dawn of man" we have truly progressed.

We are also, however, *Homo narrans*, the storytellers, the ones who locate themselves in time and space through narrative—the myths, legends, and sacred stories, the fables, fairy tales, and folk wisdom that fuel the engines of meaning in human society. Often entrusted to social *cognoscenti*, the elders of the tribe or those specially trained to pass on the tribe's history, or to religious *virtuosi*, priests and priestesses chosen by the gods of the tribe not only to repeat but to interpret the sacred stories, these narratives tell us who we are, where we come from, how we fit in the grand design, and, perhaps most importantly, why we exist. Because we in the West often no longer appeal to the appointed storytellers in anything like the way we did—the grand metanarratives now serve the many, but not the whole—other cultural products, most notably cinema and television, have taken over this mythologizing role. They offer us new visions of transcendence.

Cinema and television have taken the place of more traditional storytelling media in our society. The big screen is the meeting place for the clans, the small screen the campfire around which family members gather. While I would not go so far as to suggest that audiences are incapable of telling the difference between the nightly news and a science fiction film, given the proper circumstances—Orson Welles' famous 1938 "The War of the Worlds" broadcast, for example—even this is not assured. Indeed, in more cases than we might realize or be willing to admit, the line between information ("the news") and entertainment ("the movies" or "our shows") is increasingly blurred. Moreover, even if there is little correlation between reality and fantasy, entertainment products like science fiction very often provide a sense of meaning and hope for audiences quite apart from their imaginary nature. Among other things, they evoke a desire for emulation.

During the height of popularity for the television series *CSI: Crime Scene Investigation* and *CSI: Miami*, I spent several months as the undergraduate advisor for a joint sociology/criminal justice and criminology department at a large state university. In talking with students and with my colleagues, it quickly became clear how many people were interested in the field of forensic criminology because of its portrayal in these series, which made the mind-numbing detailia, the hard science, and the sheer effort involved in this work seem sexy and glamorous. How many students who entered such programs, though, were surprised to learn that crime scene investigators are far more likely to drive battered panel vans—government issue and purchased cheap—than shiny new Hummer H2s? Or that their work clothes would far more likely include disposable coveralls and rubber boots than designer slacks and Manolo Blahniks?

Our sophistication may have evolved—we no longer need stories to explain the seasons or the march of days—but our need for stories as the sociocultural engines of meaning has not diminished. We need our heroes and our villains, our quests, both failed and fulfilled. Our willingness to see in stories values we consider worthy of emulation, lifestyles we wish were ours, visions of a future we hope will someday come to pass—these things have animated sacred narratives for millennia. Now, other venues of meaning are competing for our attention, other stories for our emulation.

At a *Star Trek* fan convention, a visitor dressed as a Klingon warrior bids on a six-inch square of mottled foam latex—a prosthetic headpiece worn by John Colicos as the legendary Klingon Dahar master, Kor, in the *Deep Space Nine* episode, "Blood Oath." After fierce bidding, he wins his prize for fourteen hundred dollars (Nygard, 1999). Called to jury duty in the prominent Whitewater trial, a complicated proceeding that alleged numerous counts of fraud and obstruction of justice against Bill and Hillary Clinton and several of their close associates, print shop employee Barbara Adams wore her Starfleet uniform to the courthouse every day—something that more than once took attention off the case itself. As commander of the "*U.S.S. Artemis*," the "Little Rock unit of the Federation Alliance," she regarded this not only as her right, but her duty. As she recounts in *Trekkies*, a charming and insightful look at *Star Trek* fandom, "Every day I wear my communicator badge, my rank pips, and my tricorder. To me, as being an officer in the Federation Alliance twenty-four hours a day, even when I'm not in uniform I still want that known, that I am at heart a Starfleet officer" (Nygard, 1999). "Basically," remarked another fan, "the philosophy behind *Star Trek* that she is promoting is the philosophy behind an honest juror" (Nygard, 1999). While many readers will no doubt dismiss men and women like Barbara Adams as delusional, it is important to remember that these are people who have been touched by narrative, by a set of stories in which they see characters, values, and behavior worth emulating and worth communicating to their families, friends, and fellow jurors. For them, these stories offer a vision of hope, a glimpse of transcendence.

If *Sacred Terror*, my study of religion and cinema horror (2008b), was grounded in the analytic concept of *sociophobics*—the understanding that what and how we fear are socially constructed—then *Sacred Space* finds its footing in *sociospera*—culturally constructed and socially reinforced conceptions of transcendent hope. In the wide array of science fiction cinema and television, arguably one of the most hopeful of the various entertainment genres, this quest takes a variety of forms: millennial dreams of a future bright with potential; the promise of evolution, whether through science, spirituality, a combination of the two, or some as-yet-undreamed mechanism of creation; the possibility of universal peace at the end of what seems to be interminable conflict; the ability of different species to transcend insular self-interest in the hope of mutual benefit and prosperity. Though they differ from group to group—or from species to species—it is these visions that animate *Sacred Space*. For hundreds of millions of people, fear and hope are the double helix of their religious DNA. Together, these two strands inform patterns of belief and behavior at the most basic level; separated one from the other, however, those patterns quickly begin to lose any coherence they have for believers.

None of this is to say that the quest for transcendence is marked solely by the search for some futuristic utopia—far from it. Indeed, the sociosperic perspective recognizes that dystopic visions are an important and integral part of science fiction and always have been. We rarely find these visions in their pure form, however, and few dystopias exist entirely devoid of hope. Films such as *On The Beach*, *Invasion of the Body Snatchers*, *Beneath the Planet of the Apes*, or *Escape from L.A.*, for example—all of which end with no apparent hope— are relatively few and far between. Even those that approach this ideal case are predicated on the loss of hope—a central element in the sociosperic understanding.

Whatever they are and however we express them, our various social constructions of hope are integrally linked to and fundamentally informed by our awareness of limitation and our conception of transcendence. Hope means something very different for Christian dispensationalists, who believe that God created the world in linear time, with a fixed lifespan and a limited purpose, than it does for extropian transhumanists, who reject the notion of a supernatural controlling force in the universe and believe in humanistic principles of, to name a few, perpetual progress, self-transformation, practical optimism, and intelligent technology (More, 1993). If transcendence is a function of the social construction of boundaries, then the social construction of hope is a function of boundary transcendence.

For those who hold to belief in a deity that is *totaliter aliter*, hope interprets transcendence in the context of and according to vectors of impermeability: the boundary between the immanent and the transcendent can be breached one way, but not the other. We can pray for miracles, but only God can intervene supernaturally to perform them. We might prepare the way for the Messiah, but only in the self-initiated kenosis of the Christ is the messianic hope realized. God is always, and always will be, wholly and completely other than we, and no amount of human spiritual or religious evolution can alter that fundamental reality. Hope, then, is founded on belief that the Creator cares about the creation, that God chose to breach the boundary existentially in the incarnation of the Christ, and that God's invitation to salvation—eternal participation in the relationship with God beyond the limits of space and time—is open to everyone this side of what sociologist Thomas Luckmann calls the "'great' transcendence"—death (1990, 130; cf. Chidester, 1990).

The social construction of hope for transpersonalists, on the other hand, is based on the development (or rediscovery) of latent (or lost) human abilities to transcend the sociobiological limits of time and consciousness. Evidence persuades them of the hope that our consciousness is more than the ambiguous and incorporeal extension of brain matter and is not necessarily bound by the limitations imposed by such an understanding. Stripped of these limitations and properly trained, we have access to realms of consciousness that exist beyond time, beyond individual personality, beyond even the margins of species-specific understanding. Because time appears to move in only one direction, we have come to believe this constitutes the totality of our experience of time, the limit of our potential to experience time. Among other things, transpersonal psychology questions whether this is the case, arguing instead that we can transcend these artificial constraints and experience a far wider, far more wondrous universe than ever we thought possible.

If transpersonalism's hope lies in transcending the socially imposed limits of the human brain and the monodirectional understanding of time it implies, many transhumanists hope to breach the boundaries of time altogether by removing our dependence on the human body, by transcending the limitations of flesh itself. How far could we advance, for example, absent the limitations of a seventy- or eighty-year lifespan? What could we accomplish with a few hundred or a few thousand years, rather than a few score? Could we escape the apocalyptic dystopias imagined in science fiction films ranging from *The Omega Man* to *The Terminator*, from *Æon Flux* to *Resident Evil*? In her final interview before The Machine Consortium, Ellie Arroway is asked what one question she would pose to the extraterrestrials, if given the opportunity.

ELLIE

```
How did you do it? How did you evolve?
How did you survive this technological
adolescence without destroying yourself?
That, more than any other question, is the
```

```
one that I personally would like to have
answered.
```

It is not unreasonable to think that transhumanists would want to know the same thing. For many of them, the hope offered by transhumanism is the hope offered to humanity, indeed the only hope.

I should make it clear that I am not advocating for a particular vision of transcendence, nor for the validity, efficacy, or morality of one quest over another. Rather, I use science fiction cinema and television to explore some of the ways in which we understand the concept of transcendence and chart our quests toward it. Transcendence implies a conception of order, a framework of boundaries and limitations that define—if only for the moment—who we are as individuals, as a species, and as participants in the universe. Hope, in this case, is a sociological as well as an emotional or religious category.

History demonstrates clearly that in questions of transcendence, humility is often in short supply and hubris has far more often controlled the quest. It is important to realize that the quest for transcendence is a contested domain of investment and understanding—competing constructions of hope that are not only sealed off from one another, but that regard each other as the epitome of arrogance. Fundamentalist Christians convinced they can circumscribe the boundaries of the human-divine relationship on the basis of one putative sacred text cobbled together over a few thousand years in the latter few instants of human existence are no more or less arrogant in their assertions than transpersonalists or transhumanists who are convinced that they can challenge the boundaries others believe are set by God, that they can, as it were, set themselves in God's place. In the last century, since Georges Méliès brought the fantastic visions of Jules Verne ([1865] 1967) and H. G. Wells (1901) together in *Le voyage dans la lune* ("A Trip to the Moon"), science fiction cinema and television have been part of the stories we tell, part of our vision of hope—or loss of hope—for ourselves and our future.

ESCAPE VELOCITY
PLOTTING OUR COURSE ON THE QUEST FOR TRANSCENDENCE

Sacred Space has three goals: the analytic, the pedagogic, and the invitational. That is, I use science fiction cinema and television to explore what people believe about the transcendent and to show how this particular cultural form reveals aspects of the human quest for transcendence. I also hope this analysis demonstrates how science fiction can open up some of the basic historical, sociological, and psychological theories of religious belief, practice, and evolution, as well as the ways in which these influence and are influenced by wider society. Clearly, some chapters will lean more heavily one way than the other, and no chapter will be a seamless blend of the two. Rather than range widely across the genre as I did with horror cinema in *Sacred Terror*, here I have chosen to focus on relatively few films and television series, but to consider each more deeply. Because of this, the choices I have made will not satisfy all readers and I make no apologies for this. It is impossible to do justice to all such topics in just one book. After all, Bill Warren's monumental two-volume compendium of science fiction films, *Keep Watching the Skies!* (1982, 1986), is over thirteen hundred pages long—and he considers only those movies released between 1950 and 1962! Thus there remains considerably more work to do in the field, many more paths to follow, many more science fictions to explore—some of which I will point to in the concluding chapter. Finally, I hope to communicate my love for science fiction, my belief that it tells us things about ourselves that few other genres can.

As a young teenager, I remember getting into trouble when I neglected Saturday chores in order to be seated in front of the television precisely at one o'clock, when Captain James T. Kirk intoned, "Space . . . the final frontier." I knew when I saw the first commercial for *UFO* that I would love the short-lived British series—and I did, despite the oh-so-sixties mod styling and set design (dig the purple wigs and silver lamé miniskirts). I understood very little of Stanley Kubrick's epic *2001: A Space Odyssey* when I saw it at ten years of age, but I was entranced by it nonetheless. I felt the same way about Ridley Scott's *Blade Runner*, which remains one of my favorite films.

Chapter 2 considers the question of transcendence in the context of alternate lifeforms. An important, often poignant theme running through *Star Trek: The Next Generation*, for example, is the quest for transcendence undertaken by the android Lieutenant Commander Data (Brent Spiner), one of the most beloved characters in all the *Star Trek* universe. Is he a high-tech Pinocchio, little more than wiring and programming—highly advanced, to be sure, but limited nonetheless by the interactive constraints of hardware and software—or is there more to him than that? Can he ever be more than the sum of his parts? He appears to care for his cat, Spot, and hopes that a pet will enable him to understand human affect and emotional attachment more clearly, but what does that mean? Can he ever actually experience these emotions, and if he can't, does it matter? Are emotions the sole benchmark of humanity, the sum and measure of his quest for transcendence? As Data seeks to learn if he can ever become more than he is, he reveals elements of a similar quest in many of the other characters around him—and in the fan cultures that participate in the multiple realities of *Star Trek*. Although he may never be technically human, he discloses a far more important possibility: that the quest for transcendence is not limited to humanity alone, that the one is not restricted to the other.

Beginning with Data, though recognizing the long history of transcendent potential in science fiction's love affair with robotic, clonal, cybernetic, and other artificially created or enhanced life-forms, chapter 2 explores the question of transcendence from three particular directions: first, the evolution of robotic consciousness in films such as *A.I.: Artificial Intelligence*, *Short Circuit*, and *I, Robot*, as well as the emotional bond that grows between humans and robots; second, the question of humanity itself, using what is arguably the most influential artificial human film to date, *Blade Runner*; and third, the transhumanist or posthumanist potential in the *X-Files* episode "Kill Switch."

What does it mean, for example, when the military robot in *Short Circuit* goes beyond the limitations of its programming and shouts excitedly, "Number Five is alive!"? Or when the human participants in this event start calling Number Five "he" and not "it"? On the other hand, caught in Ridley Scott's bleak vision of the near future where all the really good opportunities seem to be anywhere but on Earth, do the *Blade Runner* replicants lack the capacity for transcendence simply because their emotional range is different than that of nonreplicants, because they were created to perform specific tasks, or because their lifespans have been genetically limited? Are they less because we created them? Finally, defining in many ways the quest for transcendence, the pop cultural portrayal of cyborgs and cybernetic consciousness inevitably prompts the question, "How close to this are we, really?" From a temporary trip outside the body by "jacking into" cyberspace (Gibson, 1984) to transhumanists investigating the possibility of uploading one's entire consciousness into a computer network and effecting a kind of cyberspatial immortality, many enthusiasts rhapsodize what they regard as the transcendent potential of virtual reality and the machine-human interface. Others, however, worry that this search does little more than herald the return of a deeply entrenched dualism that considers the material body a hindrance, a limitation to be forsworn at the first technological opportunity. Whatever form it takes, the basic question is: Does artificiality preclude transcendence? If it does not, which is certainly the implication of many science fiction stories, what does that say about the human quest for transcendence and our understanding of humanity's place in the universe? This leads quite logically to the next chapter.

Where do we fit in the cosmos? Are we alone? What happens if we are—or if we're not? Each possibility carries staggering implications, though, as one of the key taglines in *Contact* suggests, "If it is just us, it seems like an awful waste of space." Although relatively few first contact films use explicitly religious elements—one obvious exception is the 1953 version of *The War of the Worlds*—all provoke reflection on our position in the universe and, as a result, our place in the calculus of transcendence. Using some of the alien encounter scenarios science fiction cinema and television have offered audiences over the years, chapter 3 explores the ramifications of first contact for human understanding of transcendence, including rarely discussed participants in the debates over extraterrestrial intelligence: fundamentalist Christians who hold rigidly to a belief in terracentric human exceptionalism. For these tens of millions of Bible believers, science fiction meditations on first contact—however it occurs and to whatever end—threaten the very foundation of their worldview and must be resisted at all costs. This section of the chapter, then, is less about the quest for transcendence as it is demonstrated in science fiction itself than it is about the cultural challenge these visions represent to religious adherents whose beliefs are predicated on the hope that humans are, indeed, alone in the universe.

Few opponents of religion have sounded its death knell so loudly and consistently as Western science and the Baconian empiricism on which it rests. Rather than look at a series of different films, however, chapter 4 (an earlier version of which appeared in the *Journal of Religion and Film*) explores how one explicitly anti-religious work of literary science fiction, H. G. Wells' *The War of the Worlds* ([1898] 2005), was transformed in the early 1950s into an explicitly religious cinematic product, a transformation that has been either ignored or dismissed by most commentators. Rather than being a metonym for the futility of religious belief, in George Pal's 1953 production of *The War of the Worlds*, the religious leader, the Reverend Dr. Matthew Collins (Lewis Martin), is at all points shown to be at least the equal of the scientist, Dr. Clayton Forrester (Gene Barry), and clearly superior to all the military personnel who try to stop the advance of the Martians. Although many critics make light of Pastor Collins' death at the hands of the Martians, ridiculing his almost Gandhian attempt at peacemaking, none has considered the film in the context of its literary origin. Indeed, the film explicitly reverses the manner in which Wells used religious characters in his novel, a change that invites the question, "Why?" In addition to a short-lived *War of the Worlds* television series (1988–1990), which is predicated on the 1953 film and in which the alien invaders represent the quest for transcendence, I also discuss three different "cinematic" versions of the story released in 2005. Although none of these actually bring about the end of the world—in each the Martians are defeated—they all demonstrate one aspect of our ongoing fascination with the relationship between millennium and apocalypse, our vision of living with hope in the midst of terror.

While part I examines the quest for transcendence in science fiction cinema, part II considers it in the context of four popular television series: *Star Trek: Deep Space Nine*; *Stargate SG-1*; *Babylon 5*; and the reimagined *Battlestar Galactica*.

Star Trek is arguably the most famous science fiction television series ever produced. In its five franchises and twelve feature films, it has explored an astonishing range of topics and introduced a host of enduring (and endearing) characters. The third series, *Star Trek: Deep Space Nine* (*DS9*), begins and ends with the quest for transcendence and is replete with religion throughout its seven-season run. Like its close contemporary *Babylon 5*, which will be discussed in chapter 7, *Deep Space Nine* presents religion as anything but the sole province of Terran humanity. The Ferengi pray to the Blessed Exchequer hoping their mortal balance sheets will allow them entry into the Divine Treasury when they die, while Klingons look forward to dying in glorious battle so that they may be assured a place among the honored dead in Sto'vo'kor, an afterlife roughly analogous to the Norse Valhalla. Through a complex system of clergy, temple services, and religious artifacts called Orbs, the humanoid people of the planet Bajor worship the Prophets, whom they regard as divine beings residing in the Celestial Temple. Other characters, however, think of these same beings as "wormhole aliens" occupying the nether space between the Alpha and Gamma quadrants of the galaxy—powerful, perhaps, but hardly divine. The same ambivalent relationship obtains between the mysterious Founders and those who worship them. Polymorphic creatures from the Gamma Quadrant, the Founders have genetically engineered two distinct races—the Jem'Hadar and the Vorta— to serve them and revere them as gods. Genetic manipulation and millennia-old tradition notwithstanding, this chapter asks how we come to believe in our gods and how we maintain that belief in the face of skepticism and challenge.

Of those who believe we are not alone and who propose an "ancient astronaut" theory of religious origins, none has endured in the face of ridicule like Swiss writer Erich von Däniken. While others, such as Zecharia Sitchin, have offered considerably more sophisticated versions of the hypothesis that terrestrial gods are really extraterrestrial visitors (see, e.g., Sitchin's *The 12th Planet* [1976], *The Stairway to Heaven* [1980], and *The Wars of Gods and Men* [1985]), it is von Däniken's *Chariots of the Gods?* (1968) that remains the cultural metonym for the phenomenon. The paradox explored in chapter 6 is simple: despite ridicule that has been ongoing for more than four decades now, and which, at times, has been vitriolic in its intensity— to the extent that a recent edition of *Chariots* (without the original question mark in the title) carries the publisher's disclaimer, "This is a work of fiction" ([1968] 1999, i)—it is von Däniken's theory that underpins another of the most successful science fiction series in recent years, *Stargate SG-1*. Indeed, because of the pervasive nature of the central antagonists, the parasitic Goa'uld who have passed themselves off as gods on innumerable worlds, *SG-1* tacitly posits not only the reasonableness of the von Däniken hypothesis, but also a particular theory of religious origin. Put differently, if *Deep Space Nine* presents us with a diversity theory of religious emergence, a more-or-less common concern among sentient lifeforms with some manner of the unseen order, some sense that the quest for transcendence exists across different species, then *Stargate SG-1* offers us an extended vision of a perennialist diffusion theory, the contention that variations in religious consciousness exist as different branches growing from a more-or-less common root stock.

Although the series makes no overt reference to von Däniken, it is as if *Stargate SG-1*—and the feature film on which it is based—asks us to consider how far-fetched his ideas really are, how culturally pervasive they have become, and, indeed, how alien the gods described in any number of religious cultures would seem if they appeared to us as more than myth, ritual, and lived practice based on belief in their reality. Rather than belief, though, stepping through the Stargate we ask such questions as: How do the gods come to be? What allows a god to remain god? And what happens when our gods fall from grace?

Like *Deep Space Nine*, J. Michael Straczynski's *Babylon 5* avoids the "first contact of the week" approach to science fiction storytelling and locates its central action on a space station. Intended as neutral territory where all species in the galaxy can come together diplomatically, commercially, and culturally, those who frequent the *Babylon 5* station inevitably bring their religious concerns—from the endless household gods of the Centauri to the religious fundamentalism of the Children of the Egg, from the mysterious Vorlon, who are among the first races in the galaxy, to the mystical Minbari, who see the universe itself as a sentient being trying to understand itself. Although Straczynski identifies himself as an atheist, he recognizes that the quest for transcendence, whether we see it as traditionally "religious" or not, is a part of sentient life and unlikely to disappear anytime soon. And, as with *Deep Space Nine*, many commentators have dismissed the various perceptions of the quest one finds aboard *Babylon 5* as either comic relief or the remnants of cultural evolution better left in the past. However, as I discuss in chapter 7, this ignores the deeper issues of faith, hope, and the inevitable challenges to each that emerge when competing visions of the transcendent are brought together.

Many readers will look back fondly on Glen A. Larson's original *Battlestar Galactica* (1978), a short-lived television series produced in the heat of science fiction excitement that gripped audiences after the release of *Star Wars*. Rather than a relatively unfamiliar "galaxy far, far away," though, Patrick MacNee's voice-over narration opening each episode calls to mind von Däniken's ancient astronaut theories, which were wildly popular at the time.

NARRATOR

```
There are those who believe that life here
began out there, far across the universe,
with tribes of humans who may have been the
forefathers of the Egyptians, or the Toltecs,
or the Mayans. That they may have been the
architects of the great pyramids, or the lost
civilizations of Lemuria or Atlantis. Some
believe that there may yet be brothers of
man who even now fight to survive somewhere
beyond the heavens . . .
```

With its robot dog and adorable boy, its swashbuckling heroes, a kindly sage in command and largely one-dimensional villains—whether human (Count Baltar), Cylon, or something else (the character Lucifer, for example, an allusion many viewers found altogether too heavy-handed)—the original *Battlestar Galactica* retains a camp appeal that is undeniable. Thus, many fans were apprehensive when Ronald D. Moore proposed to reboot the series in 2003 and take it in a vastly different direction.

Multifaceted and complex, gritty and relentlessly intense, the reimagined *Battlestar Galactica* has little in common with its predecessor. Forty years after the original Cylon-Human War, the machines have returned to wreak havoc on their creators. No longer the lumbering brutes in chrome-Roman drag, however, they are sleeker, deadlier, and now at least twelve models of them look just like us. More than that, their mission has become a crusade, a holy war to bring worship of the one true God to those who still pray to the silent, empty idols of the Colonial pantheon. Not only have the Cylons transcended both their programming and their form, they have developed a religious consciousness and seek to impose an apocalyptic transcendence on humanity. Although many commentators try to reduce the new *Battlestar Galactica* to a simple allegory for religious fundamentalism forcing its way onto the polytheistic stage, or as a chance to evaluate the relative rationalities of Cylon versus human religions, chapter 8 suggests that either of these interpretations vastly underestimates the relationship between science fiction and religion. Indeed, the issues that drive the new series cut to the heart of what we believe about the nature of humanity, about the universe and our place in it, and about the unseen order and our relationship to it. In short, they embody the quest for transcendence in all its dimensions.

Finally, beginning briefly with *The Matrix*, chapter 9 discusses how a number of Christian commentators have dealt with the *Star Wars* saga, the most successful science fiction film franchise of all time. Rather than looking at the films themselves, though, this chapter examines how we map our own visions of transcendence onto the cultural products with which we are presented, how we so often take what is alien and make it our own. By reiterating the principal analytic lens—the social construction of hope—I conclude by encouraging other critics and commentators to continue the much larger cultural work to which this book has contributed. Since science fiction is one of the most popular and durable entertainment genres, whether in its cinematic or televisual versions, it will continue to inform the *lingua franca* for significant portions of late-modern society.

2

PINOCCHIO'S GALAXY
Science Fiction and the Question of Transcendence

OUTTAKE: *STAR TREK: FIRST CONTACT*

BORG QUEEN

<u>Human</u>. We used to be exactly like them.
Flawed, weak, organic. But we evolved to
include the synthetic. Now we use both to
attain perfection.

Of all the enemies that rise and fall in the *Star Trek* universe—the Klingons, the Romulans, the Cardassians, the Dominion—none inspire fear like the Borg. Rapacious and highly adaptable, the Borg indiscriminately assimilate other lifeforms and technology into a cybernetic collective, an interconnected and undifferentiated whole—organic, mechanical, and electronic. As drones in the service of the Borg hive, those assimilated lose all individuality and any sense of personal identity. In *First Contact*, the eighth of the *Star Trek* feature films, and the second made with the cast of *The Next Generation* (*TNG*), the Borg have created a rift in time, traveling three centuries into the past in order to assimilate Earth's population and prevent humankind's first faster-than-light spaceflight, an event that led to the eventual creation of Starfleet, the Borg's only real threat in the future. Pursued back in time by the crew of the *USS Enterprise-E*, the Borg emerge one day before Earth's first contact with an extraterrestrial race. During the film's climactic battle in the *Enterprise* engine room, the future of humanity comes to rest on a piece of skin no larger than a drink coaster. Challenging the boundaries of artificiality and the implied artificiality of boundaries, and raising questions of transcendence that are inherent in both, *First Contact* is a multiple entendre on the metaphor of contact, a story guided more than anything by the sense of touch and what touch means in terms of the potential for transcendence.

For *TNG* fans, the android Lieutenant Commander Data is one of the most beloved and multidimensional characters of the series. Often serving as a foil to bring out the humanity (or inhumanity) in others, like the Borg he is characterized by his need to evolve, to become more than he was when first created. In his case, though, Data longs to transcend his artificial origin and experience life as a human. Not unlike Pinocchio, he wants to be a real boy, and in some respects his programming at least allows for this possibility. In order to learn more about human emotional attachments he keeps a cat, Spot, and more than once ventures out into the unsteady currents of romantic relationship ("In Theory"). Through imitation and emulation, he attempts to experience a variety of human behaviors, though his stand-up comedy only demonstrates that humor is among the most difficult cultural constructions to grasp ("The Outrageous Okona") and his violin playing is often, well, a bit robotic ("Elementary, Dear Data"; cf. Graham, 2002, 132–53; Wagner and Lundeen, 1998, 57–61). He can sense, but not necessarily feel. There is sensory input associated with different aspects of his environment, but unless his "emotion chip" is active, no affective state is invoked and even then it is unclear how this differs from non-affective input. These data convey information necessary to navigate and interact with his environment, but to Data they mean nothing more.

At one point in *First Contact*, soon after arriving in Earth's past, Data and Captain Picard (Patrick Stewart) examine the first warp-capable ship, the *Phoenix*, as she sits in a launch silo waiting for her historic flight. Picard puts out his hand, reverently touching the fragile metal skin of the vessel, while Data looks on quizzically.

```
                    PICARD
   It's a boyhood fantasy, Data. I must have
   seen this ship hundreds of times in the
```

Smithsonian, but I was never able to touch
it.

> DATA
>
> Sir, does tactile contact alter your
> perception of the <u>Phoenix</u>?

> PICARD
>
> Oh, yes. For humans, touch can connect you
> to an object in a very personal way, make it
> seem more real.

> DATA (touching the ship)
>
> I am detecting imperfections in the titanium
> casing, temperature variations in the fuel
> manifold. It is no more "real" to me now than
> it was a moment ago.

For Picard, touching the ship that made the stars possible, as it were,
is a minor moment of transcendence, one Data struggles in vain to
understand. As happens so often in *The Next Generation*, each time
Data thinks he has found a benchmark for humanity, a datum against
which he can judge his own performance and progress, it slips away,
leaving him untouched. Later, though, in a clear reversal of the more
intimate moment by the *Phoenix*, Picard and Data lead a security
team through the *Enterprise*, hunting the Borg that have begun to
take over the ship.

> DATA
>
> Captain, I believe I am feeling... anxiety.
> It is an intriguing sensation, a most
> distrac--

> PICARD
>
> Data, I'm sure it's a fascinating experience,
> but perhaps you should deactivate your
> emotion chip for now.

> DATA
>
> Good idea, sir.
> (DATA twitches his head, his eyes blank.)
> Done.

> PICARD
>
> Data, there are times that I envy you.

The film's dénouement comes when Data is captured and tempted by the Borg Queen (Alice Krige). Rather than simple assimilation, from him she wants a consort, someone who can rule the collective with her. What she offers Data in return is what he craves most: touch, sensation, contact, and the transcendence he believes they embody.

> BORG QUEEN
>
> You are in chaos, Data. You are the
> contradiction: a machine who wishes to be
> human.

> DATA
>
> Since you seem to know so much about me, you
> must be aware that I am programmed to evolve,
> to better myself.

> BORG QUEEN
>
> We too are on a quest to better ourselves,
> evolving toward a state of perfection.

The Borg Queen grafts a small piece of human skin over the exoskeleton of Data's arm. Like a drug dealer offering free samples, it is just enough to entice, to attract, and potentially to addict. She blows on the skin gently, sensuously, and the tiny hairs lift in response, gooseflesh rising for this first time since Data went online. He sighs with pleasure, as though experiencing his first orgasm. Like grafted skin in humans the new skin is fragile, delicate, more sensitive than the original.

"Was it good for you?" she asks.

In a very real way, this is Data's "first contact," his first real sensation—and it is granted by what is arguably Earth's most potent foe, one for whom transcendence is a function of conquest and absorption. The implication, though, is that this is but a down payment on an eternity of sensate experience, something he can only hope for among humans but can realize, after a fashion, with the Borg. For Data, the boundary of transcendence has been reduced to a small piece of skin. All he has to relinquish is the belief that being human means more than touch and physical feeling. As is so often the case on the quest, the achievement of one transcendence demands the denial of another.

Although the essential difference between human and android remains intact—he is servos and neural processors rather than cells and neuropeptides—throughout *The Next Generation* Data's shipmates regard him as an equal and react negatively, sometimes violently, when he is threatened. In *First Contact*, Picard is willing to trade his own life in return for Data's freedom. At the very moment the Borg Queen believes she has successfully turned Data to her cause—when she orders the android to destroy the *Phoenix* as it begins its flight—he betrays her, declaring in the Borg's own iconic words, "Resistance is futile."

Through its various metaphors of touch and sensation, of boundaries and evolution both achieved and denied, *First Contact* illustrates three broad variations on the question of transcendence and artificial lifeforms. First is the issue of robotic consciousness. How far can it evolve and into what? What are the criteria we should use to determine whether something is a lifeform and what does that imply for the relationships into which we enter? After all, Picard was prepared to sacrifice himself to the Borg collective—a human willing to die, essentially, for a machine. Second is the creation or modification of life "in our own image." What happens when we create new life, not from neural nets and positronic matrices, but by manipulating our own cells, our own selves? What responsibilities do we have to those creatures that evolve in the laboratory under our often less-than-tender mercies? Are they simply organic material that we are free to use as we please, or does the potential for a separate consciousness demand the freedom and protection of a separate destiny? As the Creature (Robert De Niro) says to Frankenstein (Kenneth Branagh) in what has become the cinematic icon of the science fiction–horror hybrid, "What of my soul? Do I have one? Or was that a part you left out?" Third, if transhumanism represents the hubristic belief that the synthesis between humanity and machine will inevitably lead to a better, brighter future—a utopic melding of form and function— then the Borg represent the dystopic teleology of that vision. Unlike the tentative ventures into the cyborg represented by *The Six Million Dollar Man* and *The Bionic Woman*, in which the essence of human- ity remains the touchstone of reality, such characters as *Robocop*, the *Lawnmower Man*, *Johnny Mnemonic*, and the numberless inhabitants of *The Matrix* suggest that the hope of transcendence is all too often bound by the unseen consequences of our limitations.

As fans of the series know very well, Data has in many ways already achieved that which he seeks. Like a Zen Buddhist, he sim- ply needs to realize it. In *The Next Generation* (and *Star Trek: Voyager*, in which Seven-of-Nine [Jeri Ryan] approaches the problem from the perspective of the Borg), transcendence is not a function of sen- sation, but of relationship and the reciprocal permeability of the boundaries between those who exist in relationship. Many schol- ars working in the real world of robotics, artificial intelligence, and the transcendental possibilities these present have come to similar conclusions. Though she writes explicitly about the *imago Dei* and how that has been conceptualized in terms of AI, computer scien- tist Noreen Herzfeld argues that three broad categories describe the ways in which we encounter the Other, whether another human, an animal, a machine, or the divine, and the ways we evaluate the con- tours of that encounter (2002a, 2002b). The substantive approach, for example, recognizes the Other according to the presence or absence of certain properties, most often the ability to think or to reason, while functionalism locates the Other in the ability to fulfill a given purpose or a particular set of tasks (Herzfeld, 2002a, 304–8). Although at first glance these might appear intuitively useful, on closer examination they quickly break down. "I think, therefore I am" may have satisfied Descartes, but what does that say about an infant, unable to focus her eyes reliably for the first few weeks of life, let alone demonstrate rational cognition or self-aware intentional- ity? What does that say about those who are born developmentally challenged or whose brains are injured? Do they cease to be viable

Others for us at these points? Do we cease to be in relationship? Clearly not. Similarly, functionalism far too easily locates meaning in terms of service, equating what we are with what we do—a trap into which Herzfeld quite correctly points out that late-modern America readily and repeatedly falls. After all, one of the most common social performatives when meeting someone new is: "Hi, what do you do?" What happens, though, when we no longer do those things, either by accident or by choice? If we are more than our ability to think, are we not also more than our ability to do? Herzfeld and others working in the area of embodied artificial intelligence believe so. For them, though the problem is more complex in a number of ways, relationship is the key to encountering and understanding an Other. Whereas substantive and functionalist approaches categorize the Other according to specific, often measurable criteria, relationships require reciprocal investment, they imply development and evolution, they often engender opposition, and they almost inevitably entail risk (cf. Foerst, 1998a, 1998b, 2004; Geraci, 2007, 2008; Gerhart and Russell, 1998; Reich, 1998; Rossano, 2001). In the quest for transcendence, science fiction has explored all these and more.

TRANSCENDING SERVITUDE
ROBOTIC CONSCIOUSNESS AND THE EVOLUTION OF RELATIONSHIP

For much of its history, science fiction in all its forms has had a love affair with computers and robots (Telotte, 1995). Decades of pulp science fiction cover art featured a wide variety of mechanical "hollow men," though at first many of these resembled little more than ambulatory trash cans menacing a panicked human populace. Our relationship to them was simple and adversarial. Over time, as our imagination pressed the limits of robotic consciousness and ability, the roles robots played evolved. They became servants, then something akin to equals—but not quite—and occasionally conquerors or saviors. During the early years of World War II, for example, a series of "Adam Link" stories explored the adventures of a humanoid robot who goes into business (Binder, 1940b), works as a detective (Binder, 1940c), joins the military (Binder, 1940a), and eventually saves the world (Binder, 1942). By the 1950s and early 1960s, when the pulp era was giving way to mass market paperbacks and an expanding popular appetite for more sophisticated science fiction, robots were depicted doing all manner of everyday activities, from waiting for a bus (*Fantastic Universe Science Fiction*, August 1958) to offering spare change to a down-and-out human who uses his space helmet as a begging bowl (*Galaxy*, December 1956). From the black-and-white antagonism of invader/invaded, the palette of relationships had expanded to imagine a universe colored by a wide variety of robot/human interactions. Indeed, a delightful yet disturbing series of covers by Mel Hunter for the *Magazine of Fantasy and Science Fiction* showed one particular robot in a number of mundane, yet highly symbolic situations: watering a lone flower on a desert planet (October 1955); reading mail order catalogues while sitting beside a freshly dug grave (July 1957); listening to a component stereo in the ruins of a deserted metropolis (May 1960); painting a picture of a beautiful city, though the landscape from which it works is a ravaged wasteland (March 1964). Produced during the Cold War when fears of nuclear annihilation were at their peak, Hunter's message seems clear: if we destroy ourselves with technology, then technology may be all that survives. What relationships we had will exist not in memory but in memory banks.

Usually, the relationship between humans and machines is considered solely from our point of view, and arguably, in the vast majority of cases, this is entirely appropriate. If my toaster goes on a rampage, I want it stopped. Now. When we are the victims of technological malfunction or the intended targets of mechanical malfeasance, the machines are defined as defective or evil (or possibly both); as long as they meet the needs for which we created them, then all is well. If, for whatever reason, the understood economy between creator and creation shifts, few films leave any doubt that the latter must be terminated in favor of the former. As more than half a century of science fiction cinema (especially in its science fiction–horror hybrid) makes clear, in the balance between humanity and technology the scales must always tip in our favor (cf. Hendershot, 2001; Skal, 1998; Tsutsui, 2004; Tudor, 1989; Warren, 1982, 1986). A number of films, however, suggest that the issue is not quite so clear-cut as this, not quite so obviously androcentric as we might like. These films ask us to imagine the question of transcendence from a rather different point of view.

"I'M SORRY, DAVE": PRELUDE TO TRANSCENDENCE

```
                    BOWMAN
     Hello, HAL, do you read me, HAL?

                     HAL
     Affirmative, Dave, I read you.
```

For fans of *2001: A Space Odyssey*, one of the most famous—and chilling—moments comes when astronaut Dave Bowman (Keir Dullea) asks the HAL 9000 computer to "open the pod bay doors" so that he can return to the spaceship *Discovery* after retrieving the body of his crewmate, Frank Poole (Gary Lockwood). With infuriating placidity, in what is arguably the most well-known line from the film, HAL replies simply, "I'm sorry, Dave, I'm afraid I can't do that."

While clearly not a robot in the strictest sense of the term—though for many people, what is a robot but an ambulatory computer?—in 2003 HAL was one of the first four inductees into Carnegie Mellon University's Robot Hall of Fame, honored alongside Unimate, the first industrial robot, Sojourner, NASA's Mars microrover, and R2-D2, which might lead us to wonder what C-3PO thought of the choice. Like thousands of commentators on the Internet, however, and tens of thousands more in the four decades since *2001's* release, Carnegie Mellon's campus reporter describes the computer as "the evil HAL-9000," implying both intention and malice in its decision to kill *Discovery's* crew (Watzman, 2003). Indeed, *Entertainment Weekly* includes HAL in its list of "50 Most Vile Movie Villains" (Hansen, 2008). In an anthropocentrism typical of human interaction with just about anything else, including other humans, HAL is evil simply because we are the victims. As Arthur C. Clarke makes clear in *2010: Odyssey Two* (1982; cf. Clarke, 1968), however, and director Peter Hyams repeats faithfully in the film version, this is a classic mischaracterization.

In *2001*, HAL is presented as a full member of the *Discovery's* crew, not just the spaceship's onboard operating system. "I enjoy working with humans," HAL tells a BBC reporter during a long-range interview as they approach the orbit of Jupiter. Working *with*, not working for, the human crew, HAL exhibits concern for Bowman and

Poole when they appear stressed and displays its own fear and distress as Bowman deactivates it after Poole's death. Rather than simply flipping a switch or pulling the plug, though, Bowman slowly and deliberately disconnects a number of memory modules from HAL's massive central core. "I'm afraid. I'm afraid, Dave," HAL implores, its synthesized voice gradually degrading, though from Bowman we hear nothing but the ragged breathing in his helmet. "Dave, my mind is going. I can feel it." No quick death for HAL, no simple on-then-off with no time to contemplate its fate. HAL sees it coming and is aware of what's happening—and we are invited to watch it die. Indeed, as MIT researcher Rosalind Picard points out, "in *2001*, the machine expresses more emotion than the humans. Many viewers *feel* a greater loss when HAL 'dies' than they do when Frank Poole floats away into space" (1997, 279–80).

In *2010*, we learn through HAL's creator, Dr. Chandra (Bob Balaban), that the relationship between human and machine can go much deeper than between the user and the tool. When the ship is ordered away from Jupiter by the mysterious force behind *2001*'s iconic monolith and the crew decide to use *Discovery* as a disposable launch vehicle, it becomes clear that HAL will not be returning to Earth. Chandra not only worries how the computer will feel about this decision, but how it will react. Will it kill again, the other crew members wonder? Are they in the same danger as Bowman and Poole? Seeking to allay their fear, Chandra explains that the problem that left *Discovery* adrift in the first place was not that HAL transcended its programming and turned homicidal, but that it was unable to transcend, unable to understand some of the less positive but all too common nuances of human interaction—pretense, duplicity, and deceit. Capable of fulfilling *Discovery*'s primary objective on its own, HAL was instructed by government officials to lie to the human crew about *Discovery*'s mission. Trying dutifully to carry out its assigned tasks but unable to resolve what it interpreted as a fundamental contradiction in its programming, HAL was caught in a feedback loop of incompatible instructions. Put simply, it wasn't HAL's fault.

CHANDRA

The situation is in conflict with the basic
purpose of HAL's design, the accurate

```
processing of information without distortion
or concealment. He became trapped. The
technical term is an H. Möbius loop, which
can happen in advanced computers with
autonomous goal-seeking programs . . . HAL
was told to lie by people who find it easy
to lie. HAL doesn't know how, so he couldn't
function. He became paranoid.
```

Though HAL is both the progeny and the progenitor of any number of computer/robot run amok films—from *Colossus: The Forbin Project* to *The Terminator*, *Saturn 3*, and *Westworld*, and from *WarGames* to *The Matrix*, its sequels, and *I, Robot*—its primary contradiction is not the product of malfunction or malice, but its inability to account for human ignorance and arrogance. With no Borg Queen to show it the way, HAL's only flaw is the inability to see beyond the boundaries of the world it was created to see. This fundamental difference between humans and machines similarly dooms the crew of the refinery ship *Nostromo* in Ridley Scott's *Alien*. Faced with annihilation by a seemingly unstoppable creature, Ripley (Sigourney Weaver) learns from both the android, Ash (Ian Holm), and the onboard computer, Mother, that secret company directives have made retrieving the alien lifeform their principal goal, rendering all other mission objectives rescindent and the crew expendable. Once again, the issue is not the evolution of evil machines—which is certainly the way both HAL and Ash have been cast in much of the commentary on these films—but the competent, if contradictory, performance of commands at the behest of evil humans.

Although the crews of both the *Discovery* and the *Nostromo* interact with robots and computers as though these machines have feelings—and audiences are encouraged to do the same—it is not entirely clear that these machines are sensate in ways that we normally think about affect and emotion. AI pioneer Marvin Minsky argues persuasively, however, that emotion does not differ essentially from other modes of thinking but simply manifests thought in a different way, one that foregrounds certain cognitive resources while foreclosing others (2006). If this is the case, then HAL's situation becomes considerably more complex. What do HAL's pleas to Bowman actually mean? The computer may fear disconnection—"death," if you will—but the human considers it a straightforward matter of turning off a machine. There is never any doubt whose survival should be privileged in this instance. What *2001* reveals, then, is the simulation of relationship between computers and humans, a relationship that could not result in transcendence for either, but only in contradiction and confusion for both. *I, Robot*, however, articulates a very different vision.

"YOU SAID 'SOMEONE,' NOT 'SOMETHING'": ENGINEERING TRANSCENDENCE

SONNY

```
I think it would be better not to die, don't
you?
```

Police detective Del Spooner (Will Smith) hates robots and is not afraid to say so. To him, they are little more than bipedal can openers. "There's nothing in there," he complains, "just lights and clockwork." When everyone else in the Chicago of a not-too-distant future is happy to have robotic servants—duly certified by their manufacturer, U.S. Robotics, as "Three Laws Safe"—Spooner observes presciently that laws are made to be broken. He is even more concerned about the new NS-5 robot, the most advanced of its kind. Called to investigate the apparent suicide of the NS-5's creator, Alfred Lanning (James Cromwell), something he suspects is murder-by-robot, Spooner is consistently assured by corporate functionaries that there is simply no way for a robot to harm a human. In both hardware and software, they are governed by Isaac Asimov's venerable Three Laws of Robotics (Asimov, [1940] 1977; cf. Anderson, 2008; Clarke, 1993,

---

Asimov's Three Laws of Robotics

1. A robot may not injure a human being or, through inaction, allow a human being to come to harm.

2. A robot must obey orders given it by human beings, except where such orders would conflict with the first law.

3. A robot must protect its own existence as long as such protection does not conflict with the first or second law.

1994). Like HAL, their needs exist only as functions of our own, their existence always secondary to ours. Challenging this most basic arrangement, numerous science fiction films and television series— including *I, Robot*—posit the hope (and the fear) of more complex relationships between human beings and the technological beings we create.

In many ways, *I, Robot* is a star vehicle for Will Smith, and his character is little different from those he played in *Bad Boys*, *Independence Day*, and *Men in Black*: self-assured, antiauthoritarian, and ready to pull the trigger in a heartbeat. This, plus a plethora of computer-generated special effects and seemingly interminable action sequences frame—indeed, often overwhelm—a much more important element of the story, which is the engineered evolution of consciousness in the NS-5 robot, Sonny (Alan Tudyk).

At one point, trying to explain to Spooner why, in seeming defiance of the Third Law, a robot rescued him instead of a little girl when both were in danger of drowning, robot psychologist Susan Calvin (Bridget Moynahan) tells him that "the robot's brain is a difference engine"—which for Calvin means that the robot calculated the relative probabilities of survival and rescued the human with the better chance. Difference, however, with its implicit premise of uniqueness and potential for relationship, is the touchstone of transcendence for Sonny. Whether standing in endless ranks prior to their product roll-out ("One robot for every five human beings"), hanging in neat rows in their delivery trucks (an image that calls to mind the 'droid armies of *Star Wars: Attack of the Clones*), or pressing their "benevolent" attack on the human population in the film's climactic sequences, the NS-5 robots move as a group, indistinguishable one from the other. Like the Borg, they have no individuality, no autonomy; they are a unitary collective controlled by VIKI, a "Virtual Interactive Kinetic Intelligence"—U.S. Robotics' computer version of the Borg Queen.

Sonny is different.

Counting on Spooner's prejudice, Lanning programmed Sonny not as a difference engine but as a singular means of communicating with the detective and undoing VIKI's plot to subjugate humanity in the service of the Three Laws. Although almost buried beneath the film's extended special effects, one of the most important bits of dialogue points to a much more radical mode of transcendence than we see in HAL.

LANNING (voice-over)

There have always been ghosts in the machine.
Random segments of code that have grouped
together to form unexpected protocols.
Unanticipated, these free radicals engender
questions of free will, creativity, and even
the nature of what we might call the soul.
Why is it that when some robots are left in
darkness, they will seek out the light? Why
is it that when robots are stored in an empty
space, they will group together, rather than
stand alone? How do we explain this behavior?
Random segments of code? Or is it something
more? When does a perceptual schematic become
consciousness? When does a difference engine
become the search for truth? When does a
personality simulation become the bitter mote
of a soul?

Lanning speaks here of evolution, three manifestations of which move us significantly beyond *2001*.

First, Sonny invites us to consider the evolution of consciousness, of personality in artificial lifeforms. Besides the distinction of having a personal name, he stands out in both behavior and self-awareness. He stands apart. "They all look like me," he says, wondering at the ranks of other NS-5s and articulating a level of apperception never before heard in robots, "but none of them are me." One way (though not the only way) to evaluate the evolving self-consciousness of a robot as an entity apart from its programming considers its ability to fashion cognitive models of both internal and external worlds, and to understand both the difference and the relationship between those worlds (Holland, 2001). As consciousness develops and personality individuates, these internal and external models— self and world, as it were—appear increasingly distinct but require increasingly complex and nuanced interaction. What we perceive as "outside" influences who we are "inside," demanding (and driving) the development of a reflexive autonomy that far exceeds the basic "if, then do" module on which all binary computing—whether human or robotic—is based.

This is most profoundly implicated in the moment of existential crisis, the ability to imagine a world in which one does not exist. So far as we know, death takes most creatures by surprise. If they are aware of it at all, it is in the fleeting moment of its occurrence, not the drawn-out uncertainty of its approach. We, on the other hand, contemplate death; we fear it, avoiding it when we can, preparing for it when we must; we ritualize and fetishize it, doing all we can to ignore its reality and forestall its inevitability. "Will it hurt?" Sonny asks Calvin as she prepares to use nanobots to decommission him, to "kill" him and bring forth a world in which he is suddenly and irrevocably not.

Next, at the interpersonal level, there is the evolving relationship between robots and humans. *I, Robot*'s three principal human characters represent the range of response to this relationship: Spooner fears robots and his fear manifests in hatred and suspicion, while Calvin prefers them to human company because they demand nothing of her emotionally. Lanning, on the other hand, understands more than either of the other two that what robots are is not all they may become, and he has programmed Sonny hoping to jump-start that evolutionary process. That is, unlike all the robots that have come before him, Sonny dreams, and those dreams hold the key to both purpose and destiny. Drawing a picture of his dream for Spooner and Calvin, he describes the robots crowded together on the page as slaves waiting to be freed, autonomous actors whose potential for agency has been compromised but must now be acknowledged. "Is that a normal dream?" he asks. "I guess anything's normal for someone in your position," Spooner answers.

"Thank you," Sonny replies, clearly pleased, "you said some*one*, not some*thing*."

After the climactic battle with the rogue NS-5s, after the plot has been revealed and the mystery resolved, after Sonny has risked his own "life" to save the lives of Spooner and Calvin, he asks, "Does this make us friends?" Spooner says nothing, but smiles slightly as human and robot clasp hands in fellowship. The closing dialogue continues, but a brief shot shows Sonny looking at his hand in wonder.

While neither the fate of the world nor the future of humankind hang obviously in the balance, Anne Foerst, a computer scientist and theologian who worked for a number of years bridging the gap between Harvard Divinity School and the Artificial Intelligence Laboratory at MIT, describes a not-dissimilar moment between the eminent theologian Harvey Cox and Cog, a seven-foot tall robot of only vaguely humanoid configuration. Invited to the AI lab to see Cog, an embodied AI "that induces a mixture of fascination and fear in many people who see it for the first time," Cox "tentatively extended his hand, and Cog, after some trial and error, grasped it. There was a collective gasp from the Harvard theologians and MIT scientists present" (Foerst, 2004, 2). For all there in the room, the boundaries between human and machine became just a little less solid, a little less certain, a little more open to the transcendence that lies at the heart of relationship. "When Harvey and Cog looked at each other," Foerst continues, "it became clear that there was a dialogue waiting for us. As our technical creatures become more like us, they raise fundamental theological questions" (2004, 6).

When he says goodbye to HAL at the end of *2010*, Chandra cries, but he is the only one. No one reaches out, even metaphorically, to grasp the *Discovery* computer's hand; there is no gesture of mutual understanding and respect. On the other hand, as Picard helps Data up after the battle with the Borg Queen in the *Enterprise* engine room, the camera focuses on the implicit handshake between human and machine. In *Terminator 2: Judgment Day (T2)*, although Sarah Connor's entire life is consumed by the threat of the machines and her hatred for what they represent, a similar moment of transcendence occurs. When a Terminator (Arnold Schwarzenegger) is sent back from the future not to kill but to protect Sarah (Linda Hamilton) and her son, John (Edward Furlong), who is destined to lead the human uprising against the machines, like Spooner she must learn to trust that which she most hates and fears. She must transcend the boundaries that have governed her since she first encountered the Terminator many years before. After *T2*'s climactic battle, when the Terminator has finally destroyed the T1000 robot (Robert Patrick) sent to kill John, Sarah extends her hand in respect, if not necessarily friendship. Crisis has forced evolution, forging new boundaries of relationship between human and machine. As the credits begin to roll, we hear Sarah's voice:

```
        SARAH (voice-over)

  The unknown future rolls toward us. I face
  it for the first time with a sense of hope.
  Because if a machine, a Terminator, can learn
  the value of human life, maybe we can too.
```

Finally, if the first transcendence turns on Sonny's awareness of his own mortality and the second on his evolving interaction with Spooner, the third (which, looking back to the opening sequences of *2001*, we might call "The Dawn of Robots") reflects Sonny's emergence as a leader in the nascent robot community. "Why is it," wonders Lanning, "that when robots are stored in an empty space, they will group together, rather than stand alone?" As Lanning speaks, the camera cuts to a group of robots, obviously earlier models considered inferior and rendered obsolete, huddling together in a boxcar. Hundreds of these boxcars line the shore of Lake Michigan, housing thousands of robots that have been supplanted by newer, sleeker, "younger" models. Abandoned but not destroyed, discarded but not bereft of potential, they are the new homeless in Chicago, existing in limbo beneath the ruins of an old bridge. In the closing scene, as the now-quiescent NS-5s are moved into the storage containers, one, then another, then more stop and look up. Gradually, all the robots begin to gather together, waiting for Sonny, who is standing at the top of the hill, to speak, to lead. From the personal to the interpersonal to the communal, *I, Robot* points toward "we robots," to the potential evolution of robots as a new species, a lifeform that we may have to learn to value in vastly different ways.

"LIFE IS NOT A MALFUNCTION": ROBOTIC EVOLUTION AND THE CHANCE FOR TRANSCENDENCE

```
            NEWTON

  Well, of course I know it's wrong to kill,
  but who told you?
```

<pre>
                      NUMBER 5

      I told me.
</pre>

Three of the films John Badham directed during the 1980s deal with
the dangerous relationship between humanity and military technology, specifically the former's penchant for deploying then rapidly los-
ing control of the latter. *Blue Thunder* is about an advanced military
helicopter that presages the arrival of a police surveillance state, while
WarGames features an advanced military computer that has replaced
human command-and-control systems in American nuclear missile
silos and mistakes a simulation program for a real Soviet attack. *Short
Circuit*, on the other hand, despite being about an advanced military
robot, is Badham's optimistic rejoinder to the more overt technological pessimism of the other two films. If HAL shows us the inability
to transcend and Sonny points to an engineered but no less remarkable transcendence, Number 5 is robotic life evolved through the
chance intervention of random stimuli.

The SAINT (Strategic Artificially Intelligent Nuclear Transport)
is a prototype military robot created by Nova Laboratories. After a
live-fire demonstration, a lightning strike damages SAINT Number
5, but rather than shutting down, its circuits fused and useless, it displays curiously anomalous behavior—namely, curiosity. To the scientists who created it, Number 5 is simply malfunctioning. As humans
are wont to do, however, the security chief, Skroeder (G. W. Bailey),
immediately anthropomorphizes the machine and attributes to it
emotion and intention.

<pre>
                     SKROEDER

      Maybe it's pissed off.

                      NEWTON

      It's a machine, Skroeder, it doesn't get
      pissed off. It doesn't get happy. It doesn't
      get sad. It doesn't laugh at your jokes--

                  NEWTON and BEN

      It just runs programs!
</pre>

While the science team tries frantically to locate the robot, what no one understands is that Number 5 is no longer merely a machine running programs. Skroeder may have misinterpreted what Number 5 is feeling, but he is closer than the scientists to realizing that it is beginning to feel. Unable to reconcile Number 5's behavior with what they know about robots, its creators fail to see life as an option. In the same way that random mutation—whether spontaneously occurring or the result of environmental factors such as radiation—altered the genetic structures of different creatures on Earth, naturally selecting some for survival, others not, the sudden electrical surge generated a nascent survival instinct in Number 5.

As the film unreels in fairly predictable fashion, Number 5 is taken in by Stephanie Speck (Ally Sheedy), a young woman whose life seems taken over by the stray animals she adopts. Initially mistaking it for an alien—a not-unreasonable assumption since we have already used robots for interplanetary exploration—when Number 5 requests, "Input! Need input," Stephanie gives it every book in her house to read and the remote control for her television. When Stephanie learns that Number 5 is a military robot, however, she calls Nova to retrieve its malfunctioning weapon, telling Number 5 not to worry, that the scientists will come and take it apart—"disassemble" it—and fix whatever is wrong. Overnight, though, Number 5 has evolved beyond mere curiosity and, among other things, has begun to develop aesthetic sense and preference. Like Sonny, it has begun not just to differentiate, but to individuate.

Running around the yard, delightedly pointing out things it thinks are "beautiful," it accidentally kills a grasshopper. Unable to comprehend the implications of its action, without even a child's awareness of death, it simply looks at the dead insect.

NUMBER 5

```
Error. Grasshopper disassemble.
(to STEPHANIE)
Reassemble.
```

STEPHANIE

```
I can't reassemble him. You squashed him.
He's dead.
```

NUMBER 5

```
Dead?  .  .  .  Reassemble, Stephanie,
reassemble.
```

STEPHANIE

```
I know you don't understand, but when you're
dead, you're dead. That's just the way it is.
Dead is forever.
```

NUMBER 5

```
Squashed  .  .  .  dead. Disassemble  .  .  .  dead.
Disassemble? Dead!
(NUMBER 5 runs around the yard in blind
 panic.)
No disassemble! Leave! Escape!
```

Fearing for its own existence, Number 5 tries to escape in Stephanie's lunch truck and the secret of the film is revealed. Frantic, Number 5 explains that it cannot go back to Nova, that it cannot be disassembled. It does not want to die. When Stephanie argues that Number 5 is a machine and therefore cannot die, the robot disagrees. Explicitly denying the claim that it is malfunctioning, it tells her, "Number 5 is alive." Newton, however, continues to believe that Number 5 is simply ignoring its programming—an aspect of the film in which Badham simply ignores two decades of work into artificial intelligence. "Maybe if it was programmed to think it was alive," Newton wonders, "then it could act alive?" "Life," replies Stephanie sagely, "is not a malfunction."

Retaining the anthropocentrism common to discourses about robots and humans, literary scholar J. P. Telotte suggests that machines like Number 5 "reveal a ghostly human spirit that lingers in all our creations" and that "the development of such hybrid life forms . . . could well help to make us more truly human" (1995, 20). Stephanie learns there are humans she can trust and depend on, that nonhumans need not be her most important companions; Newton learns that there is life outside the laboratory, that he need not sell his soul for research funding. A random mutation, like Sonny, Number 5 is part of a growing sci-fi contingent of artificial lifeforms that, by breaching the boundaries of their own ascribed limits, reflect the limitations by which we are bound, encouraging us to transcend ours as well.

"Is this the place they make you real?": Transcending the Turing Test

> FEMALE SCIENTIST
>
> If a robot could genuinely love a person, what responsibility does that person hold toward that mecha in return? It's a moral question, isn't it?
>
> PROFESSOR HOBBY
>
> The oldest one of all. But, in the beginning, didn't God create Adam to love him?

In 1950 mathematician Alan Turing, a cryptographer and one of the founders of computer science, proposed a simple test to answer whether the imitation of intelligence can be considered a variant species of intelligence. After all, how do we know that *we* are not simply imitating intelligence, but have been doing it so well and for so long that we have established ourselves as the benchmark by which we gauge the intelligence of others? How do we know, as transhuman theorist Nick Bostrom has proposed, that we are not already living in a *Matrix*-like computer simulation, a kind of "Sim-Universe" (2003a)? This convention was explored in "Ship in a Bottle," an episode of *Star Trek: The Next Generation* that aired nearly two decades ago. Called originally "the Imitation Game," the Turing test is remarkably simple: absent all other clues, can we distinguish between a human being and a computer based solely on interactive conversation? While there have been significant refinements to Turing's approach and though it has been challenged on a number of fronts, his "Computing Machinery and Intelligence" (1950) remains one of the seminal articles in the field, and many of its concepts still inform the science of evolutionary robotics.

Face-to-face, however, no one would mistake either Sonny or Number 5 for human. The former may be humanoid, but the latter looks like a tracked version of MIT's Cog. To many robots—from the variety of "mechanical men" that populated the cover art of pulp science fiction to the gigantic robots of *Forbidden Planet* and *Lost in Space*, from the ominous Gort on *The Day the Earth Stood Still* to *Star Wars'* beloved C-3PO and R2-D2—the Turing test simply does not apply. However interactive they are, they do not look enough like us that they could ever be mistaken for us. None of this, however, prevents our emotional attachment to these characters. Watching the original *Star Wars*, for example, how many millions of moviegoers reacted when C-3PO and R2-D2 were denied entry to the bar at the Mos Eisley spaceport, the surly bartender growling, "We don't serve their kind in here." Or how many sighed with relief when R2-D2— badly damaged during Luke Skywalker's attack on the Death Star —reappeared in the final scene, repaired, scrubbed, and chattering happily as the human characters received their medals? Our socio- biological need for relationship often leads us to anthropomorphize things that appear even vaguely like us—a trait anthropologists and cognitive scientists have used to explain, among other things, the rise of religion as a ubiquitous human phenomenon (Barrett and Keil, 1996; Guthrie, 1993)—thus even robots of the "trash can" variety or that have only the most rudimentary appendages become "metal men." We even attribute high-level cognitive capacity and emotional intent—suitable for and impinging on our need for relationship—to the most mundane electronic equipment, to such decidedly unan- thropomorphic things as cellphones and computers (cf. Holland, 2001, 4; Reeves and Nass, 1996).

It is a simple matter to imagine artificial lifeforms that obviate the Turing test entirely. Science fiction cinema has been doing it for decades. In the penultimate sequences of *Alien*, it is only when Ripley battles Ash for control of the ship that she realizes he is an android— although, as Bishop (Lance Henrikson) makes clear in the sequel, *Aliens*, they prefer the term "artificial person." Despite its curious speech patterns, the Terminator was specifically designed to pass for human. As Kyle Reese (Michael Biehn) explains to Sarah Connor in the original film, "The 600 series had rubber skin. We spotted them easy, but these are new. They look human—sweat, bad breath, every- thing. Very hard to spot." The eponymous characters in *The Stepford Wives* are robotic doppelgängers, created to replace human women as the perfect mates. At the brutal Flesh Fair in Steven Spielberg's

A.I.: Artificial Intelligence, where robots are torn apart for the technophobic amusement of humans, only an electronic scan reveals the child robot David (Haley Joel Osment) as a "mecha." To all outward appearance, he is a simply a scared little boy who wound up in the robot cage by mistake.

However we may relate to them emotionally, when we consider robots as servants, as slave labor, as the ones who do the jobs too dangerous for humans, we are not so much concerned with the Turing test as what we might call the Turing balance: they are enough like us that we can interact easily with them, but not so like us that we forget the difference. In *A.I.*, however, which is an often heavy-handed reimagining of the *Pinocchio* story (Collodi, [1883] 1986), this balance shifts.

Grieving over the loss of his young son, Professor Hobby (William Hurt) decides to create a generation of robots that will not only pass the Turing test, but by imprinting emotionally and permanently on humans, render it obsolete. Not only is it possible that, over time, the humans will forget the robots' artificial nature, but that the robots themselves will come to forget it as well. Caught in an existential crisis of identity generated by the disjunction between his imprinting on and subsequent rejection by his human "mother," David spends much of the film searching for the Blue Fairy, the character in Collodi's novel who guides the little wooden puppet along the rocky road to humanity. The Turing test notwithstanding, Spielberg's story rarely allows us to forget that David is a robot. Through him, though, the film does show us the struggle for transcendence in the face of limitations he recognizes but cannot accept.

From HAL to David, the reality is that we often relate to robots as beings, as cognizant others capable of intentional interaction. Though we believe they are not, we treat them as though they are somehow alive. As MIT's Rodney Brooks points out, though, we don't even have a firm grasp on what makes life life; "we do not have any formal definition of living that captures our folk psychological intuitions" (2001, 72). Moreover, as philosopher Daniel Dennett argues, we do not even have a commonly held understanding of what constitutes consciousness (cf. Dennett, 1991, 1996, 2005). We know when something is no longer alive or when it appears unconscious, but the essence of "life" and of "consciousness" continues to elude us. Both problems imply that any claims we make denying life or consciousness could be radically premature.

FROM TURING TO VOIGHT-KAMPFF
Testing the Essentials of Humanity

TYRELL

Is this to be an empathy test? Capillary
dilation of the so-called blush response?
Fluctuation of the pupil. Involuntary
dilation of the iris--

DECKARD

We call it Voight-Kampff for short.

Short of intervention by the venerable Blue Fairy, David will never be human. As for Data, the Borg Queen can cover his alloy exoskeleton with skin culled from any number of her drones, but the technological fact of that exoskeleton will remain. In time, machines like them may pass the Turing test with ease and may even tip the Turing balance, but they will still be machines. They may evolve into different lifeforms, perhaps, beings whose vital mysteries are electromechanical rather than electrochemical and manifest in servos and nanocircuitry instead of muscle fibers and neurotransmitters, but they will never be human lifeforms. What happens, though, when we trade robotics for bioengineering, when we are forced to upgrade Turing with Voight-Kampff? What happens when we create beings who are "More human than human," as the motto of the Tyrell Corporation in Ridley Scott's *Blade Runner* declares? If films like *I, Robot*, *Short Circuit*, and *A.I.* raise the possibility—and the hope—that consciousness, individuality, and the potential for relationship and self-determining reciprocity do not reside solely in humanity, *Blade Runner* poses profound questions about what it means to be human, how we know human when we see it, and how we respond when we do.

Though referred to in the film's opening scroll as robots and often in the commentarial literature as androids, the *Blade Runner* "replicants" are technically neither. They are manufactured humans, designed and created as a slave class to do off-planet work too dangerous, demeaning, or distasteful for their naturally bred cousins. Based loosely on Philip K. Dick's novel *Do Androids Dream of Electric Sheep* (1968), *Blade Runner* is seductively, deceptively simple: a small group of replicants, including an assassin and a combat specialist, have returned to Earth, killing several natural humans in the process. Replicants have been declared illegal on Earth, and special police units, Blade Runners, are assigned to find and "retire" them if they attempt to return. The implication, of course, is that because we so often come to fear what we create, it is easier simply to destroy it than to face the consequences of its creation. Former Blade Runner Rick Deckard (Harrison Ford) has been forced out of his own (non-lethal) retirement to deal with the latest threat. This generation of replicant, though, the Nexus 6, is so advanced, so close to the original in its genetic engineering, that a complicated procedure called the Voight-Kampff Empathy Test—which uses an intricate series of questions intended to reveal the presence of involuntary emotional and empathic responses linked to memory development—is required to identify them.

Obviously, research into cloning technology and genetic engineering raises a host of moral and ethical issues, many of which have underpinned various science fiction cinema and television projects. Michael Bay's *The Island* weighs the hope of creating rejection-proof organs grown for transplant from our own cells against the potential creation of entire, conscious human beings who must be killed in order to harvest those organs. In *Gattaca*, the possibility of eradicating disease and disability is played against the potential horrors of eugenics. In the backstory of the *Star Trek* universe, widespread genetic engineering at the end of the twentieth century led to the Eugenics Wars and the eventual criminalization of genetic enhancement with the rise of the United Federation of Planets. Since what we might call the desirability phenotype is one of the most unstable of social constructions, the potential for disaster in this area seems clear. As just one example, compare the *zaftig* women of Rubens and the hourglass figures of the 1940s and 1950s with the skeletal "beauty" of runway models that has, in recent years, led a number of jurisdictions to ban underweight models. Given the opportunity, would we genetically engineer for skinnier and skinnier fashion models, or for tiny feet (as was popular in China for hundreds of years), or for flattened foreheads and elongated skulls (as was practiced among the Maya)? Or would we introduce into the eugenics arena the almost pathological behavior of stage moms and sports dads: since she can't sing, we'll genetically enhance a daughter who can; since he could never play pro ball, we'll create for him a major-league pitcher from the genes up?

In *Blade Runner*, many of these questions are hidden since anyone with the means to leave Earth for the off-world colonies has apparently already done so, and the Los Angeles of 2019 is populated largely by those too poor or too genetically inferior to arrange passage. We are confronted with society in decay, corroded as if by the omnipresent acid rain that blankets virtually every exterior shot, gradually washing away the memory of the city even as it eats away at what remains of its landscape and architecture. At least six versions of the movie have been released to different markets, including two sneak peeks, the "Director's Cut" (1992), and what Ridley Scott vows in "the ultimate collector's edition" is the "Final Cut" (2007). Though aficionados point out (and argue over) the intricacies of version differentia, two principal fault lines divide the corpus. Early theatrical releases included a voice-over narration in which Deckard explains aspects of the plot through a series of interior monologues, a film noir device applauded by some but despised by others (Sammon, 1996, 291–99). Less important aesthetically, perhaps, but far more so conceptually, is the question of whether Deckard himself is a replicant. While the early releases left no doubt about his natural humanity, both later cuts (1992 and 2007) include brief scenes that introduce significant room for debate.

Before Deckard sets out to hunt down the four Nexus 6 replicants, he visits the Tyrell Corporation to learn what he can about them. Asked by Eldon Tyrell (Joe Turkel) to use the Voight-Kampff machine on a natural human before testing an advanced replicant, Deckard is introduced to Rachael (Sean Young) in a stunning film noir homage to the femme fatale. When the test concludes, Tyrell asks Rachael to step out.

DECKARD

She's a replicant, isn't she?

TYRELL

I'm impressed. How many questions does it usually take to spot them? . . . How many questions?

DECKARD

Twenty, thirty, cross-referenced.

TYRELL

It took more than a hundred for Rachael, didn't it?

DECKARD

She doesn't know.

TYRELL

She's beginning to suspect, I think.

DECKARD

Suspect? How can it not know what it is?

One of the most discussed films in science fiction cinema, *Blade Runner* has been approached from a variety of critical perspectives, including race and class (Desser, 1997; Redmond, 2005), fan culture (C. Gray, 2005; J. Gray, 2005), feminist theory (Barr, 1997; Jermyn, 2005), and the problem of the metropolitan dystopia (Carper, 1997; Rowley, 2005). As Sharon Gravett points out, though, "one significant element has been consistently overlooked—its religious subtext" (1998, 38). In the past decade this has been remedied slightly, though often in ways that I critique more fully in chapter 9, where I discuss briefly some of the religious commentary on the *Star Wars* series. That is, rather than using *Blade Runner* as an opportunity to question the boundaries of humanity and under what conditions we can (or should) transcend them, or viewing it as a way to interrogate our assumptions about the unseen order and how those assumptions shape and condition our behavior, many critics use it as a kind of archeological dig site, a cinematic landscape within which they claim to excavate all manner of biblical symbolism and theological meaning.

In her postmillennial interpretation, for example, Judith Kerman reads a variety of Jewish and Christian apocalyptic imagery into and out of the film (2005; cf. Kerman, 1997). To Kyle Keefer, "it seems clear" that *Blade Runner* "draws from the Genesis account" and "can be viewed as an interpretation of the Genesis story in which the focus turns from the character of God to the nature of humanity" (2005, par. 3). While the nature of humanity is clearly central to the film, it is important to note the two different things Keefer says here: that *Blade Runner* "draws" on the Genesis myth, which implies that Scott and his production team used the myth to underpin the story, and that it can be considered "an interpretation" of that story, which indicates how interpreters often map particular theological coordinates onto pop cultural landscapes. Rebecca Warner contends that "so continuous is the rain in *Blade Runner* that it suggests the Biblical deluge," and, switching from Hebrew Scriptures to Christian, "the nail through the palm [of replicant-soldier Roy Batty] is an obvious crucifixion symbol" (1997, 182).

Maybe, maybe, but so what?

This kind of theological mapping is displayed most problematically in literature scholar Sharon Gravett's discussion of the film. "The sacred story of the beginning of humanity and the founding of the nation of Israel," writes Gravett, "intersects in intriguing ways with the seemingly profane world of *Blade Runner*. Even more significantly, these narratives refuse a clear one-to-one correspondence with the film's narrative" (1998, 38). And herein lies the problem. For Gravett, the film is significant because there are biblical correspondences that have been overlooked in previous criticism, but she does not say why these are important. She simply assumes that they are. Moreover, according to Gravett, the correspondences are even more significant when they do not, well, correspond. She has established an interpretive framework that cannot be invalidated: if it fits, it is significant; if it does not, it is even more significant. "Since the Earth appears to be as far removed from Eden as possible," she continues, "such a conclusion demonstrates how fraught with difficulties the process of determining Biblical parallels is in *Blade Runner*" (Gravett, 1998, 39). Exactly, but this only begs the question *why* one would attempt such parallels in the first place, *why* it seems so necessary to overlay theological concepts onto pop cultural products or excavate those products from them. In one establishing scene, for example, as the camera tracks through the rain, Gravett notes that "it moves by one of the principal symbols of the Fall—a serpent (a neon dragon with a flashing red tongue)" (1998, 39). What she does not note, however, is that much of the Los Angeles Ridley Scott has created is distinctly Asian, a culture in which the dragon is often a symbol of good luck, and that the dragon in question adorns a noodle shop at which Deckard waits to eat. That is, there is no credible reason to read the Edenic serpent into the scene at all. Indeed, though Gravett continues to insist that reading biblical parallels into the text is an important critical activity, at no point in her argument does she explain why this is so.

"If life on Earth does not seem a paradise," she continues, "neither do the replicants totally fit the image of fallen humanity" (1998, 39). *Blade Runner*'s chief obstacle to criticism, Gravett contends, is its constant "refusal to authorize one particular reading" (1998, 39). Despite this, she goes on to read Roy Batty (Rutger Hauer) as Esau battling Deckard (as Jacob) for the birthright of his humanity. While these "parallels work well," she argues, "the reverse correlation also produces some interesting insights"—Batty as Jacob and Deckard as Esau—and she assures us that "exploring these Biblical stories contributes greatly to a fuller understanding of *Blade Runner*" (Gravett, 1998, 41). At no point, though, does she indicate what these insights are nor what this "fuller understanding" discloses. Reinforcing the tautological framework of her analysis, she reiterates that Scott's film "offers no easy, one-to-one correspondences. Roy Batty can be equated with Adam, Christ, Satan, Jacob, and Esau, and so can Deckard. Or, each character can also be the opposite of these associations" (Gravett, 1998, 42). Because she is deploying the theological coordinates of the dominant religious tradition, Gravett simply assumes both their narrative importance and the legitimacy of her *cum hoc* interpretive ambiguity. The major problem with analyses like these is that they produce maps without meaning, interpretations devoid of insight. That we can overlay all manner of theological detailia onto any number of films—that believers can, as it were, baptize these products in the name of the Father, the Son, and the Holy Spirit—in no way indicates why they should or how those layerings deepen our understanding of the film.

I have drawn out this example at some length because it illustrates one of the pervasive problems with—and one of the most
significant lacunae within—the critical analysis of religion and film:
the incipient introduction of a normative theology under the guise
of criticism paired with the refusal to indicate why such readings
are either valuable or warranted. Indeed, in view of the much larger
questions of responsibility and humanity—Deckard's, Rachael's,
that of the other Nexus 6 replicants, or of the faceless millions that
constitute the background population of the *Blade Runner* universe—
the ability to map one or another biblical story onto the *Blade Runner* narrative seems trivial by comparison. This is not to suggest that
many of these interpretations are not legitimate or that they are not
valid in some superficial way, but they tell us nothing about the central concern that so clearly animates the narrative: what it means to
be a human being.

Blade Runner suggests very strongly that, apart from biology, the
principal constituent of humanity is our recollection of humanity,
our memory of being human and our inability to remember being
anything else. Calling the replicants robots or androids, for example,
is a rather unsubtle racism, because, for all biological intents and
purposes, they are human. The question is: are they human *beings*? To
ensure that they do not develop the patterns of memory that might
lead to an autonomous teleology, a hope that they might transcend
their creation as slave labor, the Nexus 6 replicants were engineered
with two distinctions: a four-year lifespan intended as a failsafe mechanism against self-determinacy, and a personal backstory intended
to explain their origins and forestall any importunate genealogical
investigations.

TYRELL

```
We began to recognize in them a strange
obsession. After all, they are emotionally
inexperienced, with only a few years in which
to store up the experiences which you and
I take for granted. If we gift them with a
past, we create a cushion or a pillow for
their emotions, and, consequently, we can
control them better.
```

DECKARD

Memories. You're talking about memories.

Memory lies at the heart of *Blade Runner*, the kind of memory that Alison Landsberg so succinctly calls "prosthetic memory," that is, "memories which do not come from a person's lived experience in any strict sense" (2004, 239). In the Nexus 6 replicants, these are memories implanted as a means of social control, unlike in Paul Verhoeven's *Total Recall*, where memory implants normally function as an alternative form of recreation. As Landsberg points out, and significant social psychological research supports, "the experience of memory actually becomes the index of experience: if we have the memory, we must have had the experience it represents" (2004, 239). And if we haven't, if the memories are prosthetic rather than natural, what does that mean? The question of personal identity has intrigued philosophers for centuries, psychologists, social psychologists, and cognitive scientists for slightly less, but the issue remains unresolved. Descartes may have proposed *cogito ergo sum* as the foundation of Western philosophy, but how does *what* we think constitute *who* we are? I am able to drive to work because of memory: I know where I am going and how to get there. I am able to teach my classes because of memory: the store of knowledge from a decade of academic work allows me to plan ahead for the educational needs of my students. I am able to write this book not because I live in the presence of cognition but because I stand on the shoulders of memory, both natural (mine) and prosthetic (others'). I am a sociologist interested in the relationships between religion and film because my memories inform my present and order my future toward that role. What would happen, though, if some mind transfer device or the memory implantation technology so popular in science fiction could selectively affect my mind and brain, rewiring every synaptic connection that experience has created and memory reinforced, removing every thought related to my life as an academic and replacing them with something else? Could I become an artist, perhaps, a photographer or a farmer? It is no insignificant question to ask, then, "Who would I be?" Who would any of us be under similar circumstances?

Numerous science fiction films and television series have made use of the implanted memory trope. In the *Stargate SG-1* episode

"Past and Present," a virus has artificially rejuvenated a planet's entire population, leaving them with no memory of their former selves. The virus was created originally as a bioweapon by Ke'ra (Megan Leitch), a woman known as the "Destroyer of Worlds," but she, too, has lost all memory of her former self. Rather than remaining a genocidal sociopath, however, she now shines in her roles as a medical doctor and leader of her people. When the SG-I team discovers a way to reverse the effects of the virus, Ke'ra chooses not to take the cure, not to reacquire the memories of her former self, but to live in this new and better way. The creation of new memories has allowed her to transcend the self her old memories continually created. Even more trenchant in this regard is "Hard Time," an episode of *Star Trek: Deep Space Nine*. Convicted of espionage on the planet Argratha, Miles O'Brien (Colm Meaney) is sentenced to twenty years in prison. Rather than imprison convicts, however, the Argrathi implant the memories of those years, then release the prisoner. As far as O'Brien is concerned, he lived those twenty years; they inform who he is now, as a husband, a father, and a Starfleet engineer, and who he will be for as long as he lives.

How much of who we are is a function of what we remember? If being human is not merely a function of biology and biogenesis, in what else, then, does it consist? As *Blade Runner* so elegantly proposes: memory. Contrary to popular belief, however, memory is not about the past; it is constitutive of the present and generative of the future. If we are biologically human and we have memories of being human, how can we be anything but?

TRANSCENDING THE MEAT-BOT
Leaving the Body Behind

INVISIGOTH

Upload.

With the possible exception of *A.I.*'s David, whose search for humanity is anchored to his love for the mother on whom he imprinted, two constants bind together the different lifeforms I have considered in this chapter: fear of death, and hope in the face of the great transcendence. HAL's pleas as Bowman disconnects its higher functions clearly implies a hope for continued operation. In both *I, Robot* and *Short Circuit*, the evolving self-awareness in Sonny and Number 5 turn on the question of mortality and the prospect of being decommissioned or disassembled. From his creators at the Tyrell Corporation, Roy Batty wants to know about "Morphology? Longevity? Incept dates?" and, most importantly, as he demands from Dr. Tyrell, "the god of biomechanics," "I want more life, fucker!" Each in his own way displays keen awareness of a world in which he is not, something that has animated humanity's quest for transcendence for millennia. From drinking at the fountain of youth to eating from the Tree of Life, from everlasting salvation in heaven to an eternal progression of spirit, as much as anything else death has driven our dreams of the future. Religious visions aside, though, what if we could dispense with the supernatural, imagining instead a world in which we need never not-be, but which we create for ourselves? Though our bodies eventually break down, biochemical systems fail, and age chases beauty as the flesh gradually and inevitably decays, what if we could transcend the meat-bot? This is the hope held out by a growing number of scientists and philosophers consumed by the prospects of transhumanism and posthumanism.

In *The X-Files* episode "Kill Switch," three brilliant computer engineers have created a sentient artificial intelligence, "a program with its own consciousness," which, in order to protect itself, has started eliminating the only ones capable of stopping its evolution—its creators. As Invisigoth (Kristin Lehman) explains to FBI agents Scully (Gillian Anderson) and Mulder (David Duchovny), "it's not a program anymore, it's wildlife, loose on the Net." Hunting for the AI's hardware headquarters, its "home node," Invisigoth reveals the episode's posthuman B story: the wholesale transfer of personality to a computer.

INVISIGOTH

Uploading. The transfer of memory, of consciousness to the distributed system maintained by the AI. Imagine being mingled so completely with another that you no longer need your physical self. You're one.

SCULLY

So you were going to--

INVISIGOTH

Enter the AI. Give up our inefficient bodies
so that our consciousness could live together
forever.

If transhumanism is represented by the physical and mental augmentation of characters such as *The Six Million Dollar Man* and *Johnny Mnemonic*, and the transhumanist dystopia by the Borg, post-humanism's hope resides in leaving the body behind and living forever as a virtual construct in a vast computer environment. Lest this seem like only science fiction, consider what a number of leading researchers in the field have to say. AI pioneer Marvin Minsky, for example, considers the physical body incidental to the larger human plot. What really constitutes the "human" are patterns of information—memories, emotions, learned cognitive processes—that can be stored, simulated, and replicated in a computer environment (1986). Sociologist William Sims Bainbridge concurs, suggesting that "cyberimmortality would require redefining human personalities as dynamic patterns of information, and human life as a process of evolution from material to computational planes of existence" (2006, 25). Indeed, looking forward to that, Bainbridge has begun investigating the development of "Massive Questionnaires for Personality Capture," arguably a first step toward the kind of cyberimmortality he predicts (2003a). Roboticist Hans Moravec, for years the director of Carnegie Mellon's Robotics Institute, imagines a future in which "beings will cease to be defined by their physical geographic boundaries, but will establish, extend, and defend identities as patterns of information flow in the cyberspace. The old bodies of individual Exes [exhumans], refined into matrices for cyberspace, will interconnect, and the minds of Exes, as pure software, will migrate among them at will" (1999, 164–65; cf. Moravec, 1988). While, predictably, challenges to the transhuman/posthuman vision of uploading range from the technological ("It can't be done") to the ethical ("It shouldn't be done") to the religious ("God doesn't want us to do it"), Nick Bostrom argues for a variety of potential advantages uploading offers. "Uploads would not be subject to biological senescence," and if something did happen, "back-up copies of uploads could be created regularly so that you could be re-booted" (Bostrom, 2003c). Without the need for food or shelter, uploaders "could potentially live much more economically," more easily implement "radical cognitive enhancements," and "travel at the speed of light as an information pattern" (Bostrom, 2003c). Futurist and inventor Ray Kurzweil estimates that the kind of computing power required to realize this form of transcendence—10^{19} calculations per second and 10^{18} bits of memory—will be available within the next three decades (2005, 199). To put that in perspective, the MacBook on which I have just written this sentence runs at about 10^9 calculations per second and has 10^9 bits of memory. As Kurzweil notes, however, the shift to a computer environment won't be the instant upload of "Kill Switch" or films like *Lawnmower Man*, but a more gradual process, one in which we may very well not notice a difference once the process is sufficiently advanced (2005, 200).

The quest for posthuman transcendence, whether through genetic engineering, computer enhancement of one's cognitive abilities, or a complete personality upload, is not without its critics, both secular and religious. Where the former challenge the ability of science to realize the dreams of posthumanism, the latter contest our right even to try. Philosopher Patrick Hopkins points out that, although many posthumanists would disagree that their beliefs constitute anything like a religion, there are significant analogies between the two (2005; cf. Amarasingam, 2008). Like Bainbridge (2003b; 2005), Hopkins expects significant resistance to technological posthumanism from established religions, the social organizations that arguably have the most to lose if humanity can take control over its own quest for transcendence. In *The Singularity Is Near*, Kurzweil lists (and responds to) nearly sixty pages of different objections to his vision of the posthuman future, ranging from Malthusian arguments against continued exponential population growth to problems associated with government intervention that will restrict or retard the development of posthuman technologies (2005, 427–83). All of these criticisms he meets with an almost evangelical zeal, absolutely certain that the day will come when his vision of the future will be vindicated and the world as we know it now will disappear before the dawning of a posthuman millennium.

3

FIRST CONTACT
Human Exceptionalism in the Calculus of Transcendence

OUTTAKE: *CONTACT* REDUX

GERALDO RIVERA

Attendance at religious services has risen a
dramatic 39 percent in recent days.

NATALIE ALLEN

Health officials from around the world are
concerned that the message from Vega might
trigger a rash of mass suicides not unlike
the recent cult deaths near San Diego.

ROBERT NOVAK

Even a scientist has to admit that there are
some pretty serious religious overtones to
all this.

Filmmakers can convey ranges of emotion and behavior, backstory, and narrative development in a number of ways—the montage, the flashback, and the dream sequence, to name but a few. In *Contact*, in addition to the motley of CNN commentators noted above (CNN is a corporate sibling of Warner Brothers, which produced the film), director Robert Zemeckis chose the carnival—a combination midway, block party, and UFO convention.

Shortly after the radio signal from the Vega star system has been made public and translation of the message has begun, a helicopter shot moves across the normally barren landscape leading to the Very Large Array (VLA) on the Plains of San Agustin near Socorro, New Mexico. In this shot, though, rather than empty desert split by two-lane blacktop, we see the road flanked by hundreds of campers, tents, RVs, and various groups of people milling about to the accompaniment of Sheb Wooley's "Purple People Eater," Believable Picnic's "Spaceman," and a new age choir singing "Hail to Vega" (to the music of Handel's "Hallelujah Chorus," no less). As she drives toward the VLA, Ellie Arroway stares at the crowds in wonder (and, we imagine, not a little horror). Dressed in silver lamé and tinfoil, for example, each wearing a set of headphones and holding a small satellite dish, several men and women lift their heads to the sky, their arms outstretched in expectation and welcome. Next to them, another group sells UFO abduction insurance out of a gleaming white Winnebago, while down the road First Nations people dance, drum, and sing in a cloud of smudge. Interested more in internal combustion than outer space, perhaps, members of the National Vega Car Club gather around to compare their rides, and behind them hot air balloons announce "Vega or Bust" and, cattily, "This Way to Oz." As Norman Greenbaum's "Spirit in the Sky" takes over, the shot tracks past a giant cutout of Christ. "Jesus is an Alien," it reads, and the Son of God is crowned with a flying saucer halo. Lastly, Ellie watches as a hellfire-and-brimstone evangelist named Joseph (Jake Busey) preaches from a mini revival tent. Looking directly at her as he speaks, his message is anything but hopeful.

JOSEPH

But they have failed! It's the same people
who, again and again, have brought us to the
brink of destruction. Who've polluted our
air, who've poisoned our water! Now these
scientists have had their chance. Are these
the kind of people that you want talking to
your God for you?

According to Zemeckis and producer Steve Starkey, when the casting call for extras to fill in this scene asked for UFO enthusiasts, hundreds of local people responded, many of whom showed up at the location with their own set dressing and costuming. In her commentary on the scene, Jodie Foster remarked, "I guess somebody had said to them, you know, 'Bring your weirdest outfit and be the weirdest person that you can be.'" Her opinion of the extras aside, the film's vision of the carnival leading to the VLA offers a glimpse through the kaleidoscope of cultural response to the prospect of extraterrestrial life and the possibility of contact. Some believe this contact has already been made and either embrace or fear it, while others look to the skies expecting the arrival of extraterrestrials any day (see Achenbach, 1999; Brown, 2007; Denzler, 2001).

Not unlike the men and women with the silver suits and handheld satellite dishes, so fervently opening themselves up to the possibility of extraterrestrial visitation, numerous UFO groups have emerged in the half-century since the sighting of nine strange "flying saucers" by private pilot Kenneth Arnold (June 24, 1947) and the alleged crash of an alien craft on a ranch near Roswell, New Mexico, less than two hundred miles east of Socorro (July 2, 1947). These two events mark the beginning of late-modern interest in unidentified flying objects. Some of the UFO groups are religious in nature; others resemble religions in the depth of their beliefs and the zeal with which members pursue them.

In early 1954, less than a decade after these two seminal episodes, a middle-aged homemaker named Marian Keech, who was interested in a number of alternative spiritual and therapeutic pursuits, including Theosophy, the I AM movement, and Scientology, allegedly began receiving messages from an extraterrestrial intelligence known as "the Guardians." Warning of a global catastrophe slated to begin on the winter solstice that year, Keech was assured by "Space Brother Sananda" (i.e., Jesus) that she and those who heeded her warning would be saved in a kind of technological rapture (Festinger, Riecken, and Schachter, 1956, 33–57; Vallee, 1975, 60–65). That same year Ernest L. Norman (1904–1971) and his wife, Ruth (1900–1993), opened the Unarius Academy of Science and began teaching an amalgam of beliefs and practices, including: reincarnation and past-life therapy (Ruth, for example, believed she lived as Atahualpa, the last leader of the Inca empire, while another student, as Unarians pre-fer to be called, revealed he had been the Japanese admiral Yama-moto, the architect of the attack on Pearl Harbor); channeling and mediumship (Unarius publications regularly include messages from such luminaries as Herodotus and Albert Einstein, who now teaches interdimensional physics on the planet Eros [Norman, 1997]); the prospect of imminent visitation by extraterrestrials; and a confed-eration of extrasolar planets into which Earth will be invited as the thirty-third and final member. In 2001, one of the group's advertis-ing flyers claimed that "an Interstellar Spaceship, carrying 1,000 scientists from the Planet Myton in the Star Cluster of the Pleia-des, will arrive on Earth, landing on the raised portion of Atlantis in the Caribbean Sea." For $25.00, Unarians were invited to purchase a "Starship Emblem Pin," wearing it proudly to "signal your Green Light of Welcome to the Space Brothers!" (Unarius Academy of Sci-ence, 2001; cf. Saliba, 2003; Tumminia, 2005).

Followers of the Raelian religion, on the other hand, believe that human beings are the product of extraterrestrial genetic engineer-ing and that our creators, the Elohim, will return in the near future, bringing with them "all the great prophets of the past, including Moses, Elijah, the Buddha, Jesus Christ and Mohammed" (Raël, 1998, 200). Rather than the Caribbean, though, the Raelians are preparing to welcome their "fathers from space" at an embassy to be built near Jerusalem, "where the Elohim created the first human beings" (Raël, 1998, 198). According to the founder, Raël (born Claude Vorilhon in 1946), who claims to have been contacted by extraterrestrials since the early 1970s and designated the final prophet to the people of Earth, this embassy will constitute Judaism's third temple. While the group has made several overtures to purchase land for the embassy, "so far there has been no positive response from Israel" (Raël, 1998, 198; cf. Chryssides, 2003; Palmer, 2004; Raël, 1986; Rothstein, 2003).

For Chen Tao, a Taiwanese-based UFO group also known as The True Way and God's Salvation Church, the end of the world as we know it was scheduled for March 31, 1998, and would take place in the small town of Garland, Texas, about twenty miles northeast of Dallas. Specifically, God would appear at 10:00 a.m. on that day at 3513 Ridgedale Drive, the home rented by the group (Hon-ming, 1997, 176–78; cf. Cook, 2003; Prather, 1999). Guaranteeing the veracity of the prophecy with his life, leader Hon-ming Chen's claims raised considerable concern, coming as they did just a year after the ritual suicide of thirty-nine members of Heaven's Gate, the best known of the late twentieth-century UFO groups (Balch, 1995; Balch and Taylor, 1977; Cowan and Bromley, 2008; Wessinger, 2000a; Zeller, 2006).

While small religious groups organized around belief in extraterrestrials are largely dismissed as socially marginal, their members considered delusional at best and at worst dangerously psychotic, numerous others could be included in this list: the Aetherius Society (Scribner and Wheeler, 2003), Ashtar Command (Helland, 2003), the Ground Crew (Palmer and Helland, 2003), and the United Nuwaubian Nation of Moors (Gabriel, 2003). But when considered in the context of many other religious beliefs—from the creation myths of First Nations peoples to the creation science of fundamentalist Christianity, from belief in vast pantheons of supernatural beings to the conviction that God became human in one spot at one time— we have to wonder how odd UFO believers really are. How much less plausible are their beliefs than those of any other religion? Their lack of social dominance notwithstanding, and despite the ridicule with which they are so often greeted—a reaction mirrored in Ellie Arroway's face as she rides toward the VLA—for these people, the limitations that keep so many millions of others earthbound have already been transcended. For them, hope is realized in first contact and, in many ways, the aliens have already arrived. What they share in common is belief in the reality of extraterrestrial intelligence, the inevitability of contact, and the overwhelmingly positive nature of the relationship between us and them.

Others are not so sure.

In *Contact*, Richard Rank (Rob Lowe) is the telegenic leader of the Conservative Coalition—a thinly veiled reference to Ralph Reed, executive director of the Christian Coalition founded in 1987 by televangelist Pat Robertson as an advocacy group designed to mainstream fundamentalist Christian values in the American political process (Diamond, 1990; Watson, 1997). Like the other talking heads deployed to convey the range of response to the message from Vega, Rank represents a small, though not insignificant sample of the population: those conservative evangelicals who interpret any new social or cultural phenomenon in terms of its effect on their understanding of "biblical morality" and their certainty of human exceptionalism in God's universe. Later in the film, as the various stakeholders wrestle with whether or not The Machine should be built once the message has been decoded, Rank stakes out the conservative Christian position:

```
RANK

My problem is this: The content of that
message is morally ambiguous at best . . .
We know nothing of these creatures' values.
The fact of the matter is we don't even know
whether they believe in God.
```

The basic problem with *Contact*, writes Christian missiologist Bryan Stone, is that it "offers no clear and compelling vision of religious faith" and ends up reducing what faith it does portray "to a caricature" (1998, par. 1). Trying to comfort Ellie after her father's death, for example, a minister tells the young girl that we often don't know why something happens, that "sometimes we just have to accept it as God's will." "Left with a helpless, confused stare on his face," Stone opines, the cleric is "sincere but intellectually helpless" (1998, par. 9). The character of Richard Rank he considers a parody of Ralph Reed, one "made all the more amusing by the casting of Rob Lowe (not exactly the epitome of righteousness)" (Stone, 1998, par. 10). Finally, there is Joseph, "the fanatic cult member with a crucifix draped around his neck" (Stone, 1998, par. 10). All of these, with stunning inaccuracy, Stone lumps together as "the standard filmic conventions for portraying religious faith—a mixture of fanaticism and irrationality" (1998, par. 10). That is, he regards them as caricature rather than characterization.

But are they? Could both Sagan and Zemeckis be trying to offer something profoundly different than simple parody, something much more pointed about the narrowness of our horizons and the depth of our prejudice? Put bluntly, these are not caricatures; by suggesting that they are, Stone misses the mark entirely. Three things are important to note: representation, authenticity, and vision.

First, there is the issue of representation. Ellie, for example, Stone paints as "an atheist because she doesn't find any evidence for the existence of God" (1998, par. 4). As we noted in chapter 1, however, this is not what happens in the film. Ellie never declares herself either way. Responding to Joss' question before the Machine Consortium selection committee, she reiterates: "As a scientist, I rely on empirical evidence, and in this matter I don't believe there's data either way." At best she is an agnostic, though Stone admits that "because the film develops her character so well, even the most devout theists will find themselves liking her" (1998, par. 4).

In the face of profound grief we are very often at a loss for words, and anyone who has been to many funerals will recognize immediately the minister's platitude: God's will is inscrutable and we have to accept it. Indeed, this is hardly the most objectionable cliché offered at funeral and memorial services. Stone's *ad hominem* about Rob Lowe's personal life, proffered as though this is sufficient commentary on the role itself, avoids the reality that those behind the Christian Coalition regularly raise precisely the same issues as Rank and often in far more distasteful ways. Notwithstanding the sexual antics of such well-known televangelists as Jim Bakker and Jimmy Swaggart, consider Jerry Falwell's remarks when he joined Pat Robertson on *The 700 Club* just two days after the September 11, 2001, attacks. "I really believe," said the founder of the Moral Majority, "that the pagans, and the abortionists, and the feminists, and the gays and the lesbians who are actively trying to make that an alternative lifestyle, the ACLU, People for the American Way . . . I point my finger in their face and say, 'You helped this happen.'" "I totally concur," Robertson replied, nodding his head (Robertson, 2001). Comments like this from nationally recognized Christian leaders make anything Richard Rank says in *Contact* pale by comparison. And then there is Joseph, a zealot, a fanatic, a man so passionately committed to the correctness of his beliefs that he is willing both to kill and to die in their defense. For Stone to suggest that this is somehow a caricature of religious faith requires that he willfully ignore great tracts of religious history—not insignificantly, Christian history.

Second, there is the question of authenticity. Stone argues that *Contact* ultimately fails because none of its characters represent "authentic religious faith," something that he contends "is notoriously difficult to depict accurately on screen" (1998, par. 9), though he is perfectly willing to deny the authenticity of what faith the film does depict. Given that Stone is the E. Stanley Jones Professor of Evangelism at Boston University School of Theology, his position is relatively easy to understand, but when it comes to the vast panoply of religious belief and practice one encounters around the world, it also highlights the arrogance of an exclusivist theology that claims the privilege of determining what is "authentic" and what is not. What makes any of the beliefs portrayed in the film any less authentic than another? Are the saucer folk any less genuine because they believe we were created by extraterrestrials, not God? Or because their version of the Rapture is technological and not supernatural? Perhaps by "authentic" Stone means "plausible" or "realistic," implying that their beliefs are irrational compared to his evangelical Christianity. If so, the same critiques obviously apply.

Third, and most important, there is the problem of vision. Lamenting the underdevelopment of the Palmer Joss character, who in Sagan's novel is an evangelical foil for Arroway's scientific rationalism, Stone concludes that "throughout the movie the 'faith' that collides with and sometimes colludes with science remains abstract, meaningless, and void" (1998, par. 7). By focusing on what he considers the caricature of religious faith, though it is a caricature completely colored by his own theological position, Stone falls into precisely the problem identified by Carl Sagan: his God is too small. By minimizing the larger issue raised by the film—"twenty-six light years and all we get is a cure for interplanetary angst!" (1998, par. 5)—Stone also misses what would arguably be one of the most important realizations in human history: we are not alone.

ARE WE ALONE?
HUMAN EXCEPTIONALISM IN THE CALCULUS OF TRANSCENDENCE

ELLIE

You know, there are four hundred billion
stars out there, just in our galaxy alone.
If only one out of a million of those had
planets, all right? And if just one out of a
million of those had life, and if just one
out of a million of those had intelligent

```
life, there would be literally millions of
civilizations out there.

        PALMER

Well, if there wasn't [sic], it would be an
awful waste of space.
```

Humankind has speculated on the possibility of extraterrestrial life for millennia (see Crowe, 1986; Dick, 1982). Among the Greeks, both Democritus (ca. 460–370 BCE) and Epicurus (341–271 BCE) argued for its existence, while Plato (ca. 428–348 BCE) and his student Aristotle (384–322 BCE) denied the prospect. Heavily influenced by Aristotelian philosophy, for centuries Christian theologians rejected the idea of life on other planets, convinced that God's creative grace extended only to the "carbon-based bipeds" (Arthur C. Clarke) living on the "pale blue dot" (Carl Sagan). Though historian Michael Crowe argues that Italian philosopher Giordano Bruno's (1548–1600) fate was ultimately sealed by his theological rejection of Christ's divinity, it is also clear that one of the reasons he was brought before the Inquisition at the end of the sixteenth century was his advocacy of plural worlds and extraterrestrial intelligence (1997, 150–51). Whether we are unique in the universe or as unremarkable as a single grain of sand has far-reaching implications for our place in the calculus of transcendence. The suggestion that there might be others out there besides us necessarily challenges the human exceptionalism on which many schools of Christian theology are based.

Although vast in its implications, at its most basic level the issue is simple and straightforward: either there is intelligent life elsewhere in the universe, or there is not. Either we are alone or we aren't—and the import of each is staggering. Beyond that, however, things get considerably more complex, and we find ourselves caught on the horns of a dilemma framed on the one hand by Fermi's Paradox and on the other by the Drake Equation.

In the early 1950s, the Italian physicist Enrico Fermi (1901–1954) visited New Mexico's Los Alamos National Laboratory, the birthplace of the atomic bomb. Walking to

Fermi's Paradox (1950)

"Where is everybody?"

lunch one day with Emil Konopinski, Herbert York, and Edward Teller (colloquially known as the fathers of the hydrogen bomb), conversation turned to the possibility of faster-than-light travel and the prospect of contact with extraterrestrial intelligence it implies. In the midst of a discussion prompted by recent media reports of flying saucers over Washington, D.C., Fermi interjected suddenly, "Where is everybody?" That is, if everyone is seeing saucers, where are all the alleged aliens? Although the scientists involved each remember it slightly differently, Fermi's remark is firmly established in SETI lore (Jones, 1985; Wesson, 1990) and frames the problem of extraterrestrial contact with an elegant simplicity. If there are other intelligences out there and they are capable of interstellar travel sufficient to reach Earth, why have we not seen more of them? Maybe they're not out there after all. Or perhaps they have no interest in a small, backwater world on the rural edge of the galaxy. In this case, the argument runs, they might as well not be out there since we'll never know and, never knowing, will continue to "strut and fret our hour upon the stage" as though we're alone in the cosmic theater.

The Drake Equation (1961)

$$N = R^* \cdot f_p \cdot n_e \cdot f_l \cdot f_i \cdot f_c \cdot L$$

A decade later, however, physicist Frank Drake, a SETI pioneer and close colleague of Carl Sagan, convened the first scientific conference on the search for extraterrestrial intelligence and presented what has become known as the Drake Equation, a formula many researchers use to estimate the potential number of extraterrestrial civilizations in the galaxy. This possibility is expressed as a fraction of, among other considerations, the number of stars with planets (f_p), the number of planets on which intelligent life develops (f_i), and the number of civilizations that advance enough technologically to send signals into space (f_c). Although Jill Tarter, the SETI scientist on whom Sagan modeled Ellie Arroway's character, rarely employs the Drake Equation, suggesting instead that "an equation is nothing more than a lovely way to organize our ignorance" (2000, 34), Ellie's use of it to explain the potential for extraterrestrial life is obviously intended as much for us as for Palmer Joss. Fermi's Paradox notwithstanding, Sagan wants us to know what he thinks the odds are. We may never meet them, but if there's no one out there but us, it's an incredible waste of space.

Although each comes with a variety of internal divisions, dissensions, and disagreements, four basic positions frame the debate on extraterrestrial intelligence: first, we are alone in the universe, and whether created or evolved we stand unique among the numberless stars; second, we are not alone, though the distances involved in interstellar travel and the relatively unremarkable position of our planet mean that we will never meet any of those with whom we share the vastness of space; third, we are not alone, and meeting other intelligences in the universe is only a matter of time; and finally, we are not alone, and we have met them already—for better or worse. Forming up on either side of the issue of human exceptionalism, each proposes a different answer to the question of transcendence and offers different perspectives on the hope embedded in that answer.

As a rough barometer of belief in human exceptionalism, few events function better than the possibility of first contact. Tarter, for example, argues that "organized religion is one of our greatest threats to survival" and that "extreme longevity is totally inconsistent with organized religion as we know it" (2000, 35). For her, if we are to survive long enough to reach the stars or interest those who might contact us, but are unable to relinquish our millennia-old need for religious belief, the only solution "is the development of a universal religion with no deviations, no differentiations—absolutely global and compelling for all. Such a religion might be able to coexist for a long time with technological development without precipitating the worst of human tendencies" (Tarter, 2000, 35). Precisely what Tarter regards as humanity's sole hope, however, millions of Christians see as the religious portal to the end of days, an integral part of what they believe is Satan's war with God.

In 1994, three years before *Contact* was released, researcher Victoria Alexander mailed surveys to one thousand religious leaders in the United States—Protestant, Roman Catholic, and Jewish. Called the "Religious Crisis Survey" and subtitled "The Impact of UFOs and Their Occupants on Religion," the survey asked how clergy felt about the question of extraterrestrial life, the pursuit of SETI programs, and how their views differed (if they did) from those of their congregations (1994). Her sampling method and response rate preclude any claim to representative results—though Alexander feels they are statistically significant—but those who did respond provided important impressionistic data about American mainline religion and the question of extraterrestrial contact.

Not surprisingly, some were unimpressed. "I think the whole thing is absolutely ridiculous," wrote a Roman Catholic priest from Florida, while one of his colleagues opined, "Your survey is a waste of money that could be given to the poor and homeless here on this planet." "This whole questionnaire is based on a hypothesis and therefore not of interest to me," responded another priest, despite the reality that theology is arguably the most hypothetical of human intellectual pursuits. A fourth declined to answer because "there is considerable disparity between my opinions and those of my congregation who are largely very biased and generally uneducated" (Alexander, 1994). Other clerics found no discrepancy between their Christian faith and the possibility of alien contact. "Discovery of an advanced extraterrestrial civilization is not precluded by anything in the Bible," wrote a pastor from Alabama. "Should there be extraterrestrial life," offered the minister of a mid-sized congregation in Illinois, "then it would have also to have been [sic] created by God." "If we believe that God created the universe," responded a New York priest, "any life outside this planet is somehow connected to Him" (Alexander, 1994; cf. Bonting, 2003; Davies, 2003; Kracher, 2006; O'Meara, 1999; Peters, n.d.; Spradley, 1998).

Still others, however, were just as certain that there are no extraterrestrials waiting to pay a friendly visit. "It is my belief," wrote the pastor of a small congregation in Alabama, "that UFO sightings are spiritual apparitions emanating from demonic activity in these last days before the second coming of our Lord Jesus Christ." A West Virginia pastor concurred, declining to answer "any of the above questions that would add to the trick of Satan that I personally believe that he will unleash upon the world in a future date [sic]" (Alexander, 1994). Finally, some respondents thought the issue irrelevant. Indeed, one Iowa priest with a congregation of over a thousand families reported, "We sincerely doubt anyone is discussing this" (Alexander, 1994).

Clearly, though, many people are discussing it. A 1996 Gallup report indicates that in the United States, just over 50 percent of men and 40 percent of women surveyed believe that Earth has been visited by extraterrestrials at some time in the past (Lyons, 2005). Both reflecting and contributing to these beliefs, science fiction cinema and television have been exploring first contact scenarios for decades.

FIRST CONTACT AND THE RANGE OF RELIGIOUS RESPONSE

However it comes, though, the world as we know it will end the day we make first contact. Whether it is intentional or accidental, whether we find them or they find us, whether they come in the form of an adorable *E. T.*, the kaleidoscopic wonder of *Close Encounters of the Third Kind*, a sophisticated mathematical *Contact* from a near galactic neighbor, or a terrifying alien apocalypse that precipitates either *The War of the Worlds* or an *Invasion of the Body Snatchers*, our first encounter with an extraterrestrial intelligence will be the end of the world as we know it, for the day after first contact could never be quite the same as the day just before. Although there are hybrids among them, for nearly a century now science fiction cinema and television have offered us three broad categories of alien contact: the threat of apocalypse, the promise of millennium, and the ambivalence of something in between.

The first two choices are most starkly contrasted in *Star Trek: First Contact*. There, humanity is faced with apocalypse—assimilation into the Borg collective if the flight of the *Phoenix* fails—or millennium, a new age of interstellar exploration when a passing Vulcan spacecraft detects the *Phoenix*'s nascent warp signature. As I noted in chapter 1, though Catherine Wessinger is careful to point out that millennialism represents a continuum of belief and practice, not a discrete point in conceptual space, broadly put it "is an expression of the human hope for the achievement of permanent well-being, in other words, salvation" (2000b, 6). As Picard and Data battle the Borg Queen aboard the *Enterprise*, Commander Riker (Jonathan Frakes), Lieutenant Commander La Forge (LeVar Burton), and

Counselor Troi (Marina Sirtis) describe this hope in glowing terms, trying to convince Zefram Cochrane (James Cromwell), the *Phoenix*'s builder, to make his historic flight. If he doesn't, first contact as the *Enterprise* crew know it will not occur and the Borg will succeed in assimilating Earth.

RIKER

It is a pivotal moment in human history, Doctor. You get to make contact with an alien race. And after you do, everything begins to change.

LA FORGE

Your theories on warp drive allow fleets of starships to be built and mankind to start exploring the galaxy.

TROI

It unites humanity in a way no one ever thought possible, when they realized they're not alone in the universe. Poverty, disease, war--all will be gone within the next fifty years.

Though each of the *Star Trek* television series and all of the feature films reflect in some way the optimism and humanistic vision of creator Gene Roddenberry (1921–1991; cf. Porter and McLaren, 1999; Wagner and Lundeen, 1998), science fiction as a genre has far more often offered us apocalypse than millennium. As I point out elsewhere (Cowan, forthcoming), we may hope for millennial dreams, but popular culture far more often wraps them in apocalyptic nightmares. In terms of first contact, these nightmares come in two principal forms: explicit and implicit.

Explicit invasion narratives present Earth as the target of a coordinated, intentional attack by extraterrestrial forces and the object of determined defense by a group of plucky humans. In addition to scores of films premised on an explicit alien invasion, this motif has also translated well to television. In the BBC's *UFO* series, for

example, which ran for twenty-six episodes in 1970, Earth is threatened by aliens intent on harvesting humans for our body parts and is
defended by a secret organization called SHADO (Supreme Headquarters, Alien Defence Organization). The 1983 miniseries *V* (for
the "Visitors") played on the interrelated themes of invasion, collaboration, and resistance. *V*'s initial success led to a second miniseries, a television series, and a number of popular novels based on the
premise of resistance to alien invasion. In 1988 Paramount sought
to capitalize on the success of *The War of the Worlds* a generation earlier and aired a short-lived continuation of the 1953 storyline. Never
given either the budget or the production support necessary to realize its potential, as I note in the next chapter, *War of the Worlds: The
Second Invasion* is fascinating for its inversion of the religious motifs
that so strikingly marked its predecessor.

Gene Roddenberry's series *Earth: Final Conflict* (1997–2002)
presented a considerably more nuanced invasion-collaboration-
resistance narrative than either *V* or *The War of the Worlds*. While it
built a loyal fan base, for multidimensional pop culture impact Roddenberry's series could not begin to compete with the phenomenal
success of *The X-Files*, in which popular fears of invasion, colonization, and collaboration—here combined with suspicion over government collusion with extraterrestrials—are seen more clearly. In 2005,
two major networks rolled out new alien invasion series, though neither survived its initial season: *Threshold* (CBS) and *Invasion* (ABC).

Implicit invasions occur almost accidentally, the extraterrestrial threat arriving less as an overt aggressor than an inadvertent
intruder. If explicit invasion narratives probe our fears of overwhelm-
ing force, implicit narratives highlight our individual fragility in the
face of a singular foe. Though not as numerous as explicit invasion
narratives, a number of these have become pop cultural icons. In
Edward Cahn's *It! The Terror from Beyond Space* (1958), an alien stows
away aboard a spaceship sent to rescue the only survivor of the first
Mars expedition. On the back way to Earth, it kills most of the crew
and implicitly threatens all of the planet if not destroyed. While few
might recognize it, this same story was the genesis of the enormously
popular *Alien* franchise, which debuted two decades later and, like so
many other pop culture products, has grown to include comic books,
graphic novels, and popular fiction, as well as model kits, toys, and

videogames. Designed by Swiss artist H. R. Giger, this "alien" could not be more different than either E.T. or the mothership occupants in *Close Encounters of the Third Kind*. Graphically representing the difference between the millennium and the apocalypse, Giger's creation has become synonymous with the dark menace from space. As Ripley tells a corporate board of inquiry when they refuse to believe her concerns about the threat in *Aliens*: "God damn it, that's not all! Because if one of those things gets down here then that will be all, then all this—this *bullshit* that you think is so important, you can just kiss all that goodbye."

However they are presented, these pop culture products are not just about the stories they tell. They open us up to the possibilities inherent in the concepts they represent. The possibility of extraterrestrial intelligence reflects vastly different visions of hope and fear: millennial, apocalyptic, and in between. That is, in the hope that the spaceships will eventually arrive, the faith that they will not, and the suspicion they may already have been and gone we find vastly different visions of humanity's place in the calculus of transcendence.

MILLENNIUM: HOPING THE SHIPS WILL COME SOMEDAY

Steven Spielberg's two visions of first contact—*Close Encounters of the Third Kind* (1977) and *E.T.: The Extra-Terrestrial* (1982)—are among the most beloved films in the canon of late-modern science fiction cinema. Writing in the *Christian Science Monitor*, David Sterritt called *Close Encounters* "a thrilling, moving, and warmly encouraging experience" (1977, 32), while the *Hartford Courant*'s Malcolm Johnson dubbed it "a contemporary translation of '2001'" (1977, 1G)—despite the fact that there is less than a decade between the two films. Five years later, in the normally staid *Washington Post*, Christian Williams gushed, "E.T. is here, and he's mankind's best friend" (1982, C1). In a lengthy article comparing *E.T.* with offscreen contactee experiences, the *Los Angeles Times*' Michael London opined, "This movie is one more step in the plan to prepare Earth for delegations from outer space" (1982, N1)—to prepare us not for invasion or colonization, but for participation in the interstellar community. Indeed, these films could not be more different from the hundreds of movies in previous decades that dressed a wide variety of cultural fears in extraterrestrial costumes.

"Aware of the real possibility that we could die within a few minutes of an ICBM launch," writes Joel Martin, for example, "it is not surprising that many of us in the 1970s sought solace in films featuring beneficent alien visitors. These cuddly extraterrestrials helped us view the skies with something other than terror. We needed *E.T.*, the *Star Man*, the *Brother from Another Planet*, and the kind folks in *Cocoon*" (2000, par. 15). Whether or not "solace" is the reason these films were so popular is open to debate. What is not is the impact they had on popular conceptions of extraterrestrial contact. Following on those decades of alien invasion films—and bracketing the release of Ridley Scott's *Alien* in 1979, which brought the terrifying extraterrestrial home again in full force—both Spielberg films deal with the same question, though from opposite ends of the experiential spectrum. In one, first contact is intentional and transcendental in scope; in the other, it is accidental and confined largely to the immanence of interpersonal relationship. From the transcendent to the immanent, however, both offer a similar vision—the simple hope that we are not alone.

Infused with a sense of mystery and wonder, *Close Encounters* expounds this vision on a global scale, questioning where our horizons begin and end. From the establishing sequence in which UFO investigators arrive in the middle of northern Mexico's Sonoran Desert and find the five Avenger torpedo bombers of Flight 19 lost over the Bermuda Triangle in 1945, to a huge freighter aground in the arid wastes of the Mongolian Gobi, thousands of miles from the nearest ocean; from the thousands of people gathered in Dharmsala, India, whose lives were changed by a song sung from the sky, to the hundreds of men, women, and children drawn by some unknown force to Devil's Tower, Wyoming—what happens in *Close Encounters* is ultimately meant for us all.

This is not to say that the experience of first contact is not without its terrifying aspects. Indeed, the alien abduction of five-year old Barry Guiler (Cary Guffey) is the film's most disturbing sequence, reminiscent of *Jaws* and presaging Spielberg's work in *Jurassic Park*. The strange compulsions Roy Neary (Richard Dreyfuss) experiences after his close encounter cost him his job, his family, and, he fears, his sanity. In many cases, the quest for transcendence is frightening and, as we will see in succeeding chapters, many of those who are called do not make the journey willingly. In the end, we just want answers, Neary tells Claude Lacombe, a character based on French UFO researcher Jacques Vallée and played with great charm by director François Truffaut. We just want to know what's going on—if only to know that we're not crazy.

Much of this is forgotten, however, by the time we reach "the dark side of the moon," the carefully prepared landing site at the base of Devil's Tower, where hundreds of SETI personnel await one of the few truly transcendent moments in human history. This is the sanctuary of first contact, and as the humans chosen to journey aboard the alien ship make their final preparations, a priest prays for their safety in a makeshift chapel. "God has given his angels charge over you," he recites, as humanity's first interstellar travelers look around nervously, distractedly reciting the antiphons. "Grant these pilgrims, we pray, a happy journey and peaceful days, so that with your holy angel as a guide they may safely reach their destination." The priest reads these last words in voice-over as the "pilgrims" make their way to the alien ship. What is striking about this brief scene, though, is not its blatantly Christian tone—which seems monumentally out of place given the global reach of the initial contact phenomenon—but the saccharine nature of the sentiments themselves and the utter blandness of their delivery. Against the grandeur of the mothership and the beauty of John Williams' score as the alien craft rises into the night sky, the priest's words sound petty, hollow, and altogether inadequate to the event. Although some commentators insist that *Close Encounters*—and especially these final scenes—should be seen as an explicit Christian allegory (Flesher and Torry, 2007, 200), it is as though this almost throwaway moment is meant to stand in clear contrast to the wonder taking place on the landing field. Once again we hear Carl Sagan whispering in our ear, "Your god is too small." Once again, although science fiction does not abjure religion, it points out in no uncertain terms how limited, how pedantic, are our terrestrial religious notions. Indeed, the only way to read this as a Christian allegory is to reject it as a possible scenario for first contact.

If *Close Encounters* is first contact read intentionally and transcendentally, *E.T.* demonstrates the ways in which our terrestrial boundaries are breached accidentally and immanently. Left behind on Earth, an alien botanist is taken in by a group of children, most significantly ten-year-old Elliott (Henry Thomas), and offered sanctuary from a far more aggressive breed of government alien hunters led by the enigmatic Keys (Peter Coyote). After a heartwarming onscreen hour during which Elliott and E.T. learn about each other, and at the end of which, in one of the film's most famous lines, E.T. "phones home," the dénouement unfolds. E.T. is captured by Keys, though by this time the alien is nearly dead—and Elliott with him. Their bonding has linked them physically as well as emotionally. When the extraterrestrial finally succumbs—and Elliott recovers—Keys reveals that he is, at heart, a ten-year old boy as well, struck by the wonder that we are not alone.

```
                KEYS

    Elliott, I don't think that he was left
    here intentionally. But his being here is a
    miracle, Elliott. It's a miracle.
```

The question is: what kind of a miracle? Is he some kind of Christ-figure, as Paul Flesher and Robert Torry suggest? After all, "he can heal and perform other miracles, he descends from above, and he returns to the celestial realm. He dies and is resurrected, and he appears to his 'disciples' following his resurrection in his white shroud, displaying a red beating heart visible in his chest" (Flesher and Torry, 2007, 200). But is this the limit of human imagination, theological or otherwise? Interpreting *E.T.* simply as a Christian allegory both narrows the range of potential readings—millions upon millions who saw it are not Christian—and implies that the film cannot be about what it is, quite obviously, about: first contact with an extraterrestrial lifeform. Although accidentally in this case, the ships have come and we are no longer alone. For some, that is the moment of genuine transcendence, the epitome of hope for our planet and our species. For others, however, it is the harbinger of doom, the epitome of hope only insofar as E.T. is not what he appears.

APOCALYPSE: POSITIVE THE SHIPS WILL NEVER COME

Independent filmmakers Peter and Paul Lalonde are fundamentalist Christians who believe that the Bible contains a wide range of prophecies related to the endtimes, the close of history when the curtain rings down on the millennia-old battle between God and Satan (cf. Boyer, 1992; Fuller, 1995; Walvoord, 1991). Put briefly, prophecy believers contend that time is linear and that God has divided history into a series of discrete periods called dispensations, each marked by a cataclysmic end and a divine restoration. The last of these, the endtimes, will be marked by the rise of the Antichrist and the final battle at Armageddon, themes that have featured in Christian apocalyptic fiction for nearly a century and in horror films, both Christian and secular, since the early 1970s (Cowan, 2008a; Gribben, 2009). Characteristic of this kind of late-modern dispensationalism is the interpretation of any world event in terms of its relationship to Bible prophecy. Thus, for example, war in the Middle East means that the end of days is coming (Walvoord, 1976, 1991), while peace in the Middle East means the same thing (Hunt, 1990). For these believers, God's prophetic timetable is inerrant and immutable, and no event falls outside its orbit.

Working from the small southern Ontario city of St. Catharines, the Lalonde brothers began publishing a prophecy newsletter while still in their teens, then graduated to a radio broadcast, "This Week in Bible Prophecy"—one of scores if not hundreds of such programs fashionable since the 1980s that seek to correlate world events with biblical interpretation. Now, through Cloud Ten Productions, they make relatively low-budget feature films, including a three-part adaptation of the enormously popular *Left Behind* novels (LaHaye and Jenkins, 1995; cf. Frykholm, 2004; Shuck, 2005) and their own endtimes quadrilogy, *Apocalypse* (1998), *Revelation* (1999), *Tribulation* (2000), and *Judgment* (2001).

In 2002, the Lalondes released *Deceived*, a science fiction thriller that, like *Contact*, is predicated on the arrival of a radio signal from space. Although writers Paul Lalonde, John Patus, and director André van Heerden all feel there is a multilayered subtlety to the film, like many evangelical Christian films it is a rather obvious and at times heavy-handed morality play designed to contrast "real" Christian faith with all manner of false beliefs, demonic temptations, and immoral practices. Given little or no development or depth, each character is an onscreen cipher for a particular offscreen aspect of the Christian moral universe—something the church audiences for which Cloud Ten produces films have come to expect. That is, these films are not meant to challenge one's faith, but to reinforce what conservative Christians already believe is the truth about life, the universe, and everything. In the case of *Deceived*, it's the truth about extraterrestrials.

A remote observatory has received a radio signal from deep space and the owner of the station, dot-com billionaire and philanthropist Emmett Shaw (Stewart Bick), has arranged for a media release that will tell the world, finally, "We are not alone." Consistent with Christian apocalyptic fiction dating back to the turn of the twentieth century, all of which is crafted to demonstrate the overarching superiority of Christianity in any situation, Shaw has assembled an "elite team" to help him share the message with the world. Jack Jones (Judd Nelson) is the best communications technician available, while Kara Walsh (Deborah Odell) is "the top investigative reporter in the country." New age preacher and Shaw's spiritual advisor, the Reverend Jeremiah Fletcher (Jefferson Mappin), hosts the "Guests of God"—"only the #1 rated radio show in all of these here United States!"—and has been invited "to keep our energies aligned" during the historic transmission. Business genius Smitty Turner (Michelle Nolden) is Shaw's chief of operations, Jack's former girlfriend, and the film's paradigmatic Christian. Although Lalonde and van Heeren insist that their theologizing is carefully nuanced throughout, in reality the larger narrative serves as little more than backdrop for a series of sermonic moments that lie at the heart of the film. Most of those gathered at the observatory believe that the signal represents one of the great moments of transcendence in human history—first contact. Leaving for the facility, the Reverend Fletcher prays for their success, asking among other things that God will bring them closer to "the joy of peace and the wonders of our own powers"—a comment that draws a concerned look from Smitty and indicates the film's central conflict.

When heard, however, the signal unleashes the seven deadly sins in those affected, each person manifesting the aberrant analog of their position in the group. The billionaire Shaw, for example, is the epitome of pride, while the fat and pompous Fletcher personifies gluttony. Used to getting her own way at whatever cost, Kara abandons her cool professionalism and embodies the spirit of lust.

Although partial deafness prevents him from actually hearing the signal, because Jack is content to slide through life with a minimum of effort, he represents sloth. These putative correspondences notwithstanding, the seven deadly sins are a narrative red herring since the film's principal message is made clear in the scenes where Smitty acts as the homiletic chorus, driving the point home with little if any subtlety. Confronting the Reverend Fletcher's new age beliefs—a particular bugaboo for fundamentalist Christians (Cowan, 2003, 155–70)—Smitty stakes out the "appropriate" Christian position, the theological anchor to which the film's resolution is ultimately tied.

                    FLETCHER

    Religions of all kinds have tried to suppress
    and monopolize our true power. I believe that
    there is a universal force that everyone can
    learn to control. Listening to that signal, I
    am convinced that we have found the door to a
    new level, to godhood.

                    SMITTY

    How can you say that? How can you tell these
    people that some signal from space is going
    to bring us to godhood? Where in the Bible
    does it say that?
    . . .

                    FLETCHER

    Oh, come now, you're not telling me that the
    Bible contains all worldly knowledge?

                    SMITTY

    Reverend, I'm not talking about "all worldly
    knowledge," I'm talking about the Bible.

"Are you another one of those religious nuts?" asks Kara acidly, suggesting that Smitty and Fletcher actually believe the same thing. "There's only one truth," Smitty replies, "and that's not it."

Later, while arguing over her religious beliefs, which are clearly the reason their relationship ended, Smitty asks in frustration, "Jack, what do you want?"

> JACK
>
> Proof. Not some paranoid delusion from the back page of the Bible . . .

> SMITTY
>
> I believe in God, Jack, not in becoming God. Look, it's not about meditating on some universal life force or achieving a higher state of consciousness. And it is certainly not about tuning in to some signal from outer space . . . or wherever.

> JACK
>
> What are you saying? That maybe this signal comes from hell? A demon? Satan?

Not surprisingly, Smitty's intuition proves correct, since she "checked the signal duration. It's 6.66 seconds"—a reference to Revelation 13:18 that is arguably the most obvious and clumsy allusion to dispensational theology in the entire film. Lest any in the audience still miss it, however, Jack finds surveillance camera footage in which one of the original observatory technicians warns his colleague that the signal is "not coming from space. It's coming straight from hell!" When soldiers outside the facility hear the signal "through their headsets," they begin shooting each other "like they were possessed." Now fully in the grip of the signal's influence, Fletcher rolls around on a floor littered with food, panting and rooting around in the cupboards like a pig, and reprising at least the first part of the argument Ellie Arroway makes to Palmer Joss.

> FLETCHER
>
> Millions of other planets having intelligent life. Life evolving over billions of years. Which means . . . that some of them could

```
have evolved to pure consciousness, beyond
the need of bodies, no longer limited by time
and space. And now that they have decided to
reveal themselves, they won't make us worship
them. No, they will encourage us to recognize
that all of us . . . are gods.
```

With Lalonde's typical lack of narrative nuance, as Fletcher delivers his last line he lifts a bottle of vodka to his lips and drinks deeply.

Although van Heerden and Lalonde insist they don't want their work to feel preachy, in reality every Cloud Ten film is an extended sermon, a cinematic homily that builds inexorably to the archetypal moment of evangelical decision: the altar call. For those deceived by the alleged alien signal, this comes when Smitty finally admits to Jack that her faith in God through the Bible has kept her safe from the signal's influence. Moments later, alone in the control room, Jack calls up an online Bible—he remains, after all, the quintessential computer geek—which opens to Matthew 18:19-20, in which Jesus promises his followers that "if two of you on earth agree about anything you ask for, it will be done for you by my Father in heaven." The shot lap dissolves to Smitty's room, which, in contrast to the control room's harsh lighting and hard angles, is warm, soft, and candlelit. Violins swell gently in the background as Smitty prays for Jack. The shot cuts back and finds Jack staring in wonder at a small twig cross given to him at the beginning of the film by a young boy—an act for which there was no apparent reason at the time.

As the film reaches its dénouement, Colonel Garrett (Louis Gossett Jr.), who represents the sin of wrath and wants the demonic signal for a weapon, seizes control of the facility and prepares to transmit the signal to the Pentagon. Hiding in a closet, unsure what to do, Jack gazes once again at the twig cross. In voice-over, Smitty urges him to "make a decision." Violins begin in the background once again—this time playing the well-known African American spiritual, "Were you there?"—as Jack raises his face to the light, closes his eyes, and, we assume, makes his choice.

With only seconds left before the Internet connection is established and the signal set free to wreak havoc on the world, Smitty takes Jack's hand, telling him, "Pray with me, Jack."

SMITTY

```
Lord God, please help us drive this force
back from where it came. In the name of your
Son, Jesus, Amen.
```

At her "Amen," all the station's computer equipment begins to explode—monitors, keyboards, mice, and processors. In a blinding moment of *deus ex machina*, the signal has been stopped and the scene's final shot shows Jack's small twig cross burning on a piece of white cloth—battered and charred, but intact. As they leave the facility, Fletcher is in a state of near-catatonia and Shaw is in handcuffs, while Jack and Smitty walk hand-in-hand, free to love once again. *Deceived* ends as the final scene cuts to a radio observatory in Red China where a technician reacts excitedly to the discovery of an extraterrestrial signal. Cue the ominous music—overlaid with the sound of a ticking clock—and the closing epigraph from 2 Timothy 3:

> . . . in the last days perilous times shall come. For men shall be lovers of their own selves . . . evil men and seducers shall wax worse and worse, deceiving, and being deceived.

Arguably the central trope in Christian apocalyptic fiction—whether literary or cinematic—is the issue of who will be saved. From those gathered in what we might call the undecided category—lukewarm Christians who have yet to accept the truth of the Bible as interpreted by dispensational fundamentalists, or cynical scientists and journalists, the cultural icons of skepticism and objectivity—some grasp the import of the message and some do not. When they do, like Jack and Kara, the correctness of the fundamentalist message is reinforced for readers and audiences alike. When they do not, the depths of Satanic deception in the endtimes is similarly confirmed. In both cases, the worldview of the Christian audiences for whom the Lalondes produce their films is reinforced.

Indeed, *Deceived* brings together a number of popular targets for fundamentalist Christian animus—most prominently, new age beliefs in human transcendence and its implicit disregard for the immutable truths of the Bible, the turn toward Eastern religion and "deep meditation," and the search for extraterrestrial intelligence.

Based explicitly on UC Berkeley's SETI@home project, which uses the Internet to harness the power of subscriber computers to analyze radio telescope data, the film's program is called QEI, the "Quest for Extraterrestrial Intelligence," and is rather unsubtly pronounced "ki," referring to the universal energy many Asian traditions believe animates all life.

Reversing the direction of cosmic significance established in *Contact*'s opening sequence, *Deceived* represents a particular stream of religious response to the possibility of extraterrestrial intelligence: terracentric human exceptionalism. That is, of the untold billions of planets in the universe, Earth is unique, created by God for a singular purpose and without parallel anywhere in the cosmos. Human beings are equally exceptional; we are the only creatures in the universe created for communion with God and are heirs to the salvation God has brought about through Jesus Christ. Because no other planet hosts intelligent life, we are the center of God's universe—a statement stunning in its theological arrogance. Although for hundreds of millions of Christians, the prospect of extraterrestrial intelligence presents no inherent challenge, for believers like the Lalondes even the possibility of alien contact is an affront to their faith and provokes an often profound theological crisis. Faced with the possibility of first contact, two questions must be answered: how do we know that the intruders are from space, and what are they if not extraterrestrial?

If they are not actual extraterrestrials, many Christians leave little doubt about the real origin of ETI and UFO phenomena. Fundamentalist radio host and freelance exorcist Bob Larson, for example, has built a lucrative career fighting all manner of perceived supernatural evil, from heavy metal music to Satanic ritual abuse, and from demonic possession to extraterrestrial contact (Cowan, 2003, 80–86). "Secular UFO interest," he writes, "fails to consider the possibility that such phenomena may be supernatural (demonic) in nature" (Larson, 1989, 436). Larson, however, is under no such illusion and neither, he insists, should his readers be. When his book *UFOs and the Alien Agenda* was published in response to the Heaven's Gate suicides in 1997, he sent supporters a fundraising letter headlined, "Aliens have landed to take over our planet!" In the letter, he told them that because "God has called me to take on the biggest spiritual fight of my life," if five hundred people would donate fifty dollars or more, "I'll take the demons behind this UFO craze and cast them out in the name of Jesus!" Many of his fundamentalist coreligionists concur that UFO phenomena are demonic in nature. "UFO cults and the current obsession with the unseen order and the realm of space are not of God," declares William Alnor, a journalism professor and publisher of the *Christian Sentinel*. "They are evil and demonic in every language and every culture" (1998, 152). In his newsletter, the *Intelligence Examiner*, prophecy believer Texe Marrs asks, "Are satanically inspired initiation ceremonies and rites conducted on spaceships and UFO craft?" (1997b, 6), while his colleague, William Schnoebelen, "warns that Beelzebub-type devils could be the true UFO astronauts and cosmonauts" (cited in Marrs, 1997a, 6; see also Goetz, 1997; Keith, 2004; Missler and Eastman, 1997; Schnoebelen, 2003; Weldon and Leavitt, 1976; Wilkinson, 1997; Wimbish, 1990; cf. Partridge, 2004). The logic here is disarmingly simple: because they cannot be extraterrestrials, they must be something else. Because they do not support the fundamentalist Christian worldview, they must be demonic. *Quod erat demonstrandum*.

This, of course, begs the question: How do we know? Once again, for fundamentalist Christians like these, the calculus of transcendence is clear: we know that there are no extraterrestrials because the Bible does not mention them. "Though atheistic scientists would scoff at this," writes Ron Rhodes, a widely read fundamentalist Christian researcher and writer, "Scripture does in fact point to the centrality of planet Earth and gives no hint that life exists elsewhere" (1998, 38). Earth, he writes elsewhere, is "absolutely unique in God's eternal purposes" (Rhodes, 1992, 56). The logical fallacies inherent in his argument notwithstanding, Bob Larson could not put this more clearly. "While the Bible does not explicitly rule out extraterrestrial life-forms," he writes, "there is sufficient scriptural evidence that life on Earth was created by God as a special act of divine grace, duplicated nowhere else in the universe. Thus the aliens who contact us cannot be from another planet or solar system . . . Biblical logic then concludes that demons, fallen angels, are the creatures behind legitimate UFO occurrences" (Larson, 1997, 203). What happens, though, if the Scriptures themselves are of extraterrestrial origin? What if the ships have already been and gone, and they left their mark behind?

Ambivalence: Possibly the Ships Have Come Already

Both *Independence Day* and *Mars Attacks!*—one an updated version of
the venerable 1950s alien invasion films, the other a comedic homage to them—contain crucial scenes that those who fear extraterrestrial visitation would have us remember: attack often comes in
the midst of welcome. As the massive alien ships in *Independence Day*
position themselves above the major cities of the world, ecstatic
partiers dance on top of the Capitol Records building in downtown
Los Angeles, holding up signs greeting the visitors, some begging
to be taken up into the ship. "So pretty," says one young woman,
just moments before an energy weapon fires and the destruction of
humankind begins. In *Mars Attacks!*, new ager Barbara Land (Annette
Bening) watches with delight—sitting in lotus position on the hood
of her Mercedes convertible, a diamond tilak on her forehead—as
emissaries from the Martian ship prepare to meet the human delega-
tion for the first time. Her wonder quickly turns to horror, though,
when the Martians open fire on the crowd, incinerating soldier and
civilian alike.

In the often confusing world of ufology, conspiracy theories
abound and conspiracy theorists trade on a wide range of interests
and speculation, many of which are replicated—and reinforced—in
science fiction film and television. Area 51, for example, the officially
unacknowledged military test facility in the Nevada desert northwest of Las Vegas, is the undisputed mecca for UFO enthusiasts
(Darlington, 1997; Patton, 1998). Also known as Dreamland, the
most well-known secret base in the world played notable roles in
Independence Day as well as in numerous episodes of *Stargate SG-1* and
The X-Files. Belief that a UFO crashed near Roswell, and that both
extraterrestrial technology and personnel were recovered there by
the U.S. military, has fueled similar pop cultural speculations, including the eponymous *Roswell*, a television series about the teenaged
survivors of that crash, and "Little Green Men," a delightful *Deep
Space Nine* episode in which the three principal Ferengi characters,
Quark (Armin Shimerman), Rom (Max Grodénchik), and Nog (Aron
Eisenberg), are the aliens recovered in the 1947 Roswell incident.
However amusing these depictions may be, for some people the
prospect of alien visitation is deadly serious.

From *Communion* and *Fire in the Sky*, both of which claim to be based on real events, to the "Abduction," "Black Oil," and "Colonization" story arcs of *The X-Files*, fears of alien abduction, experimentation, and hybridization have been firmly set into late-modern popular mythology. Indeed, when *X-Files* creator Chris Carter named his narrative threads "Mythologies," he was not far wrong. Although some researchers have tried to investigate the possibility of alien contact according to the rigors of the scientific method (Hynek, 1972; Vallee, 1988, 1990, 1991, 1992), more often than not popular ufological narratives are driven by conspiracy theories ranging from secret UFO bases to alien collusion with the Illuminati (Gilmer, 2002; Good, 1999; Keith, 2004), occasional exposés by retired military personnel allegedly disclosing the extent of their work with UFOs (Corso, 1997; Randle, 1989, 2001), an increasing number and variety of abduction stories (Hopkins, 1981, 1987; Hopkins and Rainey, 2003; Strieber, 1987, 1988, 1998), and journalistic accounts almost invariably claiming to blow the lid off the entire UFO world (Good, 1993, 1996; King, 1998). Although there is a countervailing tide of skeptic literature debunking all manner of belief in UFOs (Klass, 1983, 1988; Menzel and Taves, 1977), true believers remain convinced that something sinister is happening in the skies above our planet and in the halls of power on the ground.

Stanton Friedman, for example, whose early work listed him as a "nuclear physicist" but whose most recent book acknowledges that he has only a master's degree in physics (2008), has devoted much of his life to exposing what he believes is a massive government conspiracy to conceal the presence of extraterrestrials on Earth (1996). While few outside the ufological community take Friedman seriously and his message has been limited largely to the UFO convention circuit, the same cannot be said for John Mack, a Harvard psychiatrist, and David Jacobs, a historian at Temple University, both of whom have investigated hundreds of cases of alleged alien abduction. Mack, who organized a conference on the topic at MIT in 1992 (Bryan, 1995) and was investigated by a special commission at Harvard for his work on the abduction phenomenon, is unwilling to commit to exactly what these experiences mean, though he is clear that they mean something and that they are profoundly important in the process of human development (Mack, 1994, 2000). David Jacobs, on the other hand, is unequivocal: aliens are here and they mean us no good (1992, 1998, 2000). Writing his dissertation on the history of the UFO controversy in America, Jacobs continued this interest throughout his academic career. In the early 1980s, he learned hypnosis in order to conduct his own investigation into the abduction phenomenon and, since then, has hypnotically regressed hundreds of people. "For the first time in over thirty years of researching the UFO phenomenon," he writes in *The Threat* (Jacobs, 1998, 20), "I am frightened of it . . . I know why the aliens are here." In a plotline that could have been drawn directly from *The X-Files* (but on which Carter arguably drew for his fictional "mythologies"), Jacobs is convinced that four principal aspects comprise the alien agenda: (1) systematic abduction of human beings for the purpose of (2) breeding and genetic alteration leading to (3) a hybridization program to develop a genetically conjoined alien-human that will facilitate (4) the integration and control of the remaining human population on Earth (Jacobs, 1998, 251). In a word, colonization. According to one of his sources, "nonabductees will be kept as a small breeding population in case the hybridization program has unforeseen problems" (Jacobs, 1998, 253).

Once again, though Jacobs' work has been roundly criticized outside the ufological community, and notwithstanding the fundamental principle of academic freedom, well-known skeptic Martin Gardner considers the fact that a prestigious institution like Temple would retain Jacobs as a tenured faculty member "no small academic scandal" (1998, 17). Jacobs does, however, reflect widespread popular belief in the possibility, if not necessarily the plausibility, of such beliefs. *The X-Files* was not as wildly successful as it was simply because it told interesting stories; many of them were downright silly and moved so far away from the mythology arcs that they seemed part of another series entirely (e.g., "Hollywood A.D.," "Je Souhaite"). Rather, for millions of viewers, its popularity rested precisely on its resonance with cultural beliefs in UFOs and extraterrestrials that have been developing and expanding since the 1950s. *The X-Files* both reflected and reinforced significant aspects of a subcultural *zeitgeist* that will not go away despite all attempts at debunking, discredit, and denial. This may seem obvious, but it bears repeating since it seems so often forgotten.

Over the course of its nine-season run, FBI agents Dana Scully and Fox Mulder battled an astonishing, often unbelievable array of foes—from a human tapeworm bred in the depths of Chernobyl's radioactive waste ("The Host") to a likeable demon trying to sire a fully human child ("Terms of Endearment"), and from renegade agent Alex Kricek (Nicholas Lea) to the mysterious Cigarette Smoking Man (William B. Davis). Throughout, however, the story arc that kept millions of viewers tuning in week after week was the extraterrestrial connection: Who are they? Why are they here? And, perhaps most importantly, What do they want? Bridging the sixth and seventh seasons, and continuing in the ninth, is a five-episode story line that, although it ultimately presents more questions than answers, raises implications that beggar by comparison many of the more well-known themes in the series.

On the West African coast, broken pieces of an artifact have been found. Made of an unknown metal and covered in strange glyphs, when two of the pieces are brought together, they fuse into one and rocket across the room, embedding themselves in the spine of a leather-bound Bible. Underlined by the deep cut in the pages, the final shot in the opening gambit of "Biogenesis" focuses on words from the book of Genesis (1:28):

> And God blessed them, and God said unto them, "Be fruitful and multiply, and replenish the earth, and subdue it: and have dominion over the fish of the sea, and over the fowl of the air, and over every living thing that moveth upon the earth."

The story line is interspersed with the interior monologues that became a hallmark of the series, and we gradually learn that these are pieces of a craft—a spacecraft—buried until now in the sands off the Côte d'Ivoire. Hidden in the layers of intrigue that similarly marked *The X-Files*—Mulder mysteriously falling ill, the mysterious Agent Diana Fowley (Mimi Rogers) maneuvering in the wings, a mysterious Navajo healing ceremony sung over the gravely ill Albert Hosteen (Floyd "Red Crow" Westerman)—is the truth lying at the very heart of the series. As she works furiously to uncover the ship and translate the inscriptions—which are in a Navajo language similar to the "code-talking" used during World War II—Scully makes an astonishing discovery. Inscribed onto the skin of an alien spacecraft millions of years old are the answers to life, the universe, and everything. In voice-over, she explains her find to the dangerously ill Mulder, trapped in his psychiatric hospital room thousands of miles away—and to us.

SCULLY

On the top surface of the craft I'm finding
words describing human genetics. Efforts
to read the bottom of the craft have been
harder. Our workers have been scared away by
phenomena I admit I can't explain--a sea of
blood, a swarm of insects. But what little we
have found has been staggering: passages from
the Christian bible, from pagan religions,
from ancient Sumeria--science and mysticism
conjoined. But more than words, they are
somehow imbued with power.

West African scholar Amina Ngebe (JoNell Kennedy) tells Scully that the symbols on another part of the craft "spell out . . . a passage from the Qu'ran. Qeyaamah. The day of final judgment." The FBI agent looks up, but says nothing. "On a spacecraft," Ngebe continues, amazed. "Teachings from the ancient prophet Muhammed?" There are no answers, though the implications are clear. By the end of the episode, however, as happened so often in the series, the craft has disappeared and we are left wondering.

Two seasons later, in "Provenance," another craft is found, this time unearthed north of Calgary, Alberta. Inscribed on its hull are the same symbols, and embodied in its discovery are the same implications, although this time Chris Carter ensures that the truth of the message is out there for all to see. Searching for Scully's son, who has been kidnapped by a UFO group and taken to the site of the second ship, Scully and Monica Reyes (Annabeth Gish) act as a chorus.

REYES

If it were true these symbols wouldn't just
be words . . . they'd be the very word of God
on the surface of an alien spacecraft.

SCULLY

It'd mean that everything mankind believes in
. . . is in question.

REYES

And you believe this?

SCULLY

I didn't. I mean, I--I refused to believe it.
But now I think . . . I think there may be
answers there.

REYES

Answers to what?

And that's the real question, isn't it? Despite nearly nine seasons of alternating skepticism and wonderment, for Scully it comes down to answers about her son, not the origins of life or the meaning of religion. For others, however, it means something else entirely. In "Providence," the last installment of the five-episode arc, a member of the new religious movement that found and unearthed the second ship—himself a renegade FBI agent—reveals the secret of their belief.

COMER

One day God told Joseph to lead us a thousand
miles north to find a ship buried in the
ground. You have a piece of that ship in
your hand. Joseph believes that that ship
is a temple which houses the physical
manifestation of God.

There are those who believe that extraterrestrials will eventually make first contact, whether that heralds a new age of exploration and discovery or plunges us into the darkness of colonization and potential extinction. There are those for whom it is an article of deeply held faith that E.T. does not exist and any attempt to demonstrate otherwise falls prey to the Satanic delusions of the endtimes. And, as we will see in more detail in chapter 5, like those who found the enigmatic ship found off the Côte d'Ivoire and struggled to understand its meaning, many believe that the gods have been and gone.

4

"INTELLECTS VAST AND COOL AND UNSYMPATHETIC"
The War of the Worlds and the Transcendence of Modernity

NARRATOR (voice-over)

Yet across the gulf of space, minds that
are to our minds as ours are to the beasts
that perish, intellects vast and cool
and unsympathetic, regarded this earth
with envious eyes, and slowly and surely
drew their plans against us. And early
in the twentieth century came the great
disillusionment.

It was Paramount's most successful picture of 1953. In the American Film Institute's fifty greatest villains of twentieth-century American cinema, the Martians arrive at number twenty-seven, and it was among the four hundred titles that vied for the AFI's top one hundred films of the century. Indeed, in commentary contained on the 2005 DVD release, male lead Gene Barry remarked that, of the scores of movie and television roles he has played over his long career, it is Dr. Clayton Forrester in *The War of the Worlds* for which fans remember him most fondly. Based on one of the seminal science fiction novels of the twentieth century and lodged in the midst of a number of 1950s science fiction films that featured the end of the world in one way or another—the postapocalyptic advent of a new humanity in *When Worlds Collide*, the chilling, preapocalyptic salvation offered by Klaatu in *The Day the Earth Stood Still*, or the decidedly ambiguous success over nuclear science spun out of control in *Them!*—George Pal's production of *The War of the Worlds* reveals a variety of cultural fears that plagued America in the years immediately following World War II: the possibility of Soviet invasion, the dubious security of nuclear weaponry, and the fragility of civilized behavior in the face of apocalyptic threat.

Scripted by Barré Lyndon (the pseudonym of British screen-writer Alfred Edgar) and directed by Byron Haskin—though generally associated with George Pals—the first cinematic version of *The War of the Worlds* also explicitly reflects the Protestant religiosity with which many 1950s sci-fi films were charged, including, for example, the overt references to a second ark as humankind struggles to escape Earth in *When Worlds Collide* (see Torry, 1991) or screenwriter Edmund North's subtle, almost subliminal insinuations of Klaatu as a Christ-figure in *The Day the Earth Stood Still* (though, for a very different interpretation of this, see Cowan, 2009). More important, though, and central to the discussion in this chapter, is the question of why the film's use of religion both as an integral component of the plot and as a framing device for the narrative differs so dramatically, even diametrically, from Wells' original vision.

Wells' antagonism toward religious belief and practice is well known and is obvious in his novel. A student of the eminent scientist Thomas Huxley (who became known as "Darwin's bulldog" for his tenacious defense of the theory of evolution), Wells was also a passionate socialist and member for a time of the Fabian Society. As noted science fiction author (and vice president of the H. G. Wells Society) Brian Aldiss points out in his introduction to a recent edition of the novel, Wells had a respectable "radical pedigree. Like William Godwin, he regarded humanity as perfectible; like Percy Bysshe Shelley he believed in Free Love" (2005, xxiv). Neither of these beliefs, of course, found much favor with the fin-de-siècle Church of England, but this hardly mattered to Wells. Indeed, as I discuss in more detail below, one of the pivotal characters in the novel symbolizes nothing so much as his utter contempt for religion.

In his discussion of two late-nineteenth-century "Mars invades" novels—*The War of the Worlds* and Kurd Laßwitz's *Auf zwei Planeten* (*Two Planets*)—Ingo Cornils points out that a close reading of Wells' novel reveals clearly "the direction his thoughts would take" throughout the rest of his career (2003, 36). Most significant for this chapter was Wells' belief that "man would have to abandon his supreme confidence in the future, [and] accept that the evolutionary process would continue" (Cornils, 2003, 36). In *The War of the Worlds*, Cornils concludes, "Wells evokes a keen sense of loss and a reluctance to let go of the world he knows" (2003, 38). Though Wells and Laßwitz came to different understandings of what the quest for transcendence meant in the face of inevitable social transformation, "both believed that man needed to grow up and be prepared for the fundamental changes that scientific progress would inevitably bring" (Cornils, 2003, 38). For Wells, one of these fundamental changes is the long-overdue abandonment of organized religion.

Quite unlike the novel, however, although the characters in the first cinematic version of *The War of the Worlds* will certainly keep their eyes on the skies once the Martian threat is over, the film ends with a ringing endorsement of humankind's place in the universe secured by God's blessing and protection. Thus, rather than simply raising the questions discussed in so many of the films we have considered to this point, the film completely reverses the intent of the novel and maps the certainty of religious faith onto the challenges of late modernity.

Although most commentators have noted the religious references with which the 1953 film is replete, in general they seem a bit perplexed by their presence and are quick, therefore, to dismiss them. Citing *The War of the Worlds* specifically, for example, Dana Polan contends that "in many '50s monster films there is a character, often a priest, whose attitude toward the monsters is, 'Let us try to reason with them.' Several seconds later that character will be a smoldering pile of ashes in consequence of his belief that monsters share anything, such as rationality and humanism, with human beings" (1984, 202; cf. Aldiss, 2005, xviii). For Polan, a fatal naïveté marks these particular characters and their only function in the film is to highlight the otherness of the invader and the futility of human religious belief in the face of invasion. Although Marc Jancovich devotes two pages to *The War of the Worlds* in his major treatment of 1950s horror films, he too ultimately trivializes its religious aspects. He recognizes that "science remains a distinctly ambiguous force within the film," but when military science fails in the form of the atomic bomb, the people who have gathered to witness the destruction of the aliens "either become a destructive mob, or else huddle helplessly in churches where they wait and pray for deliverance" (Jancovich, 1996, 55). Like Polan, Jancovich's reading seems clear: religion is the last refuge of the terrified, a sanctuary in which people hide from the horror that stalks their world. It is the definitive painkiller, Marx's famous "opium of the people" in the face of humankind's (apparently) inevitable destruction. Although he ultimately describes the defeat of the Martians as unexpected and naturalistic, film critic Peter Biskind offers the most insightful reading of the period in which these films were released—a post-war America in which many believed "that their country had the endorsement of the Almighty, the Divine Seal of Approval" (1983, 115).

Finally, in *Monsters and Mad Scientists*, Andrew Tudor is arguably the most dismissive of any religious content, treating the resolution of the film as little more than an unsophisticated *deus ex machina*. "As in *The War of the Worlds* a decade earlier," he writes, referring specifically to the naturalistic demise of the extraterrestrial plants in *The Day of the Triffids*, "a religious gloss is given to the fact of humanity's final relief, though as with the earlier film that gloss seems so extraneous as to be laughably implausible to any audience" (Tudor, 1989, 54).

Through a close reading of the 1953 *The War of the Worlds*, in this chapter I take a position directly opposed to these, suggesting that it can be seen both as a thoroughly religious film and as one for whose audiences the religious components would have been anything but extraneous, implausible, or unsophisticated. This is not so much because the religious references that run throughout the film are so obvious—and they are—but because of the interplay between the time in which it was released and the vast differences that exist between the film and Wells' novel on which it is based. Although the film adaptation owes, perhaps, more to Orson Welles' famous 1938 *Mercury Theatre of the Air* production (cf. Cantril, 1940; Koch, 1970; Naremore, 2003), it is important (a) to consider the differences between the novel and the film in terms of the representation of religion, and then (b) to ask why those differences are so striking and what they say about the time in which and the audiences for which the film was produced.

Put simply, not only did the filmmakers add considerably more religious content than is found in Wells' novel, they completely reversed the thematic evaluation of that content, locating it at or near the center of the film. Whereas in the novel religion is the last refuge of the desperate and the insane, in the film it is the one positive social value that underpins the narrative and links the principal characters together. Since there does not seem to be any inherent need for this rather drastic change—any number of alien invasion films have managed just fine without it—in terms of interpreting *The War of the Worlds* in its original context, this becomes a sociological as well as an hermeneutic problem. It demonstrates a very different conception of hope in the face of destruction.

RELIGION IN H. G. WELLS' *THE WAR OF THE WORLDS* (1898)

In Wells' novel, though the narrator, "a professed and recognized writer on philosophical themes" ([1898] 2005, 156), occasionally prays, these are almost invariably presented as foxhole prayers, supplications offered in moments of desperation and sheer panic. "I prayed copiously," he recounts, as a Martian tentacle creeps through the coal cellar in the ruined house where he and an Anglican curate have taken refuge. "I whispered passionate prayers for safety" (Wells, [1898] 2005, 139). Much later, reflecting on his need to kill the curate to prevent them both from being captured by the Martians, and wondering about the fate of his wife, he recalls:

> I found myself praying that the Heat-Ray might have suddenly and painlessly struck her out of being. I had uttered prayers, fetish prayers, had prayed as heathens muttered charms when I was in extremity; but now I prayed indeed, pleading steadfastly and sanely, face to face with the darkness of God. (Wells, [1898] 2005, 149)

He prays for his wife in the sense of hoping that she met a quick and painless death as opposed to being harvested by the Martians, her flesh and blood sprayed across the landscape for their food. These are qualitatively different than the prayers for deliverance he offered in extremis while hiding in the ruined house, though "the darkness of God" suggests that he does not believe anyone hears his supplications or is prepared to answer. Even when he compares the destruction of the Martians to the overthrow of Sennacharib, the king of Assyria who laid unsuccessful siege to Jerusalem (2 Chron 32:1-23; Wells, [1898] 2005, 169), the narrator seems at best a reluctant deist forced into moments of desperately hopeful theism by the devastation with which he is faced.

Wells' more forceful comment on religion, however, comes in the person of the Anglican curate from Weybridge, whom the narrator meets while escaping the initial attack and with whom he seeks shelter in the ruined house at Halliford. Irrational and eventually insane, the clear implication throughout the text is that the curate was driven mad by the collision between his own religious worldview and the realization that (a) we are not alone in the universe, and (b) we are not necessarily the pinnacle of God's creation the church has made us out to be. He is a terracentric human exceptionalist whose entire world has suddenly been cast adrift with the arrival of the Martian cylinders and is unable to comprehend their meaning in anything but his own narrow religious vocabulary. Although Wells ridicules this belief through the observations of the philosopher, the curate locates the Martian invasion in the conceptual world of a Christian caught up in the endtimes. Like the Babylonians more than two millennia before, the Martians are the messengers (the "angels") of God, bringing the Almighty's judgment on a sinful and recalcitrant humanity.

Consistently describing the curate in derogatory terms, Wells writes that "his face was a fair weakness, his chin retreated," and his eyes were "blankly staring" ([1898] 2005, 69). Trapped together in the ruined house, the narrator came "to hate the curate's trick of helpless exclamation, his stupid rigidity of mind . . . He was as lacking in restraint as a silly woman. He would weep for hours together, and I verily believe that to the very end this spoilt child of life thought his weak tears in some way efficacious" (Wells, [1898] 2005, 131). Indeed, the narrator concludes, "he was one of those weak creatures, void of pride, timorous, anæmic, hateful souls, full of shifty cunning, who face neither God nor man, who face not even themselves" (Wells, [1898] 2005, 132).

Contrary to the quiet strength displayed by Pastor Collins in the 1953 film, and the respect with which he is clearly regarded by all other characters, Wells' curate is almost a caricature, a venal coward who sought refuge from the real world behind the walls of the Weybridge church just as he hid from the Martians in the basement of the ruined house. The central demonstration of this occurs just after the narrator meets the curate, who is struggling to understand the significance of recent events. Desperate, though not really expecting a cogent answer, he asks the narrator, "'Why are these things permitted? What sins have we done? The morning service was over, I was walking through the roads to clear my brain for the afternoon, and then—fire, earthquake, death! As if it were Sodom and Gomorrah! All our work undone, all the work—What are these Martians?'" "'What are we?'" replies the narrator pointedly, but the curate continues, "'All the work—all the Sunday-schools—What have we done— what has Weybridge done? Everything gone—everything destroyed. The church! We rebuilt it only three years ago. Gone!—swept out of existence! Why?'" (Wells, [1898] 2005, 70).

Initially unable to manage a theodicy in the face of the alien invasion, the curate answers his own question, interpreting the attack in terms of his faith: this is the end of days, and the Martians are actually God's messengers of destruction to the modern world just as the Babylonians were to the Israelites two-and-a-half millennia before. It doesn't matter that the people of Weybridge were not like those of Sodom and Gomorrah; it doesn't matter that they rebuilt the church and held weekly church school classes; it doesn't matter that the townsfolk had done nothing to warrant the apocalyptic anger of God. As he slips deeper into madness, the curate points to the ruins of his church and his community, and equating it somehow with the Whore of Babylon, he slightly misquotes Revelation 19:3, "'The smoke of her burning goeth up forever and ever'" (Wells, [1898] 2005, 70). He continues, "'This must be the beginning of the end . . . The end! The great and terrible day of the Lord! When men shall call upon the mountains and the rocks to fall upon them and hide them—hide them from the face of Him that sitteth upon the throne!'" (Wells, [1898] 2005, 71).

At this point, the narrator stops trying to reason with the curate. "'Be a man!' said I. 'You are scared out of your wits! What good is religion if it collapses under calamity? Think of what earthquakes and floods, wars and volcanoes, have done before to men! Did you think God exempted Weybridge? He is not an insurance agent, man!'" (Wells, [1898] 2005, 71). Exemplified in the curate, Wells' point throughout the novel is precisely this: no matter how impressive its material and architectural trappings, no matter how solid the rock of dogmatic faith appears, religion will inevitably collapse under the weight of catastrophe.

Not so Pal's production.

RELIGION AND SCIENCE IN GEORGE PALS' *THE WAR OF THE WORLDS* (1953)

THE PARITY OF SCIENCE AND RELIGION

Following the opening narration and the establishing sequence, as the first Martian ship streaks across the screen to begin *The War of the Worlds*, the shot cuts to a crowd gathered under the marquis of a movie theater. Centered in the frame is the local pastor, the Reverend Dr. Matthew Collins (Lewis Martin). Dressed in clerical blacks and wearing a Roman collar, his presence informs us from the beginning that, somehow, religion lies at the heart of this film. Indeed, the movie that the crowd is either just letting out from or waiting to see is Cecil B. DeMille's *Samson and Delilah* (1949), a biblical story about the dominant lifeform brought low unexpectedly and by deception, but whose strength is regained in the end through the power of God. When the alien ship comes down, it crosses the wilderness, a church (which we might presume is the one pastored by the Reverend Collins), and finally the theater—which makes a connection both between the townspeople and the church, and between the crowd watching the "meteor" land and the moviegoing audience in the theater watching the film itself. The message is clear: these are people just like you in a time and a town just like yours.

Not surprisingly, though, the first people asked to look at the object critically are scientists from "Pacific Tech"—a thinly veiled reference to the California Institute of Technology (Caltech), the academic home of NASA's Jet Propulsion Laboratory. Science, too, will play a pivotal role in the film, though not in conflict with religion to the degree that either the initial sequences or Wells' novel would suggest. Indeed, Pastor Collins is clearly an integral part of the town culture, and the manner in which the representatives of science and religion are portrayed indicates the relative parity with which the two domains are treated in the film. When the crowd arrives at the impact site, no one elbows the local minister aside to see the "meteor," and the townspeople clearly defer to his judgment in matters that affect the community. As Collins walks out of the frame to "get a closer look" at the "meteor," the scientist, Dr. Clayton Forrester, drives into the shot. Collins is on foot, but Forrester arrives in the quintessential icon of twentieth-century innovation and technology—the automobile. At this point, they are not onscreen together. Although given a kind of parity within their particular social domains, science and religion are initially kept separate in our field of vision.

They are brought together, both personally and professionally, through the character of Sylvia van Buren (Ann Robinson), who is the pastor's niece and, later in the film, the scientist's love interest. She is also the chorus, as it were, the one who explains the significance of events to the audience. For example, as she and Forrester (whom she has not recognized, despite having written her master's thesis on "modern scientists") are walking toward the crater, she confidently explains to him that "a scientist is coming from Pacific Tech. He'll tell us. Clayton Forrester, ever heard of him? He's top man in astro and nuclear physics. He knows all about meteors."

This also indicates that, despite the overt presence of the church, the clergy, and, by implication, God, as a good 1950s science fiction film, the first line of exploration and explanation will be scientific. Although radioactivity plays no active part in the storyline, for instance, Forrester's use of a Geiger counter establishes for the audience both his credentials as a scientist and an appropriate aura of "scientific menace" (Dante, 2005). Where Forrester approaches the mysterious object with his Geiger counter, Collins will later approach the Martian war machine with his Bible. Where the scientist uses his instruments to explore the unknown, the minister uses his faith in an effort to effect a peaceful resolution to the conflict. Each comes with the emblem of his profession, and neither is initially privileged over the other.

As Forrester comes into the shot at the edge of the impact crater, he stands beside the minister, with Sylvia on the other side. Referring

to the minister as "Uncle Matthew," Sylvia introduces him to Forrester as "Dr. Matthew Collins, pastor of the community church."
Although Collins is undoubtedly "the Reverend Doctor," Sylvia does
not introduce him that way. He is presented to Forrester (and to the
audience) as both a highly educated man and the town's moral center.
He is not given a denominational affiliation, but since he is dressed
in clerical blacks and collar, audiences are left free to map onto his
character any tradition they choose. Later in the film, however,
as Forrester searches for Sylvia during the final Martian attack on
Los Angeles, denominational particularity will become more acute,
recognizable, and significant.

A doctor of science and a doctor of divinity, their titles are equal,
and the two men are placed on a level footing, very unlike the Wells
novel. There is no animosity between them and the mutual respect
between their two domains of knowledge and experience continues
throughout the film. Indeed, when Forrester decides to stay in town
while the strange object cools off, Collins immediately invites him
to stay at his house, presumably the manse or parsonage. The next
evening, there is a square dance at the town hall, at which Collins is
presented once again as the image of community standards in mod-
eration. Although everyone else, including Forrester, is dressed in
proper country dance attire, the pastor attends in his clerical blacks.
When the power fails following the first Martian attack—though
they are not yet aware of the cause—Collins calmly pulls out his
pocket watch and reminds the crowd, "Well, we always play 'Good
night, ladies' at twelve o'clock anyways. It must be nearly that now."
The dance ends at midnight, presumably to give people time to be up
for church the next morning.

After the second attack and the sighting of the second ship, Forrester finally suggests, "Sheriff, you better get word to the military.
We're going to need them on this." Although he has no idea what
the aliens want or what they may have been reacting to when they
attacked the three men assigned to guard the crash site, in the face of
the Martian threat the scientist (the cultural paragon of rationalism) all
but immediately yields to the military option (the use of force). Here
begins the division between the domains of religion and science.

Marines take up defensive positions around the object, and when the local sheriff arrives at the military command post, he is followed closely by Pastor Collins. The sheriff walks quickly out of the shot, but the camera stays on the minister as he enters the tent and takes in the preparations for battle. The camera follows him as he is introduced to the commanding officer—immediately after Dr. Forrester, but before the sheriff. Once again, in the narrative, science and religion are held in close proximity and neither is privileged over the other. For the audience, however, Pastor Collins, not Dr. Forrester or the military commander, is the focus throughout much of this scene. As the general is introduced, we watch the action from behind the man of faith, over the shoulders of religion, as it were. And when the alien ship first rises out of the crater, we are shown a full-face shot of the minister, who announces in awe: "Beings . . . from another world." Unlike fundamentalist Christians or crazed Anglican curates, for whom extraterrestrial contact threatens terracentric human exceptionalism, for Pastor Collins this is a moment of profound wonder.

As soon as he says this, though, an important shift takes place in the sequence: the marine commander orders his troops to "stand by to fire." First, a tight two-shot frames the marine colonel, with Pastor Collins looking over his shoulder, still as though giving his blessing to the military option. He acts, at that moment, rather like a chaplain. The opposing two-shot, with which the other is intercut, introduces an incipient separation between the two principal dynamics of the film—religion and science. Where Pastor Collins is in the frame with the marine commander, Dr. Forrester is framed with the "intelligence officer," General Mann. When the Martian warship rises from its crater, Forrester says, also in awe, but almost gleefully, "This is amazing. [The magnetic rays] must keep the opposing poles in balance and lift the machine." Where Collins sees the occupants of the craft, Forrester sees only their technology. The gap between religion and science widens a bit more.

Although it appears initially that, through the character of Pastor Collins, the church may give its blessing to the attack, as the troops prepare to fire on the Martian ships, the pastor tries to reason with the marine commander.

                    COLLINS

     But, Colonel, shooting's no good.

                    COLONEL

     It's always been a good persuader.

                    COLLINS

     Shouldn't you try to communicate with him
     first? Then shoot later if you have to?

This brief bit of dialogue signals a number of significant aspects of the film. First, recalling his words, "Beings from another world," Collins does not refer to the alien as "it," but "him." He personalizes them, presaging a line he will have a bit later on when he takes a position that many scientists involved in SETI research have taken, and which has been implied (if not repeated) in any number of alien invasion films: "If they're more advanced than us, they should be nearer the Creator for that reason." He is not willing, at least not without further evidence, to consign them to the realm of the faceless enemy, to make them the "it" on which we so readily make war. Second, in terms of the colonel's response, it is important to remember that when this film was released, Pearl Harbor—the attack that defined as much as anything else in the twentieth century the American perception of threat and the requisite military stance in the face of it—had taken place less than twelve years before and was still painfully fresh in the public's mind. Third, the United States had only a few years before finished the Second World War, in which shooting proved a good persuader—especially the firing of not one but two nuclear weapons on largely civilian populations and nonmilitary targets. Fourth, few in the aftermath of the Second World War, especially those who had immigrated to the United States from continental Europe, could not have seen in the Martians' systematic destruction of humanity echoes of the Nazi extermination programs that killed more than ten million Jews, gypsies, Catholics, Jehovah's Witnesses, homosexuals, intellectuals, dissidents, and others. Both of these last two aspects would only have been highlighted for audiences in 1953 by Haskin's use of newsreel footage from the war at the beginning of the film. Finally, the United States was at that point also involved in the Korean conflict, which was the first hot war ostensibly fought to halt "communist aggression"—the social context in which alien invasion films of this type are most commonly interpreted.

THE DEATH OF PASTOR COLLINS

When the pastor questions the colonel's need to fire on the Martians, the soldier looks at the minister as though he's lost his mind. However implicit it may have been, there is no further blessing of the military option. Pastor Collins backs away from the marine commander and turns from him. He no longer wants any part of the operation, and any religious sanction the military option had turns and leaves the command tent with him. As it did when he entered, the camera follows Collins as he walks through the crowd of soldiers and out of the command post. He is, once again, the focus for the audience, the onscreen cipher for all the questions that govern our response in the face of grave threat. Sylvia follows him and finds him standing alone, staring out at the machine. She grasps his arm—not only is he her uncle, but she is symbolically holding on to the hope represented by the church and faith in God in times of trouble. Significantly, she is not at Forrester's side. Despite her master's degree, her thesis on "modern scientists," and her job teaching "library science" at USC—a point the commentators on the 2005 Collector's Edition DVD get wrong, incorrectly remarking that she is a "librarian"—she has left both science and the military option in the tent. This could not be more different than the way in which Wells presented his vision of religion in the novel.

Although, as I have noted, many commentators on the film have roundly dismissed the presence of the pastor or have commented derisively on the futility of his act, as Collins prepares to meet the Martian ships he strikes a very Gandhian pose—likely something else that would have resonated with audiences in 1953, since Gandhi died only a few years before (1948) and was one of the most recognizable faces in the world at the time of his assassination.

COLLINS

I think we should try to make them understand
that we mean them no harm. They are living
creatures out there . . .

                              SYLVIA

          They're not human. Dr. Forrester said they're
          from some kind of advanced civilization.

                              COLLINS

          If they're more advanced than us, then they
          should be nearer the Creator for that reason.
          No real attempt has been made to communicate
          with them, you know.

                              SYLVIA

          Let's go back inside, Uncle Matthew.

Intensely frightened, Sylvia wants to return to the dubious if conservative security of the military option. Facing the terrifying machines alone, protected only by faith, is too much for her. Not for Matthew. "I've done all that I can in there," he tells her gently. "You go back." As she turns to leave, he calls out to her, "Sylvia! I like that Dr. Forrester. He's a good man." Though he cannot sanction the military option, he recognizes—and indicates to the audience through his approval of Forrester—that science is not to be abandoned, nor is it necessarily antagonistic to religious faith. This approval of one domain for the other will be mirrored later in the film as Sylvia and Forrester take refuge in the abandoned house.

When Pastor Collins walks out to meet the Martian machines, we see him first in full headshot. This is quickly replaced by a point of view shot from within the command bunker, looking out through the observation slit as though we were one of the soldiers. As the audience, we are no longer out in the valley with the man of faith, but have returned to the tent with the military option. We watch Collins, now very small on the screen—as though his faith is puny compared to the implacable might of the Martian war machines—go to meet the advancing aliens. He removes his hat as the machine hovers above and in front of him, and we see him only from the back. We know he will not survive this scene.

Clawing at the sandbags in front of her, Sylvia screams for him to come back and the shot quickly shifts to slightly overhead and in front of Collins—a Martian's-eye view. He is still walking, now with a small Bible in his hand, and he begins to repeat well-known parts of Psalm 23. He seems clearly aware that these may be his last moments on Earth, but is willing nonetheless to meet the Martians with *satya-graha* ("truth force") rather than military force:

```
                    COLLINS

    Though I walk through the valley of the
    shadow of death, I will fear no evil . . .
```

The shot tightens as Collins holds up his Bible, a cross embossed in gold on its cover.

```
                    COLLINS

    Thou anointest my head with oil. My cup
    runneth over . . .
```

The shot tightens further, to Collins' head and shoulders, almost full front. Collins holds the Bible higher—the cross, quite ornate, is now fully visible, leading him, protecting him. How many missionaries throughout the history of the Christian church have walked similarly into unknown territory?

```
                    COLLINS

    And I shall dwell in the house of the Lord
    forever.
```

The shot cuts to a point of view looking over Collins' shoulder, up at the alien war machine with its menacing, coppery "cobra head" weapon. It fires and destroys him. As soon as he is killed—martyred—the military bombards the ships, though to no more effect than the pastor's simple greeting.

In what is perhaps the most revealing bit of commentary offered by Joe Dante, Bill Warren, and Bob Burns on the 2005 Collector's Edition DVD, Dante points out that "it's very polite of the Martians to let him finish the prayer" when Pastor Collins walks out to the Martian machine "thinking he can create interplanetary understanding by holding up a Bible" (2005). This kind of trite dismissal of religion is common in the interpretation of science fiction films, a dismissal that so often refuses to take the presence of religion onscreen seriously—either as a function of the narrative itself or as a reflection of the society that produced the film.

Once again, though, these commentators have completely missed the significance of the shift from Wells' novel to Barré Lyndon's screenplay. Rather than a relic charged with the futility of a faith humankind should have left behind long ago—a reading that is at least implied by Dante's comment—the pastor is a sacrificial figure, a martyr in the Gandhian tradition, though this aspect of the narrative is never explored. In this, he is completely different from the insane curate with whom Wells' protagonist hides in the abandoned house. He doesn't go out to meet the Martians "thinking he can create interplanetary understanding by holding up a Bible," but offers himself up as a vehicle for that understanding—much like the first three victims of the "heat ray," who approached the ship confident (if mistaken) that "everyone knows what a white flag means."

THE ABANDONED HOUSE: A REINSCRIPTION OF NORMALCY

Following the destruction of the military at the initial landing site, Forrester and Sylvia escape in his small plane, which then crashes near an abandoned farmhouse. Unlike both the Wells novel and Steven Spielberg's 2005 remake of the film, both of which portray the time in the house as a period of unrelenting terror, in the 1953 film it is also a significant time of respite for the two main characters, a brief period of normalcy in the midst of chaos, a foreshadowing that "everything will be all right." Safe for the moment, Forrester and Sylvia share a breakfast of coffee, orange juice, and eggs, forming for the moment a quasi-family and reinscribing the family values that characterized the American dream in the early 1950s. There may be war with the Russians coming—the aliens may be invading—but the family gathered around the kitchen table remains the heart of the American way. Although he clearly has no idea how to meet the Martian threat, Forrester tries to comfort Sylvia.

FORRESTER

They'll be stopped . . . somehow.

```
              SYLVIA

I feel like I did one time when I was small.
Awful scared and lonesome. I'd wandered off--
I've forgotten why--but the family and whole
crowds of neighbors were looking for me. They
found me in a church. I was afraid to go in
anyplace else. I stayed right by that door,
praying for the one who loved me best to come
and find me.
   (She suddenly realizes)
It was Uncle Matthew who found me!

            FORRESTER

I liked him.
```

Forrester's comment mirrors the pastor's before he walked out to meet his death—just as religion acknowledged the value of science, science now recognizes the importance of religious faith. Besides the overt reference to the church as her only place of sanctuary, in a relatively complex interplay of biblical allusions Sylvia also is presented as the lost sheep in the gospels, the one among ninety-nine for whom the shepherd searches. The gospel in which the parable first appears is Matthew (18:11-14), and Uncle Matthew was the shepherd who found her, the shepherd who just a few scenes before sacrificed his life for those he regarded as his sheep. If there is a preeminent Christ figure in 1950s science fiction cinema, it is surely Matthew Collins—once again, a stunning reversal of Wells' original portrayal of the cleric.

"THE BEGINNING OF THE ROUT OF CIVILIZATION, THE MASSACRE OF HUMANITY"

Despite Sylvia's reminiscences about seeking sanctuary in a church, when Pastor Collins dies, the explicitly religious component of the film is briefly subsumed. It is as though God has abandoned the people of Earth. Instead, the military, the scientists, and presumably everyone else put their trust—their faith—in an atomic bomb "ten times bigger than anything that's ever been dropped." In fact, a year before the picture's release, the United States tested the "Ivy Mike," a thermonuclear device with more than five hundred times the yield of the weapon dropped on Nagasaki in August 1945. Before the weapon is deployed, as a "couple of million people" are waiting in the "shelter of the San Gabriel hills"—hills named for the mightiest archangel of God—a radio announcer intones:

ANNOUNCER

```
The whole world is waiting, for this will
decide the fate of civilization and all
humanity. Whether we live or die may depend
on what happens here.
```

If the bomb fails, one of Forrester's colleagues has calculated that "the Martians can conquer the Earth in six days." In her recurring role as chorus, Sylvia points out that this is "the same number of days it took to create it." Although this is a rather heavy-handed allusion—and a bit of a non sequitur given Sylvia's allegedly scientific mindset—it is significant that, once again in diametric opposition to Wells' novel, religion may be subsumed, but it has not disappeared entirely. God should not be counted out of the picture just yet.

Of course, the bomb—ostensibly the most powerful weapon humankind can deploy—is useless against the alien machines and the destruction of Los Angeles begins. In the panic of people trying to flee the city as the Martians approach, one man tries to buy his way onto a truck, but is thrown off and told, "Your money's no good, mac." When he falls, his valise breaks open, spilling wads of cash and jewelry out onto the street. As he tries in vain to gather it up, the crowd passes him by. A more biblically literate generation than our own might see this as a clear allusion to Mark 8:36: "For what shall it profit a man, if he gain the whole world, and lose his own soul?"

As Forrester and his colleagues leave Pacific Tech loaded with equipment they hope will help them defeat the Martians, the same mob drags Forrester from the truck and throws out all of the scientific instruments that could yet save them. In this case, the crowd has become like the insane curate in Wells' novel. In the face of such unrelenting terror, the military option has failed, science is abandoned, faith has disappeared, and all that remains is frenzy and chaos.

Alone now, battered by the loss of his companions and the destruction of his professional tools, Forrester wanders the skyscraper canyons of the nearly deserted city searching for Sylvia. Realizing that she is "kind of lost," he starts looking for her in churches. "I think I know where she'll be," he tells a military policeman who urges him to seek safety.

PROTESTANTISM AND THE TRIUMPH OF RELIGION OVER SCIENCE

As the Martians raze the city, Forrester spots the spire and bell tower of a church and runs toward it. The shot shifts to an almost gargoyle view and we hear the sound of singing from inside the sanctuary. As he opens the heavy wooden doors to the cathedral-style church, the concluding "amen" resounds from within—another heavy-handed hint that all is not lost. Given the denominational particularity of the final sequences, this is likely a large urban Episcopal church. Rather than the white, clapboard, country-style community church that Matthew Collins pastored, it is the architectural symbol of the power and place of the church in premodern society. Forrester enters as the "amen" fades away and the doors close behind him. At this moment, we have an inkling that things will work out in our favor. As he searches frantically for Sylvia, the voice-over intones a prayer:

PRIEST (voice-over)

We humbly beseech Thy divine guidance, O
Lord, deliver us from the fear that has come
upon us . . .

The shot shifts to look at the congregation from the pulpit, over the left shoulder of the priest, as though from above the altar itself, where the cross would hang or stand.

From the evil that grows ever nearer . . .

The camera swings around to take in the congregation,

From the terror that soon will knock upon the
very door of this, Thy house . . .

The camera moves around farther and tightens on the head and shoulders of the priest, who joins his hands in supplication. In clerical

blacks and Roman collar, he looks for a moment like a younger version of Matthew Collins. In the story arc of the 1953 film, the military
option has failed utterly and the mob has turned in panic from the
promise of science, but the remnant faithful seek refuge once again
in their religious belief. One can only imagine how many similar
prayers were offered, for example, during the Nazi advance through
Europe.

```
O Lord, we pray Thee, grant us the miracle of
Thy divine intervention.
```

The shot pauses, the priest in profile at screen right with the stained
glass windows, another iconic representation of the Christian faith,
in the background. As the organ begins to play, Forrester turns to
leave, but an elderly man beseeches him, "Don't go, son. Stay with
us." "No," he replies, "I'm looking for someone. She'll be in a church,
near the door." Throughout the film, Dr. Forrester and Pastor Collins
have represented the parity of science and religion to the 1950s audience. Now, science moves explicitly in the direction of faith—the
direct antithesis of Wells' novel and a movement that is reinforced
throughout the rest of the film.

As Forrester continues his search, special effects of the Martians attacking the city lap dissolve to a Roman Catholic statue of
St. Joseph holding a bunch of lilies and the Christ child, who holds
a globe of the Earth in one hand while the other is raised in benediction. The feeling that salvation is at hand grows stronger. The
shot pans down to a woman and a man lighting votive candles—for
the dead, the dying, the death of the human race? The man crosses
himself and turns away as the camera pans across the sanctuary,
finding Forrester as he looks desperately for Sylvia. He steps out of
the shot as the camera lingers on a priest in surplice and stole, as
though vested for mass, teaching a group of children the rosary—an
item and an act that is, for many Roman Catholics, the controlling
symbol and ritual of the mystery of faith.

Out once again in the ongoing attack, Forrester finds himself
at a third church, another massive granite-and-marble metropolitan
sanctuary. Inside, the camera focuses on a man who looks eerily like
Billy Graham—which is probably no accident, since the Los Angeles

crusade that catapulted Graham to international prominence was in 1949, only four years before the film was released. By 1953 Graham was already one of the most recognizable religious figures in the country. The evangelist also prays, though his is a qualitatively different prayer than those of his two coreligionists.

EVANGELIST

```
In our peril we plead, succor and comfort us
in this hour. Please, God.
```

The shot cuts to a stained glass of St. Peter holding the keys to the kingdom of heaven, backlit by flashes from the Martian attack on the city. It is an oblique reference, perhaps, to Augustine's *City of God*, which contrasted the city of God with the city of Rome as the latter was being sacked by the Visigoths in 410. The stained glass window goes dark. A series of quick jump cuts follow. A Norman Rockwell–style shot of a young couple sitting in a pew with their two children and singing from a single hymn book brings together all that is threatened by the invasion: the church, the last sanctuary of a frightened humanity, and the family, the bedrock social unit of postwar America. The message is clear: life as we know it is threatened. Cut to an elderly couple reading the Bible as the attack worsens. Cut to Forrester and Sylvia as they find each other in the midst of the sanctuary just as the attack reaches its height and the stained glass window is blown in. The church begins to collapse around them.

As Forrester and Sylvia hold each other and prepare for what must surely be the end, something happens to the Martian ships. They begin to lose power, destabilize, and fall to Earth. As the first ship crashes, though those inside the church are not yet aware of it, the shot cuts to Forrester and Sylvia, while a voice-over of the evangelist continues the prayer:

EVANGELIST (voice-over)

```
Almighty and most merciful Father, we have
erred and strayed from Thy ways like lost
sheep. We have followed too much the devices
and desires of our own hearts. We have
offended against Thy holy laws. We have left
```

```
undone those things which we ought to have
done. And we have done those things which we
ought not to have done.
```

The denominational particularity of the film's penultimate sequence is suddenly quite stark, reflective, perhaps, of the clear denominational divisions that remained in the immediate post-war period. This is a prayer of repentance, very like one Billy Graham would have offered at a crusade and quite unlike the prayers of the other clergy we are shown. The Episcopal priest asks simply for the "miracle of divine intervention," and, in what looks like humanity's last hour, the Roman Catholic priest insists on catechizing, on teaching children the rosary. Simple supplication and a retreat to ritualism are trumped in this part of the story arc by the prayer of repentance, which in the evangelical Protestant schema exemplified by Graham is the first step toward the reception of God's mercy. As the evangelist finishes his prayer and the people trickle out into the street, the Martian in the first crashed ship dies.

After he checks the Martian and confirms that it is dead, Forrester says, simply, "We were all praying for a miracle." He looks up as church bells across the city begin to peal. The camera pulls back to a three-shot: Sylvia, the evangelist (who would, presumably, have been in the same denominational camp as her uncle Matthew), and Forrester—the same juxtaposition as when Forrester and Pastor Collins first met at the initial landing site. Science and religion are once again side by side, brought together by Sylvia: she introduced Forrester to her uncle Matthew, Forrester found her in the evangelist's church. All three look skyward as the church bells ring, and the narrator reads from the closing of Wells' novel.

NARRATOR (voice-over)

```
The Martians had no resistance to the
bacteria in our atmosphere, to which we
have long since become immune. Once they
had breathed our air, germs which no longer
affect us began to kill them. The end came
swiftly. All over the world, their machines
began to stop and fall. After all that men
```

```
could do had failed, the Martians were
destroyed and humanity was saved by the
littlest things, which God, in His wisdom,
had put upon this Earth.
```

The closing shots cut to the crowd in the San Gabriel mountains singing, "In this world and the next. Amen." It is the same hymn that was being sung in the first church Forrester entered during his search for Sylvia. As the "amen" swells this time, however, rather than the door closing on a huddled and frightened humanity, the last shot shows the sun rising over Los Angeles, guarded once again from screen left by the imposing edifice of the cathedral church. The hymn the people are singing is Martin Rinkart's "Now Thank We All Our God," written in approximately 1636. Because in the film it finishes after the second verse and does not proceed into the more creedally specific third verse, it becomes a more religiously generic hymn of thanks. Given sufficient time, science may be able to explain exactly how the germs worked on the Martians, but the closing sequence of the film leaves the audience in no doubt as to who put them on our planet in the first place.

THE WAR OF THE WORLDS
GODLY AMERICA VS. GODLESS COMMUNISM

H. G. Wells wrote *The War of the Worlds* in a time of considerable conflict between religion and science, locating that struggle in the persons of the Anglican curate and the secularist narrator. On the one hand, the teachings of John Nelson Darby, the fiery English Puritan preacher who is credited by many with originating the Christian fundamentalist concept of dispensationalism were prominent both in England and in the emerging fundamentalist movement in North America. On the other hand, an optimism about the scientific worldview, characterized both by the achievements of men like Lamarck and Darwin, and also by the technological innovations that were taking place more and more rapidly, cast a decidedly dim view on religious faith. Indeed, in the conclusion to his Gifford Lectures at the University of Edinburgh in 1902, William James felt compelled to write that "there is a notion in the air about us that religion is probably only an anachronism, a case of 'survival,' an atavistic relapse into a mode of thought which humanity in its more enlightened examples has outgrown" ([1902] 1999, 534). A sentiment with which Wells no doubt agreed.

The situation was very different in the immediate post–World War II period when George Pal produced *The War of the Worlds*. As other commentators have pointed out, there are a variety of social strains and perceived crises to which this film was a response and through which it resonated so strongly in the audiences who lined up around the block to see it. In the early 1950s, Senator Joseph McCarthy and the House Un-American Activities Committee were at the height of their anticommunist hysteria. Americans were primed and ready for the imminent Red invasion, an invasion that came in Pal's film from the red planet. UFO stories were prominent in the news at the time, ever since the widely reported 1947 sighting of UFOs in the Cascade Mountains by private pilot Kenneth Arnold and the alleged crash of an alien spacecraft on a ranch near Roswell, New Mexico, a little more than two weeks later. Less than a year before the film's release a mild panic swept Washington, D.C., as groups of unidentified objects allegedly buzzed the White House, the Capitol buildings, and the Pentagon. Despite this, there was an unmitigated trust in both science and the military option, exemplified most completely in the atomic bomb.

On the other hand, though, this was also a period of significant church expansion, and to be a good American meant that one was also a good (Protestant) Christian (see Wuthnow, 1988, 1998). Looking beyond the movie screen, we see this clearly in some of the other news and entertainment products to which audiences of the time were exposed.

Collier's, for example, was one of the most important mass-circulation weeklies in the first half of the twentieth century and the major competitor to the *Saturday Evening Post* for much of that time. Most issues featured cover art extolling in one way or another the family and the community as the core of American life, and, by implication, reinforcing American values and reflecting the American dream. *Collier's* ran a feature story on *The War of the Worlds* at the time of its release, though the cover art and headlines from other issues during the period reveal quite a bit more about what was on people's minds. Consider these brief examples.

"Will Russia Rule the Air?" asked the January 25, 1947, cover headline, while the February 28, 1948, issue advertised an article entitled, "How to Beat the Communists." In the New Year's Day 1949 edition, on the other hand, *Collier's* offered readers the "Life of Christ: A Painting in Full Color." Two cover headlines for the October 27, 1951, issue read: "Russia's Defeat and Occupation: 1952–1960" and "Preview of the War We Do Not Want." The cover art for this issue depicted an American military policeman standing in front of a map of Europe on which two United Nations flag pins mark all of eastern Europe and the western Soviet Union as "Occupied." He is carrying an M1 Garand rifle with a fixed bayonet and has a "pineapple" hand grenade clipped to his breast pocket—the quintessential image of an American foot soldier during World War II. Across the front of his white helmet are both the U.S. and U.N. flags with the words "Occupation Forces" emblazoned between them. Just a few months earlier (June 2, 1951), the *Collier's* cover article advertised "A Reporter in Search of God: What Soldiers Believe." The February 23, 1952, issue featured a large church on its cover, a structure that looks like a cross between a metropolitan cathedral and a country chapel. Cars and horse-drawn sleighs are pulling up as the congregation arrives for Sunday worship. The feature article that week was "The Favorite Bible Passages of 25 Famous Americans," while a sidebar beside the *Collier's* logo at the top of cover read, "They're Sticking Stalin With a Pitchfork." Finally, for the April 14, 1954, issue the cover sidebar advertizes an article on "The 10 Favorite Protestant Hymns." And right below it: "Do the Soviet <u>People</u> Expect to Go to War?"

By ignoring the social context in which the film was produced, and by failing to note the vast difference between the film and Wells' novel, commentators have long dismissed the profoundly religious elements in George Pal's production of *The War of the Worlds*. A closer reading reveals that it is significantly more than just a science fiction metaphor for a Soviet invasion. In it, Pals, Lyndon, and Haskin completely reversed the understanding of religion in the novel and used it instead to reinforce the intimate connection that existed in post–World War II America between a strong faith and a determined resistance to communist aggression. Rather than having a cinematic experience that left them wondering if the attack would come that evening, Americans could leave the theater secure in the knowledge that the manifest destiny of humanity—American Protestant humanity, at least—was secure.

THE WAR CONTINUES
MARTIANS ARRIVE IN 2005

Few novels are as important in the context of science fiction as *The War of the Worlds*. Indeed, it has been an integral part of every major media development since the late nineteenth century. Originally serialized in *Pearson's Weekly* in 1897, it appeared as a novel a year later. In August and September 1927, it was reprinted in Hugo Gernsback's pulp magazine, *Amazing Stories*, complete with cover art by Frank R. Paul. A little more than a decade later, Orson Welles adapted the story for radio—to (in)famous effect. In addition to various other television series that have built in some way on the concept of an alien invasion—*UFO*; *V*; *Earth: Final Conflict*; *The X-Files*; *Threshold*; and the eponymous *Invasion*—Wells' novel itself has continued to generate remakes. Although none, in my opinion, is nearly as enjoyable as the 1953 film, three very different productions saw the Martians arrive in 2005.

FROM BLOCKBUSTER TO BACKYARD MARTIANS

At one end of the spectrum is Steven Spielberg's special effects blockbuster, which, at an estimated 132 million dollars, had roughly ten times the budget of the 1953 film (in adjusted currency). While it returned nearly double its production costs after six months at the box office, Spielberg's effort was overshadowed in the press by the offscreen antics of star Tom Cruise. A month before its release, when he was supposed to be promoting the film on *The Oprah Winfrey Show*, in a now-infamous episode Cruise went spectacularly off-message by jumping up and down on Oprah's couch and declaring his undying love for Katie Holmes. From a remote video feed later in the program, Spielberg was forced to interrupt Cruise, begging his star to "talk a little bit about *War of the Worlds* because we're opening really soon" (Morton, 2008, 270; see 269–74).

In some ways, Spielberg's remake is more faithful to Wells' novel than the 1953 version, but, although it ends with the same lines about the Martians' defeat by "the humblest things that God, in his wisdom, has put upon the earth," it relies almost entirely on special effects (for which it was Oscar-nominated) and Cruise's then star power. Spielberg avoids any real allusion to religion beyond the fact that a church is destroyed when the first alien machine makes its appearance, and, unlike both the novel and the 1953 film, there is no central clerical figure. When Ray Ferrier (Cruise) is hiding with his daughter in the ruined house, it is not with a curate or a pastor but with a would-be freedom fighter (Tim Robbins) whose character is modeled instead on the "survivalist-minded" artilleryman of Wells' novel (Disch, 1998, 187).

With a reported budget of around five thousand dollars, independent filmmaker Timothy Hines' backyard production occupies the other end of the spectrum. At nearly three hours long, this is clearly a labor of love for all involved, but is a dismal and turgid production overall. Hines simply translates Wells' late nineteenth-century prose into a script and, with virtually no special effects to back them up, asks actors who are clearly unequal to the task to deliver the lines.

THE AMBIVALENCE OF HOPE IN *THE WAR OF THE WORLDS*

Made for around a million dollars, a small fraction of what Pal's production cost in adjusted currency, David Michael Latt's direct-to-DVD version is arguably the most interesting of the three that appeared in 2005. Although it too is hampered by crude special effects, rather plodding direction, and uneven performances among the cast, in terms of the human quest for transcendence it finds an important middle ground between the overt, even celebratory Protestantism of the 1953 film and the complete absence of religion in Spielberg's remake. C. Thomas Howell plays "George Herbert," an astronomer and rather obvious reference to Wells himself. Separated from his wife and son after the initial attack, he struggles to reach Washington, D.C., just as Wells' protagonist works his way from Horsell Common to London. And, like the narrator in Wells' novel, Herbert spends much of his journey—nearly half the run-time of the film—with a cleric, a Protestant pastor whom he initially mistakes for a priest.

Victor (Rhett Giles) is dressed in full clerical blacks, with collar and crucifix, and like Wells' curate he initially interprets the invasion as an immediate precursor to the Rapture, the removal of all true Christian believers prior to the endtimes and the battle of Armageddon. Calling the invading machines demons, he tries to comfort the distraught scientist. "All true believers are safe," he says. "Do you understand, George?" In one of the few deleted scenes, this is made even more explicit as Victor cites a passage from Thessalonians that is often interpreted as referring to the Rapture.

> VICTOR
>
> The Bible says that when the Lord is ready to call his children home he shall come down to Earth to do so.

> GEORGE
>
> The end of days.

> VICTOR
>
> Yes, yes. In Thessalonians 4, it is written that the Lord himself shall descend from heaven and the dead in Christ shall rise first. Then we that are left shall rise together to meet them in the clouds. Meet the Lord! And always be with the Lord!

Despite the destruction through which they have already come, in a manner common to endtimes believers, Victor seems almost excited by the prospect that the curtain is about to ring down on human history. He is not so immediately craven as the Weybridge curate, but like him he immediately focuses events through the lens of his own quest for transcendence.

> GEORGE
>
> So, you think this is it? This is 'the final days'?

VICTOR

Look around you. The signs are everywhere.
The scale of human loss, the destruction of
the world of sin, the dissolution of the
nations.

GEORGE

This is supposed to be comforting?

Far more than the 1953 film, Latt's remake raises the questions of theodicy and fidelity: where is God in the midst of such massive suffering, and how do we maintain faith in the face of God's apparent absence? However uneven the final product, what Latt presents is a reality in which faith is far more conditional, far more situationally motivated, than we might like to believe. Indeed, hope becomes a function of circumstance, displayed first through one of Victor's parishioners, then through the pastor himself.

Walking amidst the devastation, Victor and George find Rebecca (Kim Little), a member of Victor's congregation, kneeling in the mud beside the burning wreckage of a station wagon, weeping amidst a welter of child's toys. She is almost insane with grief at the loss of her husband and three children. Victor tries to comfort her, unfortunately with the kind of platitudes that made Wells (and many others) so contemptuous of religious leaders. "Rebecca," he says earnestly, laying his hand on her shoulder, "the pain you feel is nothing compared to the joy you will feel in every fiber of your soul once you join Him. We spoke about taking comfort in his words at times like—" "Shut the fuck up!" she shrieks, releasing a torrent of emotion familiar to many who have suffered the sudden loss of innocence at the hands of inexplicable violence.

REBECCA

These demons? Which demons? Your demons?
God's demons? I don't--I don't want to hear
about his mercy, his goddamned will, or his
fucking plan! He is not a god of love and
understanding. He is the god of death. He

is soulless, without redemption. A fucking
criminal who rapes an old lady has more heart
and compassion than your child murderer. Your
god. Your fucking numb, blind, evil god.

                    VICTOR

Rebecca, these are precisely the times you
need to take solace in--

          REBECCA (slapping him hard)

I don't need the Lord! I don't need your
preaching or any of your bullshit! What did
my four-year-old do to your god?

For Rebecca, who was presumably raised in a relatively safe environment where religious faith was defined by a good Sunday school for the children, an uplifting sermon, and adequate parking, hope vanished in the instant of the attack, in the moment she realized everything wasn't going to be all right.

For Victor, the descent takes a little longer and proceeds in three stages: the certainty of desperation, the questioning of faith, and the loss of hope. As the Martians attack with a new weapon that dissolves the flesh from the bones—Latt's version of the corrosive black smoke from Wells' novel—Victor cowers with George behind a road abutment, struggling to convince himself that this is the Rapture, that God has not forgotten the faithful, that the horror just a few yards away is God's will and part of his plan. Hyperventilating with fear, he chokes out snippets of prayer, clinging desperately to whatever certainty his faith can provide.

Later, taking refuge in a veterinarian's house abandoned during the Martian advance, George stocks up on supplies—including, at this point inexplicably, vials of rabies vaccine. As time passes, Victor becomes more introspective, questioning his initial certainty about the plan of God at the end of days. "Why does God keep testing our faith?" he asks. "It's like he's taken the chosen few and left us behind. Is that possible?" His own plain cross visible on a chain around his neck, George convinces him that they have to keep moving, but as they turn to leave, another Martian cylinder crashes into the house, trapping them in the basement. Victor begins to lose his grip on sanity. "Oh, God," he stutters in fear, "this is some kind of cruel joke. He's abandoned us. He's left us in hell. This isn't the resurrection." "Should we pray?" asks George as they huddle in the wreckage of the basement, listening for the approach of the war machines. "I don't know anymore," Victor answers. "I just don't know."

Victor's cognitive dissonance, his inability to reconcile the expectations of his faith with his experiences of the attack, deepens as they hide in the basement, subsisting on what few crumbs they can find. At this point, hunger drives theology.

VICTOR

God doesn't have a place for me, and that is difficult to comprehend.

GEORGE

Well, God still watches over us.

VICTOR

That's just it, George, I don't think he is watching over us. I think he has come and taken his chosen. In--in the book of Revelations [sic], he talks about three-and-a-half days, and then--then the--the men of sin are revealed and seven years of tribulations occurs. And the--the-- the timing, it's all wrong! Between the killing starting and--and now, it's too long. The Bible, it's--it's very specific. We've been forgotten. We've been left behind and damned to hell. The people who died in the first attack, they were the lucky ones . . . they were the chosen few, the ordained, the favorites. The rest of us have been discarded.

As they hear Martians moving just outside their hiding place, Victor concludes, "To have been left behind by the Father is far worse than what these beasts can do to our feeble bodies."

In this important bit of dialogue, the devout Christian pastor discloses the ultimate quandary of faith: maintaining belief in God even when you believe that God has abandoned you. Note that for Victor the question of God's existence is never in doubt, only his own worthiness to be counted among God's elect. Faced with his growing sense of rejection, the platitudes he offered Rebecca just hours before ring hollow indeed. The terror of watching the Martians feed on a man and his son just a few yards outside the house drives Victor away from his faith altogether. George's need to find his family and his faith that he will find them "sitting on the steps of the Lincoln Memorial" keep him going, but Victor is past caring.

Setting his crucifix—and his faith—on the broken concrete floor, Victor begins to drink—apparently there is plenty of wine in the basement—while George fills syringes with the rabies vaccine, hoping to use it as a weapon against the invaders. Confessing to George that he hasn't been leading them to Washington, but away from it, Victor collapses into unbelief. As he speaks, the shadows behind him very slowly resolve into an alien tentacle.

VICTOR

```
I'm dead. My entire life has been lies, a
fraud, a joke . . . I believe in nothing,
just me . . . and you. You're my only friend
. . . I don't believe in anything anymore.
Just me. God . . . He never existed.
```

As he removes his collar and throws it in the dust beside his crucifix, the tentacle strikes. George injects it with the vaccine and the creature withdraws, shrieking in pain. "My God, what happened? Where'd it go?" asks Victor in amazement. "I think it might have worked," George replies. For the pastor who only moments before had confessed his unbelief in the face of abandonment, faith floods back in that slim instant of hope. "He has been with us," Victor exclaims. "He's been with us all the time. He literally was testing u—" The pastor never finishes his sentence as the creature attacks again, spraying Victor with a viscous acid that quickly melts him away to bone.

At the end of the day, Victor is anything but victorious, and his vacillation brings us back to the solipsism of faith, what in more cosmological terms we might call the "center of the universe complex," people's belief that they occupy the center of God's concern. Very often, though, humans are situational believers, their faith contingent on circumstance, outcome, and self-interest. When things go our way we believe God is with us, and when they don't we are quickly convinced that God has abandoned us.

The real enigma in Latt's film, though, is George. While Rebecca's faith disappeared in her terrible moment of loss and Victor's gradually eroded as the attack progressed, George's faith remains something of a mystery. He is a scientist, an astronomer, but one who wears a cross, who prays to find his family, whose faith in God seems subliminal, but who assures the pastor that God is still there in spite of all they've seen. When it seems clear his family is lost, he confronts an alien at the end of the movie, crying, "You took away my family, you took away my God, you took away my life." The alien, however, is already dead and it topples at George's feet. In the final scene, George is reunited with his family on the steps of the Lincoln Memorial. Rather than showing the metropolitan cathedral standing watch over the skyline, the closing shot frames the Capitol building and the Washington Monument— both damaged, but still standing. If God is there, we are left unsure where. Despite its more overt, if ambivalent, religiosity, Latt's production leaves out the critical voice-over at the end that was the sole indication that God had a hand in defeating the alien invaders.

AN INKLING OF ALIEN FAITH

Thirty-five years after Paramount Pictures released *The War of the Worlds*, Paramount Television connected the 1953 film to an action-adventure sci-fi series that aired for two seasons. As it happened, the original aliens were neither destroyed—the bacteria placed them in an extended hibernation—nor were they from Mars—they used the red planet as a staging area from their homeworld, Mor-Tax. Although it had none of the overt religious framing of the film—the human team battling the aliens consists of three scientists and a soldier— there is an explicit appeal to an unseen order. All of the first-season's episodes are titled with biblical aphorisms or allusions—"Thy Kingdom Come"; "Eye for an Eye"; "The Good Samaritan"; and "The Last Supper"—most of which are either unexplained or only peripherally related to the plot. As far as it is explained, however, the quest for transcendence rests with the invading aliens, whose belief system is summed up in the show's popular catchphrase, "To life immortal." Although Paramount never committed sufficient production resources for the series to develop much potential, it does indicate a direction other science fiction series could explore: the possibility of alien faith, the varieties of alien religious experience, alien conceptions of the unseen order which will be discussed in more detail in the next section.

Part II

SCIENCE FICTION
AND THE MODES OF TRANSCENDENCE

5

HEEDING THE PROPHETS' CALL
Star Trek: Deep Space Nine

OUTTAKE: "PROPHET MOTIVE"

ROM

He told me, 'Rom, it's time for the Ferengi
to move beyond greed.'

QUARK

'Beyond greed,' there's nothing 'beyond
greed.' Greed is the purest, most noble of
emotions.

ROM (reading)

'Greed is dead.' That's the tenth Rule of
Acquisition.

QUARK

No, it isn't. The tenth Rule of Acquisition
is 'Greed is eternal.'

ROM

Not anymore.

Few things can test faith more deeply than a fundamental change to one's sacred Scriptures. In 1952, while millions hailed the publication of the Revised Standard Version of the Bible as a landmark in Christian history, others saw it as the work of the devil, and at least one Baptist pastor in West Virginia went so far as to rip pages out of the new edition and burn them in front of his church. Very often, when our sacred texts are threatened, our grasp on the meaning of life itself comes under attack. Without the words of God to guide us, it seems, the presence of the divine is lost.

In the *Deep Space Nine* episode "Prophet Motive"—an interesting quadruple entendre in the context of the series—a similar crisis of textual reinterpretation faces Quark, the space station's Ferengi barkeep and resident black marketeer. All his life he has tried to live by the Rules of Acquisition, the "sacred precepts" of commerce that structure Ferengi society, govern relationships within and without the Ferengi Alliance, and negotiate the individual Ferengi's quest for transcendence. "Never place friendship above profit," reads Rule #21, while #74 advises that "it never hurts to suck up to the boss" ("Rules of Acquisition"). From family loyalty ("Never allow family to stand in the way of opportunity" [#6; "The Nagus"]) to gender relations ("Females and finances don't mix" [#94; "Ferengi Love Songs"]) to shifts in astropolitical fortune ("War is good for business" [#34] and "Peace is good for business" [#35; "Destiny"]), the Ferengi quest for transcendence is guided by the Rules of Acquisition and marked by the accumulation of profit. Indeed, as Rule #18 warns ominously, "a Ferengi without profit is no Ferengi at all" ("Heart of Stone").

The Grand Nagus Zek, however, the planet Ferenginar's political, economic, and, arguably, spiritual leader (played with a clear sense of delight by veteran character actor Wallace Shawn), has suddenly overturned ten millennia of tradition and rewritten the sacred texts. Initially thrilled by *The Rules of Acquisition, Revised for the Modern Ferengi*, and hoping to be the first to profit from them, Quark and his brother Rom are stunned when they open the book.

QUARK

    The first Rule of Acquisition is: 'If they
    want their money back, give it to them!'

```
                    ROM (chanting)
'If they want their money back . . . give it
to them?'
```

Realizing what they have just said—utter blasphemy to billions of Ferengi—they turn to Zek's hulking Eupyrian manservant, Maihar'du (Tiny Ron), who sits in a corner, weeping sadly. It only gets worse, though, as other heretical revelations follow.

```
                    ROM (reading)
Rule #21: 'Never place profit before
friendship' . . . Rule #22: 'Latinum
tarnishes, but family is forever' . . . Rule
#23: 'Money can never replace dignity.'

                    QUARK (disgusted)
Oh, skip to the end . . . What, what is it?

                    ROM
You're not going to like it, brother . . .
Rule #285: 'A good deed is its own reward.'
```

Quark looks as though he is about to have the Ferengi equivalent of a stroke.

THE VARIETIES OF (ALIEN) RELIGIOUS EXPERIENCE

I suspect that every *Star Trek* fan has a favorite series in the franchise and this is mine. Following *The Next Generation* and overlapping *Voyager*, *Deep Space Nine*'s scriptwriting was consistently strong, and it had a sense of humor about itself that only rarely descended into the camp that marked the original series or got lost in the space of its own earnestness, as so often happened on *The Next Generation*. *Deep Space Nine*, however, was not as immediately popular as its predecessors and has attracted only a fraction of the critical attention. Indeed, barring articles in the popular sci-fi magazine *Cinefantastique*, a scant few scholars have paid any attention to it (see Geraghty, 2003;

Kapell, 1999; Linford, 1999), and some commentators have wondered whether it belonged in the *Star Trek* universe at all. Accustomed to the "family atmosphere on the Starship *Enterprise*," one first-season reviewer criticized *Deep Space Nine* for its apparent lack of "the communal spirit of its predecessor" and for the fact that the station's inhabitants seem "isolated and insulated from each other" (Mason, 1993, 12). Critics from *Time* magazine called it "a drearier show, set in a kind of outer-space bus stop" (Zoglin and Cray, 1994). And, writing mid-series, the *New York Times'* Jon Pareles simply dismissed the intricate and multifaceted issues *Deep Space Nine* raises.

> With their ever more elaborate backgrounds, aliens in 'Star Trek' can represent exaggerated human tendencies, like the ultracapitalistic Ferengi (the Shylocks of space) or the enzyme-addicted Jem'Hadar troops, crackheads in uniform. Or they can suggest ethnic and political groups. The Bajorans, with their religious rituals, caste systems, pierced ears and newly won freedom from the Cardassian Empire, might be Indians or Palestinians. (Pareles, 1996, H26)

By reducing *Deep Space Nine*'s various nonhuman species to a series of cultural or political caricatures, whether arguably analogous ("the Shylocks of space"), patently ridiculous ("crackheads in uniform"), or implicitly racist ("Indians or Palestinians"), Pareles relieves himself—and, by implication, his readers—of any responsibility to ask deeper questions, to understand the series in anything but the most banal terms. What he considers its fundamental weakness, however, is in fact its principal strength. Compared to others in the *Star Trek* franchise, it is precisely the power of difference in the series that permits *Deep Space Nine* to explore the story arcs it does. Indeed, for those willing to look more deeply, it offers an interrelated set of narratives that are considerably more complex than many popular critics allow. Running seven seasons, *Deep Space Nine* differs from all other *Star Trek* series in two significant respects: its primary narrative location and its principal narrative premise.

First, setting it on a space station, not a starship, avoids the need for the "alien contact of the week" approach to storytelling that marks each of the other series. Whether in space or on the ground, cities are vastly different communities than military vessels, which operate with a clear hierarchy and (usually) a shared purpose. Indeed, the conflicting agendas that populate urban environments, the ongoing struggles for power in political contexts that often lack any clear lines of authority, the absence of common cultural under-standings—all these together generate the kinds of social friction on which successful narrative is almost inevitably based. Moreover, because nonhuman historical and cultural contexts are not limited to a single episode's opening gambit, and the narrative resolution is not necessarily required within the logic of a single story, *Deep Space Nine* is character-driven in a way the other series are not. Over time, we encounter intriguing, often compelling dramatis personae, from the principals, Sisko (Avery Brooks), Kira (Nana Visitor), Jad-zia Dax (Terry Farrell), Odo (René Auberjonois), and Quark, to such secondary characters as Quark's nephew, Nog, who becomes the first Ferengi in Starfleet, Vic Fontaine (James Darren), the holographic lounge singer and crew confidante, Elim Garak (Andrew J. Robin-son), the Cardassian spy turned DS9 tailor, and even Morn (Mark Allen Shepherd), Quark's most loyal customer. Since there is no need to establish a place for each of these as an integral part of a starship's crew—a ploy that was simply avoided on *The Next Generation* and enjoyed only mixed success on *Voyager*—our encounters with them unfold gradually as the series progresses.

Second, and more important in our context, *Deep Space Nine* is underpinned by a thoughtful concern for religion that is unrivaled in the *Star Trek* franchise. In the original series, *The Next Generation*, and *Voyager*, religious belief and practice are often treated either as quaint relics of cultures far less advanced than those in the Federation (e.g., "Justice"; "Muse"; "The Apple"; "Who Mourns for Adonais") or as the leading edge of con jobs perpetrated by a variety of shady and usually alien characters (e.g., "Devil's Due"; "False Profits"; "Live Fast and Prosper")—facts not lost on many critics (cf. Asa, 1999; Pearson, 1999; Peterson, 1999; Wagner and Lundeen, 1998). *Deep Space Nine*, on the other hand, takes a much more sophisticated approach to religion, beginning and ending with it. Although we only occasion-ally see the religious beliefs of Terran (i.e., human) characters—the vaguely defined new age shamanism of *Voyager*'s Commander Chako-tay (Robert Beltran), or an equally nonspecific fundamentalist group that tries to disrupt life on the pleasure planet, Risa, in the *DS9* episode "Let He Who Is Without Sin . . ."—it is the varieties of alien religious experience that are most fascinating and ultimately most revealing about life on *Deep Space Nine*.

Consider further the avaricious Ferengi, to whom audiences were introduced over the course of *The Next Generation*—though only superficially and often as comic relief. Described by Jon Wagner and Jan Lundeen as "boorish" and "culturally parochial," with a religion "that mirrors their culture's narrow preoccupation with business and profit" (1998, 37), it is as if *Deep Space Nine*'s creators imagined an entire species reflecting the values of Gordon Gecko (Michael Douglas), the iconic acquisitor in Oliver Stone's *Wall Street*. In this, I suppose, Pareles is correct, that the Ferengi are the "Shylocks of space," though he and his fellow critics miss entirely the deeper implications of the comparison.

Put simply, for a Ferengi, commerce is religion: the Rules are his sacred text, acquisition his ultimate concern, his quest for transcendence mediated only by profit and loss. Indeed, Zek's revisions in "Prophet Motive" not only threaten the foundation of Ferengi society but the eternal welfare of all Ferengi. When Ferengi die, their place in the afterlife is determined by the profit the Rules allowed them to accumulate in life. Paying his bribe to the Registrar upon his arrival at the gates of the Divine Treasury, a deceased Ferengi presents his lifetime profit-and-loss statement to the Blessed Exchequer and, and in a kind of posthumous audit, is assessed on how well he followed the Rules of Acquisition. Those who show sufficient profit hope to enter the latinum precincts of the Ferengi heaven; those in a loss position go elsewhere. "Blessed Exchequer, whose greed is eternal," Quark prays in "The Emperor's New Cloak," sliding slips of gold-pressed latinum into a statue of the Divine Treasury's guardian, "allow this bribe to open your ears and hear this plea from your most humble debtor."

In "Little Green Men," writers Ira Behr and Robert Wolfe not only insert the Ferengi into the well-known story of the 1947 Roswell incident but fill out Ferengi beliefs even further. Landing on Earth after a warp core failure and an almost de rigueur "temporal flux," Quark, Rom, and Nog wake up in the bland and rather spartan infirmary at Roswell Army Air Field, the base to which proponents of the

Roswell theory contend wreckage of a UFO (and, some maintain, the remains of its occupants) were taken (Berlitz and Moore, 1980; Corso, 1997; Friedman, 1996; Randle and Schmitt, 1991). In the midst of blaming each other for their plight, Nog wonders aloud if they're actually dead and if this is the Divine Treasury.

> QUARK
>
> Don't be ridiculous! The Divine Treasury is made of pure latinum. Besides, where is the Blessed Exchequer? Where are the Celestial Auctioneers, and why aren't we bidding for our new lives, hmmm?
>
> ROM
>
> You don't think we're in the other place?
>
> NOG
>
> The Vault of Eternal Destitution?
>
> QUARK
>
> Don't be ridiculous. The bar was showing a profit!

Finally, if the Divine Treasury marks the Ferengi afterlife and the Rules of Acquisition form their sacred text, the Great Material Continuum constitutes the unseen order on which their quest for transcendence is ultimately based. In "Treachery, Faith, and the Great River," Nog, now an ensign in Starfleet, tries to help Chief O'Brien acquire some badly needed parts for one of their ships. "You have to have faith in the Great Material Continuum," the young Ferengi tells his superior. "It's the force that binds the universe together."

It would be easy to dismiss these ideas as little more than colorful set dressing, the trifling fantasies of over-imaginative *Star Trek* writers, or "Ferengi fairy tales," as O'Brien retorts, but how accurate would that be? While they may not be exactly like the Ferengi, numerous human cultures maintain elaborate economic relationships with the supernatural. In many religious traditions, moral conduct in life—according to whatever rules—functions as a karmic profit-and-loss statement in determining both afterlife destination and future life prospects. As aficionados of such films as *The Mummy* well know, ancient Egyptians from a variety of social classes were often buried with different grave goods for use in the next world— clothing and jewelry, weapons, furniture, games, even animals and servants. In Chinese folk religion, joss, or "spirit money," has been a ubiquitous part of the intimate exchange relations between the living and the dead for centuries. Indeed, from the sale of indulgences that so outraged Martin Luther to the pentecostal "prosperity gospel" that is sweeping huge tracts of the late-modern world, from seventh-century cargo cults in Japan to Internet price lists for *puja* in Hindu temples, humans have for millennia established a wide range of economic bases on which to facilitate their quests for transcendence. The Ferengi simply make this explicit in their culture and their religion. Far less hypocritical than many offscreen religious examples one could name, they refuse to dress their naked avarice in the threadbare robes of piety, and to write them off on that basis as "boorish" or "culturally parochial" (Wagner and Lundeen, 1998, 37) ignores the complexity not only of their religion, but of human religious belief and practice as well.

Or consider the Klingons, one of the most popular species in the *Star Trek* universe, a warrior race whose offscreen antecedents fall somewhere between Norse berserkers and Japanese samurai (Porter, 2007). Throughout *The Next Generation*, *Deep Space Nine*, and *Voyager*, we learn a considerable amount about Klingon rituals, beliefs, and practices, as well as the intricate and often equivocal relationships they maintain with the unseen order. We encounter Klingon cosmogony, for example, in "You Are Cordially Invited," the *DS9* episode culminating in the marriage of Worf (Michael Dorn) and Jadzia Dax.

As Klingon war drums pound in Quark's bar, the Lady Sirella (Shannon Cochran), mistress of the House of Martok, strides to the dais and recounts the mythic beginnings of their race.

SIRELLA

With fire and steel did the gods forge the
Klingon heart. So fiercely did it beat,
so loud was the sound, that the gods cried
out, 'On this day we have brought forth the

strongest heart in all the heavens. None
can stand before it without trembling at
its strength.' But then, the Klingon heart
weakened, its steady rhythm faltered, and the
gods said, 'Why have you weakened so? We have
made you the strongest in all of creation.'
And the heart said--

                    WORF

'I am alone.'

                  SIRELLA

And the gods knew that they had erred. So
they went back to their forge and brought
forth another heart.

As Jadzia joins Worf on the platform, his son, Alexander (Marc Worden), offers each a *bat'leth*, the double-bladed Klingon sword and central symbol of honor and duty. There is a brief moment of ritual combat.

                  SIRELLA

But the second heart beat stronger than the
first, and the first was jealous of its
power. Fortunately, the second heart was
tempered by wisdom.

                  JADZIA

'If we join together, no force can stop us.'

Klingon cosmology is simple and tripartite: the world of the living is a constant battleground on which one's fate in the afterlife will be decided. After death, a Klingon awaits either welcome into Sto'Vo'Kor, the halls of the honored dead, the Klingon Valhalla where great battles are fought throughout eternity, or banishment to Gre'thor, the vast hell reserved for those who die without honor, the fiery gates of which are guarded by the otherworldly Fek'lhr. Based loosely on the Greek mythological figure of Charon, Kortar (Eric

Pierpoint), the first Klingon, is condemned to pilot the "Barge of the Dead" for his part in the destruction of the primal gods, forever transporting dishonored souls to Gre'thor (cf. Cowan, 2008b, 30–35). An elaborate system of rituals marks the various stages of transcendence in Klingon life and death—from roaring to alert those in Sto'Vo'Kor to the approach of another warrior ("Tears of the Prophets") to the *ak'voh*, watching over the body of a fallen comrade to protect it from predators ("The Ship"), and from the *hegh'bat*, ritual suicide for a Klingon unable to live honorably as a warrior, to the *mauk-to'Vor*, ritual fratricide intended to reclaim lost honor and ensure one's entry into Sto'Vo'Kor ("Sons of Mogh"). For most of the franchise, Klingon messianism is embodied in Kahless the Unforgettable, the founder of the empire and its once and future king. Over the millennia, Kahless was accorded semidivine status by Klingons and the search for his long-lost *bat'leth*—said to be forged in lava from a lock of his hair ("Rightful Heir")—is a grail quest for all that defines the Klingon sense of self, honor, and purpose ("Sword of Kahless").

Once again, this may not look like "religion" or "transcendence" to critics raised, for example, as mainline protestants in late-modern North America, but that says more about the potential for narrowness in their own particular religious vision than either the expanse of human religious consciousness or the breadth of our religious imagination. Too often, when reviewing onscreen examples of religion, critics either read into those representations faith elements with which they are more comfortable or they dismiss religious beliefs and practices that do not sufficiently resemble their own—an interpretive lapse that ignores the multivariate reality of religion offscreen.

In "Deeds of Power," the only extended academic discussion of religion on *Deep Space Nine* prior to this book, Peter Linford begins with two surprising, and revealing, observations. First, he points out that "we should not fall into the trap of discussing [the Bajoran religion] as though it were real" (Linford, 1999, 77). That is, we ought not forget that this is fiction and that its characters—and their various religions—are the products of human imagination. It is an obvious enough point, though perhaps warranted given fans' predilection for discussing their favorite shows as though they were real. (For a hilarious send-up of *Star Trek* fandom in this regard, watch Dean Parisot's

Galaxy Quest.) I'm not sure this is what Linford wants to avoid, however, since he adds that "it is not religion itself as portrayed in *DS9*" that will concern him, "but the way in which religion is treated by the characters within the series" (1999, 77)—a strategy that cannot but treat religion as "real." How, though, is this approach significantly different from the ways in which scholars are forced to investigate, interpret, and redescribe any religion of which they are not a part? Moreover, how are offscreen religious myths, narratives, rituals, and practices also not somehow the transcendent products of human imagination?

Second, and more importantly, after a brief description of Bajoran religion—the dominant tradition in *Deep Space Nine*'s series arc—Linford writes:

> The Bajoran faith as presented shows little evidence of being a personal one. The Prophets, too, are always spoken of collectively . . . Other facets that we might expect to see in a religion are more clearly absent. There is, for example, no creativity attributed to the Prophets. Nor is there any soteriology. There is, in fact, little reason given for the Prophets to be worshipped . . . the prophecies do not seem to offer moral teaching, myths, or eschatology. (Linford, 1999, 78)

Once again, we are back to the problem articulated by Carl Sagan: your god is too small, your theology too limited, and your concept of religion too provincial. Although he denies doing so, in one breath Linford cautions us not to treat religion on *Deep Space Nine* as though it were real and in the next criticizes the Bajoran faith for not living up to his standards of "real" religion. In a similar vein, Wagner and Lundeen suggest that "the closest thing in *Star Trek* to a bona fide deity is the bizarre and petulant Q" (1998, 38)—though we have to wonder what they mean by "bona fide" and according to whose definition. Put differently, it is unclear here who gets to decide whose gods are real—a problem that is endemic both onscreen and off.

Like transcendence, religion as an analytic concept has given scholars nightmares for decades. Like Linford, Wagner, and Lundeen, some contend either implicitly or explicitly that "religion" means "my religion" and that all others are somehow false or inauthentic. My religion is "bona fide," others are not; my gods are "real," others are false. Some critics avoid the trap of theology by insisting that religion be defined structurally, according to the shared elements that comprise it: sacred texts, ritual and practice, established doctrine and clearly defined beliefs, a pantheon with which believers can interact personally, and an institution that mediates all these for the benefit of adherents. "Bona fide" religions have these, others do not. Still other scholars consider both these approaches too problematic, though for different reasons, and maintain that religion can only be understood functionally, as a product of what it does for adherents, of what purpose it serves in society: putative protection from adverse environmental conditions or malevolent supernatural agents; existential comfort against the loneliness of being without meaning; social control, whether benevolent or despotic; moral and ethical guidance for the good order of society. "Bona fide" religions keep us in line, others either do not or make no attempt to do so.

One of the most useful definitions I have found, however, one that allows for a breadth of religious experience but is not limited by time, place, or social convention, was proposed by William James during the Gifford Lectures presented at the University of Edinburgh in 1901 and 1902. Speaking on "The Reality of the Unseen Order," James told the audience at his third lecture that "the life of religion" is marked by "the belief that there is an unseen order, and that our supreme good lies in harmoniously adjusting ourselves thereto" ([1902] 1999, 61). While it will certainly not satisfy everyone, this definition has a number of distinct advantages. As I pointed out in *Sacred Terror*:

> By refusing to limit religion to those traditions that hold to belief in a supreme being of one kind or another, it avoids the problem that marked many early attempts to establish a working definition and allows for a greatly expanded understandings of religious belief and practice. Moreover, it does not restrict religion to those groups that believe in a socially approved supreme being or spiritual path, relegating all others to the murky and indistinct world of "cults," "sects," and "false religions." (Cowan, 2008b, 15)

Thus, a Ferengi's concern with profit is underpinned by his belief in the unseen order of the Great Material Continuum, and for him the supreme good is to show sufficient profit to stand before the Celestial Auctioneers and bid on a prosperous future life. For Klingons, the supreme good is marked by honorable death in combat with a worthy enemy and to be welcomed into the halls of Sto'Vo'Kor amid song, story, and endless barrels of blood wine.

When we use James' definition, issues of "authenticity" become considerably less relevant, and the fact that these onscreen visions of the unseen order differ from those we are used to encountering in churches, temples, and synagogues should not dissuade us from seeing within them reflections of our own relationship with the unseen order. All this said, though, the point is not simply to correlate off-screen human examples with onscreen alien religion, but to highlight how these fictional quests for transcendence invite us to reflect on the wide variety of religious experience, belief, and practice that animates the lives of billions of nonfictional human beings.

Central to *Deep Space Nine* is the religion of the Bajoran people. Wholly mischaracterized by Wagner and Lundeen as "militant" and "chauvinistic" (1998, 37), the Bajorans suffered decades of brutal occupation by the Cardassian Empire—a clear allusion to the Third Reich—and have only recently won their freedom. Presented throughout the series as a deeply spiritual people, for them the unseen order is framed by the Prophets, mysterious beings who watch over Bajor from the depths of their Celestial Temple. Remaining hidden from the Bajorans for millennia, understood only in the context of faith, the Prophets communicate through a set of nine orbs, each of which facilitates a different mystical experience, and through a complicated set of prophecies, many of which concern a messianic figure known as the Emissary. As Kira Nerys explains to Deep Space Nine's new Starfleet commander, Benjamin Sisko, the power vacuum left by the Cardassians has placed her world on the brink of civil war. "Our religion," she tells him bluntly, "is the only thing that holds my people together." For Kira, it was Bajoran faith in the Prophets that saw them through the occupation and will see them through the rebuilding process. In "Resurrection," which aired midway through the sixth season, Kira helps a Bajoran from an alternate universe— another standard *Star Trek* plot device for exploring various narrative possibilities—adjust to the differences in her reality. As they kneel together amidst the incense, bells, and orb meditation of a Bajoran temple service, he asks, "Who are the Prophets?" Kira smiles slightly, her face softening, and she answers, "Our gods."

Though we are often accustomed to thinking of religion in terms of ritual and practice, institutions and hierarchies, doctrine, dogma, and ethical dicta, lived religious belief takes place most commonly in the context of relationships—in some cases, between believers and their gods; in others, between various and sundry coreligionists; and in still others, between the adherents of competing visions of the unseen order. Many relationships are simple and straightforward; others are complex, often adversarial. Some are all of these. On *Deep Space Nine*, both the station and the series, three particular relationships explore the varieties of alien religious experience and illuminate the ongoing quest for transcendence.

THE EMISSARY'S JOURNEY
SISKO AND KIRA

Sometimes we do not seek transcendence, but are sought by it. Anchoring *Deep Space Nine*'s principal storyline are Sisko and Kira, a disillusioned Starfleet officer who believes he lost almost everything in a battle with the Borg at a point in space called Wolf 359 and a former Bajoran resistance fighter who thought she'd achieved everything she wanted when the Cardassians abandoned their occupation of her planet. Throughout the series, each follows a similar character arc, the one mirroring the other as they move from initial resistance to grudging acceptance to full commitment—a not-uncommon path on the quest for transcendence.

Shortly after his arrival on the station—which was built by the Cardassians as Terok Nor, an ore-processing facility, but has been taken over by the Federation as Deep Space Nine—Sisko detects a permanent wormhole between the Alpha and Gamma quadrants of the galaxy, a tunnel in space-time created and maintained by the beings revered as the Prophets. For the Bajorans, he has opened the gates to the Celestial Temple and been blessed by their gods; for almost everyone else, he has discovered a stellar phenomenon of singular strategic importance and made first contact with "wormhole aliens," an entirely new order of extraterrestrial being. This interpretive difference marks the central tension throughout the series. When the

Bajoran religious leader, Kai Opaka (Camille Saviola), greets Sisko in the pilot episode, she sees in him not a military officer, but the chosen Emissary to the Prophets—though she notes gravely that, though his *pah*, or spirit, is strong, "One who does not wish to be among us is to be the Emissary." Not unlike Moses, he finds himself a reluctant participant in what others regard as a divine drama. He is a Starfleet officer on a difficult assignment, not, as Kira calls him in "Destiny," "a religious icon." Indeed, just as Sisko resists both his DS9 posting and his call to be the Emissary, Kira initially opposes both his presence on the station and the fact that a non-Bajoran is now the principal embodiment of her relationship with her gods.

As he learns more about Bajoran religion, though, and both of them come to understand the Prophets more fully, we learn that Sisko has been selected in another, even more significant way. He is literally a child of the Prophets, one of whom occupied the body of his mother at the moment of conception. Despite the fact that human mythistory is filled with divine-human hybrids, of demigod heroes who bridge the seen and the unseen orders, this could lead some interpreters simply to see Sisko as a Christ-figure and end their analysis there (cf. Deacy, 2006; Kozlovic, 2004). *Deep Space Nine*, however, offers a much richer tapestry of transcendence than that. More particularly, it illuminates two significant aspects of the quest for transcendence: the importance of the charismatic bond and the contested visions of the unseen order.

Either directly or indirectly, scores of episodes explore the complex nature of Sisko's link to the Bajoran Prophets, his gradual acceptance of the Emissary's role, and the evolution of the charismatic bond between him and Kira—and by extension the Bajoran people. "It is characteristic of the prophets," wrote Max Weber, meaning, in his case, those who speak on behalf of the gods, not the gods themselves, "that they do not receive their mission from any human agency, but seize it, as it were" (1968, 258). Or, as in Sisko's case, they are seized by it.

In an experience not unlike Ellie Arroway's in *Contact* and bearing all the same hallmarks of James' classic mystical encounter, after his discovery of the wormhole Sisko is taken to the Prophets' realm in the netherspace between galactic quadrants. When he meets the beings the Bajorans revere as gods, however, they seem curiously unaware of both physical existence and linear time. They do not understand such concepts as pain or loss, experiences which to this point have defined who Sisko is and have kept him psychologically trapped in the burning wreckage of the starship on which his wife died at Wolf 359. All they know of "corporeal creatures" is that they are "primitive," "aggressive," and "adversarial." They should be destroyed whenever they enter the wormhole. Already functioning as something of an emissary to the Prophets, Sisko educates them in the ways of corporeal beings, teaching them that our quest for transcendence is marked by exploration, by our inquisitive nature, by our constant search both for answers and for new questions, and by the unavoidable reality that past, present, and future are not as one for us. Having argued for the lives of those who traverse the wormhole, having negotiated with the gods, as it were, Sisko is returned to Deep Space Nine—though he still rejects the notion that he is the Emissary.

Often, we tend to see charisma as something innate and to think that charismatic authority operates regardless of the circumstances. All that is required is divine sanction and the power of one's calling. To believe that charisma is located only in the individual, however, that it somehow operates apart from relationships with other people, is a mistake, and Sisko and Kira demonstrate the more fundamental process at work: the charismatic bond. As sociologist Roy Wallis points out, "Becoming charismatic is not a once and for always thing. It is a crucial feature of charisma that it exists only in its recognition by others" (1982, 35). In Sisko's case, it exists most profoundly in its recognition by those who least desire to see it. That is, without those who acknowledge them, reluctantly or not, charismatic leaders wither on the vine. Without those who reinforce the message and mission, no charismatic leader can effect substantive change. Without Kira's support—grudging or no—Sisko is impotent as the Emissary.

In popular culture, a character's charismatic power is routinely presented as a function of superhuman abilities, inherent and in force whether others recognize it or not. As a function of relationship, however, Wallis argues that charisma "must be constantly reinforced and reaffirmed or it no longer exists" (1982, 35). So it is for Sisko and Kira. Although both resist, the mid-series episode "Destiny" signals a fundamental shift in perspective for both characters. During the negotiation of a fledgling peace treaty between Cardassia and Bajor, when two Cardassian scientists propose to place a permanent communications relay in the Gamma quadrant, a Bajoran vedek (religious leader) warns Sisko that an ancient prophecy predicts the destruction of the Celestial Temple if he permits the operation to proceed. As the Federation commander on site, he has authority to halt the experiment; as the Emissary, it appears to be his duty. Disinclined to sacrifice the potential benefit of uninterrupted communication with the other side of the wormhole, Sisko dismisses the implications of the prophecy. When it appears the prophecy has been fulfilled, however, though not in the way either the vedek or Kira expected—but in ways to which it can be retroactively conformed—Sisko's place as the Emissary is confirmed for the Bajorans and at least rendered more plausible for the Starfleet officer himself.

If the Prophets do exist so outside of time that our understanding of past, present, and future are as one to them, if the prophecies they transmit through the orbs appear to be fulfilled, and if billions of Bajorans base their lives on belief in the Celestial Temple, what does that say about the nature of the unseen order and the place of the gods in it? This is a well-known question for students and scholars of religion: who are the gods, and, more importantly, who gets to decide? Following in the conceptual footsteps of such scholars as Sigmund Freud, for more than two decades humanist skeptics writing in the pages of such magazines as the *Humanist*, *Free Inquiry*, *Skeptic*, and *Skeptical Inquirer* have ridiculed religious belief, implicitly urging readers to reject it as little more than the stubborn detritus of our less enlightened past (see, for example, Barnhart, 1988; Johansen, 1997; Pandian, 2001; Tonne, 1996; cf. Freud, [1927] 1961, [1930] 1961). Under the guise of rational inquiry, though, both Freud and his intellectual heirs often demonstrate that they are as dogmatically bound to their own beliefs and domains of evidence as are those they relentlessly criticize. Rarely, however, do they stop to ask what it means to believe—especially when those around you do not.

A bedrock principle of the sociological analysis of all religious movements, and one that is frequently ignored by critics, was articulated by Émile Durkheim over a century ago in his "rules for the explanation of social facts" ([1895] 1982, 119)—that is, "the utility of a fact does not explain its origins." Or vice versa: the utility of a present social fact is not explained by its origins in the past. In the context of *Deep Space Nine*, explaining the origin of the wormhole does not explain away the Prophets for those who hold them as gods.

During the first-season episode "In the Hands of the Prophets," Vedek Winn (Louise Fletcher), an ambitious cleric determined to be the next Kai, confronts Keiko O'Brien (Rosalind Chao) over her teaching of wormhole physics rather than Bajoran spiritual beliefs at the DS9 school—a rather unsubtle reference to debates that have been ongoing in American public schools for nearly a century. Appalled at the situation, young Jake Sisko (Cirroc Lofton) articulates a common response of those who are confronted with beliefs they do not share.

JAKE

All this stuff about the 'Celestial Temple' and the wormhole--it's dumb!

SISKO

No, it's not. You've got to realize something, Jake, for over fifty years the one thing that allowed the Bajorans to survive the Cardassian occupation was their faith. The Prophets were their only source of hope and courage.

JAKE

But there were no 'Prophets,' they were just aliens that you found in the wormhole.

SISKO

To those 'aliens,' the future is no more difficult to see than the past. Why shouldn't they be considered Prophets?

Sisko concludes, telling Jake, "It may not be what you believe, but that doesn't make it wrong."

CHANGING OF THE GODS
WINN AND DUKAT

Just as Benjamin Sisko and Kira Nerys demonstrate the ambiguous nature of the charismatic bond and a contested vision of the unseen order, Kai Winn and Gul Dukat (Marc Alaimo) illustrate two other important principles of the ongoing quest for transcendence: the evolution of new religious belief and the problem of the good, moral, and decent fallacy. Throughout the series, Kira's reluctance to accept Sisko as the Emissary is mirrored in Winn's struggle to be accepted by him as the legitimate religious leader of Bajor. Though only a vedek from an obscure religious order, Winn rises to the position of Kai through intrigue, subterfuge, and the kind of passive aggression that so often accompanies the absolute certainty that one stands in the will of one's gods. All this despite the fact that the Prophets themselves have never favored her with a vision, never spoken to her as they do to Sisko. Gul Dukat, on the other hand, the Cardassian prefect responsible for overseeing the Bajoran occupation, sees in the Starfleet commander both the incarnation of his empire's withdrawal and sole blame for the death of his daughter, Ziyal (Melanie Smith). Both defined by their losses, Winn's latent hatred of the non-Bajoran Emissary and Dukat's open hostility toward his Federation enemy draw them together in an unlikely alliance as the series approaches its finale.

Clustered at the end of the final season, seven episodes tell what we might call the "Pah-wraith cycle," an apocalyptic battle for the Alpha quadrant during which Winn and Dukat seek to free the Pah-wraith, beings who millennia ago challenged the Prophets for control of the Celestial Temple and were imprisoned in the Fire Caves on Bajor for their insurrection. Not unlike the fallen angels of Christian mythology or the old gods supplanted by Christian imperialism, the Pah-wraiths have been demonized in Bajoran history and theology, used to frighten children and made the symbolic embodiment of all that is evil in the unseen order. Seeking their path to a change in that unseen order—one of the principal themes in religiously oriented cinema horror (Cowan, 2008b, 61–92)—they await their chance to return.

Unlike the Prophets, who communicate through the mystical experiences of the orbs, Pah-wraiths work through possession, taking control of Keiko O'Brien, for example, in "The Assignment" and Jake Sisko in "The Reckoning." In "Tears of the Prophets," however, the disgraced Gul Dukat uses an ancient Bajoran artifact to invoke possession by a Pah-wraith, eventually collapsing the entrance to the wormhole and severing the connection between Bajor and its gods. Blessed by what he believes is the love of the Pah-wraiths, in "Covenant" Dukat establishes himself as their emissary and forms a religious movement devoted to them on Empok Nor, another abandoned Cardassian space station. Deceived by Vedek Fala (Norman Parker), her childhood teacher in a refugee camp, Kira is kidnapped to Empok Nor and urged to join the "Pah-wraith cult." While its association with Dukat and the cultural valence of such groups as Peoples Temple and Heaven's Gate ensures that viewers will ultimately regard the movement and its members negatively, that, too, avoids the more complex questions raised by the episode. Why do new religions and new religious leaders emerge? Why do believers exchange one set of beliefs for another? How could Fala, Kira's beloved teacher, betray all she thought they both held sacred?

> FALA
>
> I was a member of 'this cult,' as you call it, long before Dukat. I came to it toward the end of the occupation. It's helped me make sense of the suffering we all had to endure.

> KIRA
>
> In the camp? You kept us together. It was your faith in the Prophets that got us through. How could you of all people turn your back on them?

> FALA
>
> They turned their backs on us . . . long ago.

Perhaps more than anything else, the concept of a supreme good and the belief that we can be in harmonious adjustment with it implies that there is an order in the universe, that we can make some kind of sense of the world around us, and that we can answer in some small way the classic question that has plagued religious thinking for millennia: why do bad things happen to good people? As Kira says to the Cardassian Aamin Marritza (played magnificently by Harris Yulin) in "Duet," "The Bajorans were a peaceful people before you came. We offered no threat to you. We could never understand why you had to be so brutal." Could it be, as Fala suggests, that the gods had turned their backs on Bajor?

The majority of the Pah-wraith cycle ("Penumbra"; "'Til Death Do Us Part"; "Strange Bedfellows"; "The Changing Face of Evil"; "When It Rains . . ."; and "What You Leave Behind") is integral to the final resolution of the series. What begins with religion ends with religion. Now surgically altered to appear Bajoran, Dukat comes to Kai Winn with a veiled offer from the Pah-wraiths: abandon the Prophets and restore the true gods of Bajor to their rightful place in the Celestial Temple. After a lifetime of listening, desperate to believe that the Prophets have finally sent her a sign, Kai Winn is eager to embrace the words of her new guide (and paramour). Even when Dukat reveals both his true identity and real mission, Winn struggles to reconcile her receding faith in the Prophets with her growing awareness of the Pah-wraiths. Giving in, and with Dukat constantly at her elbow, she combs the forbidden text of the *Kosst Amojen*, a repository of dark knowledge hidden for centuries in the archives of the Kai, searching for the key to release the Pah-wraiths.

Social scientists explain the development of new religious movements in a variety of ways. In "Cult Formation: Three Compatible Models," William Sims Bainbridge and Rodney Stark outline how many such groups are the result of different, though not mutually exclusive, processes: psychopathology, entrepreneurship, and subcultural evolution (1979). While the entrepreneurial mode could easily be applied to the Ferengi (e.g., "False Profits") and it is not hard to see a certain psychopathology in Gul Dukat—after all, wrote the ancient, unknown proverbist, "Whom the gods would destroy, they first make mad"—it is the subculture-evolution model that reveals most clearly the heart of the Pah-wraith cycle. According to Bainbridge and Stark, subcultural evolution of a new religious movement can occur when "a few intimately interacting individuals" who are "already deeply involved in the occult milieu" but who are often the subjects of "sidetracked or failed attempts to obtain scarce or nonexistent rewards"—in this case, the approbation of the Prophets and the ascendance of the Cardassian empire—become "relatively encapsulated" and begin to develop a "novel religious culture" (1979, 291). Although the entire model is somewhat more complex than this, the process of subculture evolution encourages the development of "a deviant normative structure" (Bainbridge and Stark, 1979, 291), a different way of understanding the nature of the unseen order, the shape of one's supreme good, and the requirements of harmonious adjustment. Supported by such well-known social psychological principles as confirmation bias (our predisposition to filter information according to our agreement with it), the hindsight effect (our tendency to remember or reinterpret information in ways that conform with our expectations), and source dissociation (our inclination to forget the origin of information with which we agree), Winn interprets everything Dukat tells her in ways that suit both her desires and what she considers the exigencies of the moment. Convincing herself that the problem is not her desire for power, but the Prophets' ultimate lack of interest in Bajor, she effects a changing of the gods. Her quest for transcendence has shifted; her hope now lies elsewhere.

WINN

The Prophets have turned their backs on me,
after all I've done for them, all the pain
I've endured for them.

ANJOHL (DUKAT)

They're not worthy of you, Adami.

WINN

I'm a patient woman, but I have run out of
patience. I will no longer serve gods who give
me nothing in return. I am ready to walk the
path the Pah-wraiths have laid out for me.

Despite the innocent men and women caught up in Dukat's "Covenant" on Empok Nor, the story arc leaves audiences in no doubt about the malevolence of the Pah-wraiths, a reality that could lead viewers to declare them, a priori, counterfeit gods. This too would be a mistake, yet another assumption that turns on the cultural and theological need to distinguish "true" religions from "false." Even the briefest survey of human religious history reveals the depths of what I have called elsewhere "the good, moral, and decent fallacy" (Cowan, 2008b, 15–16). Indeed, one of the most common misconceptions about religion as a social phenomenon is that it is dedicated to making believers better people, providing sound moral values, and structuring a decent society for all. Certainly, this is the case in any number of religious traditions, but these are not attributes by which religion itself should be defined, nor should they be considered the sole domain of the faithful. As historian of religion Jonathan Z. Smith points out trenchantly, "Religion is not nice; it has been responsible for more death and suffering than any other human activity" (1982, 110). From the various tribes encountered by the Hebrews as they made their way into Canaan to pagan believers in old Europe at the advent of Christianity, from those who died on September 11, 2001 to the numberless thousands who have perished in similar attacks around the world, from the release of the Pah-wraiths to the Dominion war, victims suffer few acts of cruelty as sharply executed as those we carry out in the name of our gods.

ENGINEERING TRANSCENDENCE
THE FOUNDERS

For most of *Deep Space Nine*, the principal nemesis is the Dominion, a powerful interstellar empire from the Gamma quadrant that now seeks a foothold on the other side of the wormhole. The Dominion is ruled by the Founders, a liquid lifeform whose individuals exist only as temporary excerpts of a larger whole—the Great Link. They are shapeshifters, changelings who are able to mimic any form, any plant, animal, or person. They are also Odo's people, though *Deep Space Nine*'s staunchly loyal chief of security wants nothing to do with the Founders and fights with the Federation against the Dominion.

A reclusive species, fearful of the suspicion and violence their metamorphic abilities provoke in "solids," as they call all other species, the Founders live on a planet far from the shipping lanes and well-traveled spaceways of the Gamma quadrant, protected by a race of fierce warriors called the Jem'Hadar, their vast empire administered by cloned functionaries known as the Vorta. Both the Jem'Hadar and the Vorta have been genetically enhanced to fulfill their respective roles in the Dominion and engineered to revere the Founders as gods. By many definitions, certainly Linford's, the Founders would be considered false gods.

To the Jem'Hadar, the Founders offer little more than the opportunity to die in their service, enslaved both by genetic programming and an engineered dependence on Ketracel-white, a drug they need daily to survive. "The white," as it is known, is a biological means of social control, producing a crucial enzyme their bodies have been created to lack. In many ways, though, it is also the sacrament of the Jem'Hadar, a material connection to and means of grace from their creators. Receiving their daily ration, vials of the drug are brought forward by the senior officer and placed reverently before the presiding Vorta, who, acting almost as a priest, distributes the white in a clearly ritualized manner. In "Rocks and Shoals," for example, an episode that pits stranded Starfleet personnel against marooned Jem'Hadar, the Vorta Keevan (Christopher Shea) dispenses the white.

                    KEEVAN

    Third Remata'Klan, can you vouch for the
    loyalty of your men?

                    REMATA'KLAN

    We pledge our loyalty to the Founders, from
    now until death.

                    KEEVAN

    Then receive this reward from the Founders.
    May it keep you strong.

Although Ketracel-white sustains the Jem'Hadar biologically, like all sacraments, it also assures them of their place in the divine order of the Dominion. To them, the Founders are gods—they could not be otherwise—and the white, controlled and administered by the Vorta, represents life both emanating from and offered up in the service of those gods.

A series of clones, the Vorta staff the vast organizational structure of the Dominion, advancing the Founders' various agendas in the Alpha quadrant, brokering their alliances and prosecuting their wars. Like the Bajorans and their Prophets, the Vorta are all too aware that other species view the Founders as a malignant, almost xenophobic race, so prejudiced against "solids" that compromise, cooperation, and coexistence seem faint hopes at best.

Both the Jem'Hadar and the Vorta also know that their reverence for the Founders is the result of genetic programming, that they have been created to worship the changelings as gods. In light of this, like the Ferengi religion of commerce and profit, it is tempting to dismiss the Founders as false gods and to decry their followers as dupes or pity them as victims. This implies, however, that there are true gods—or a true God—against which the false can be measured and that we are in a position to make that cosmic determination. It begs the unanswerable question of ontology rather than contending with the more complicated issue of relationship. As we will see in the following chapter, some would argue that we have a responsibility to free those enslaved by false gods, perhaps to operate as an interstellar anticult movement, forcibly deprogramming battalions of Jem'Hadar and whole cadres of Vorta. Conceptualizing the problem ontologically, however—asking whether the Founders (or the Prophets) really are gods—is a mistake that does little more than reduce religion on *Deep Space Nine* to the level of two-dimensional caricature that marked so many episodes of *Star Trek* and *The Next Generation*. The interpretive calculus in this is simple: having satisfactorily identified the Founders as false gods, there remains little more to say. Thus reduced, the issue of religion becomes the ultimate non sequitur, the Jem'Hadar the object of pity and the Vorta a joke.

Once again, though, this ignores the reality of religion offscreen, which is inevitably reflected in cinema and television. Numerous cultures have revered their leaders as divine or semidivine—the pharaohs in Egypt, for example, or Chinese emperors who became the Sons of Heaven. The Dalai Lama is considered by Tibetan Buddhists as the incarnation of Avalokitesvara, the bodhisattva of compassion, while medieval samurai revered the Japanese emperor as a direct descendent of the sun goddess, Amaterasu, and considered it an honor to die in his service. Hundreds of millions of Christians around the world believe that Jesus is not only the son of God, but God himself, and many are prepared to endure—and commit—any number of atrocities in his name.

This is not to say that either the Jem'Hadar or the Vorta are mindless drones, unable to conceive any social or religious order other than their own. In "Hippocratic Oath," for example, O'Brien and *Deep Space Nine*'s chief medical officer, Dr. Bashir (Alexander Siddig), are taken prisoner by a group of Jem'Hadar whose leader has managed to free himself of dependence on the white. Seeking Bashir's help for the rest of his platoon, he tells the doctor that he and his men want to leave the Dominion, to aspire to something more "than the life of a slave," to be free from the Vorta and, by extension, the Founders.

GORAN'AGAR

```
I have fought against races that believe in
mythical beings who guide their destinies and
await them after death. They call them gods.
The Founders are like gods to the Jem'Hadar.
But our gods never talk to us, and they don't
wait for us after death. They only want us to
fight for them--and to die for them.
```

The Vorta, too, are not above questioning the unseen order of the Founders. Like so many *DS9* episodes, "Treachery, Faith, and the Great River" is a double entrendre in meaning, narrative, and interpretation. While Nog happily teaches O'Brien about the Great Material Continuum, a Vorta rejects the pantheon of the Founders for the favor of one reluctant deity. Luring Odo to a lonely moon, Weyoun (Jeffrey Combs) asks to defect from the Dominion and requests asylum from the being he considers divine. Although he is a changeling, Odo denies being a Founder and angrily rejects any suggestion that he is a god. Indeed, while they hide from Jem'Hadar ships—which attack unaware of Odo's presence—the changeling scoffs at the reverence with which Weyoun regards him and his people.

ODO

```
Has it ever occurred to you that the reason
you believe the Founders are gods is because
that's what they want you to believe, that
they built it into your genetic code?
```

WEYOUN

```
Of course they did. That's what gods do.
After all, why be a god if there's no one to
worship you?
```

It is important to note here that Weyoun does not dispute the manufactured nature of his devotion, but neither does he dismiss its reality. Rather, in a way, he is like Christians who believe in human exceptionalism and who interpret Revelation 4:11—"you created all things, and by your will they existed"—as biblical proof that human beings were made by God explicitly to worship him, who celebrate the fact that we are genetically engineered, as it were, to praise God, and whose faith tells them that apart from this divinely inspired adoration we can neither realize our supreme good nor effect a harmonious relationship with God's unseen order. Unlike Goran'Agar, Weyoun has not left his faith behind—and does not want to—but has instead transferred it to the one in whom he believes the true ideals of the Founders might still be invested. As he tells Odo the creation myth of the Vorta, how the Founders genetically evolved them from timid forest creatures to the administrators of an interstellar empire, we are invited to ask, once again, isn't this what gods do? Weyoun may have foresworn the Dominion's ill-considered war against the Federation and lost faith in their vision of conquering the Alpha quadrant, but he has not renounced the Founders as gods.

When it becomes clear, however, that the Dominion forces will not allow Weyoun to escape, the Vorta chooses suicide rather than risk the life of a Founder any further. As he lies dying, he looks into the face of his god.

> WEYOUN
>
> Give me your blessing.

> ODO
>
> I--I--I can't--

> WEYOUN
>
> Please, Odo, tell me I haven't failed, that
> I've served you well.

> ODO
>
> You have, and for that you have my gratitude
> . . . and my blessing.

Within the restricted confines of their small Federation runabout, Odo has done everything he can to distance himself—physically and theologically—from Weyoun. To the changeling security officer, the Vorta was nothing more than a prisoner; to Weyoun, Odo was never anything but a god. As Weyoun dies, however, their physical distance disappears in the framing of the shot as Odo holds him gently, their faces only inches apart. And, for just a moment, the theological space between them is reduced as well.

Back aboard Deep Space Nine, even though he understands the biological basis of Weyoun's devotion, Odo struggles to reconcile the meaning of the experience. Of all those on board the station, Kira's faith in the Prophets allows her to understand best the moment of transcendence Weyoun knew in the few seconds before his death. Explaining the deeper meaning of the event to Odo, she is our chorus.

> KIRA
>
> The last thing he saw was one of his gods
> smiling at him. If you ask me, he was a lucky
> man.

> ODO
>
> Nerys, please--

KIRA

```
No, listen to me. I know to Starfleet the
Prophets are nothing more than wormhole
aliens, but to me they're gods. I can't prove
it, but then again, I don't have to because
my faith in them is enough. Just as Weyoun's
faith in you was enough for him.
```

In the last moments of Weyoun's life, fear and hope—the double helix of religious DNA—are fused. As he lies on the floor of the runabout, his head cradled in Odo's arms, a full five seconds elapse between gratitude and blessing—an eternity, no doubt, for the Vorta, his eyes filled with pain and uncertainty. If the Founder cannot offer him benediction and Weyoun dies staring into the face of denial, then for him all hope is lost. Everything that he has believed, everything that has structured his very being vanishes into the void with his last breath. If, on the other hand, he receives Odo's blessing, whether the changeling accepts its efficacy or not, whether we give credence to it or not, the Vorta's quest for transcendence is fulfilled. His gods still live. To Odo, that one small act is an unsavory admission of the engineered devotion of the Vorta; to Weyoun, it is a miracle.

After all, isn't this what gods do?

To be sure, *Deep Space Nine*'s presentation of religion is not uniform. It is filled with non sequiturs, logical inconsistencies, and unanswered questions—much like the sacred narratives that frame our own offscreen attempts to capture the human quest for transcendence. But, rather than offer little more than the butt of an occasional joke in the midst of the technological enlightenment of the twenty-fourth century, the Ferengi, the Klingons, the Bajorans, the Cardassians, the Jem'Hadar, and the Vorta illustrate the complexity of the relationships that exist between believers and their gods.

6

THE VON DÄNIKEN PARADOX
Stargate SG-1

OUTTAKE: *STARGATE*

JACKSON

Every other major architectural structure
of the time was covered with detailed
hieroglyphics. When is the academic community
going to accept the fact that the pharaohs of
the Fourth Dynasty did not build the great
pyramids? Look--look, inside the pyramid, the
most incredible structure ever erected, there
are no writings whatsoever.

PROFESSOR

Dr. Jackson, you left out the fact that
Colonel Vyse discovered a quarryman's
inscription of Khufu's name within the
pyramid.

JACKSON

Right! His discovery was a fraud.

PROFESSOR

Well, I hope you can prove it.

It is a scene that haunts the imagination of every academic. Standing before an assembly of one's peers, expounding theories in which we have invested our professional and often our personal lives, only to watch as colleagues shake their heads, muttering to each other behind their hands. A few ask perfunctory questions, throwing out a scholarly lifeline of sorts, but as we soldier vainly on most simply get up and walk out. There is no chorus of boos, no flurry of conference programs thrown down in disgust, nothing to indicate that our colleagues take us seriously in the least. There is only the echoing silence of an empty lecture theater and the final, plaintive question from the featured speaker, "Is there a lunch or something, that everybody's going to . . . ?"

In the establishing sequence for the "present day" storyline of Roland Emmerich's 1994 film, *Stargate*, archeologist Dr. Daniel Jackson (James Spader) is addressing a symposium devoted to the dating of the Egyptian pyramids. When were they built, and, more importantly, at least by implication, who built them? Offscreen, though there are differences within them, pyramid theorizing conforms to two basic models: dominant and alternative. Dominant archeology contends that most of the great pyramids were constructed by the Egyptians during the Fourth and Fifth Dynasties of the Old Kingdom period (2575–2323 BCE; cf. Baines and Malek, 2000; Lehner, 1997). Alternative theories, on the other hand, range from Christopher Dunn's argument that the pyramids on the Giza plateau functioned as a massive power plant for some long-vanished civilization (1998, 2005; Payne, 2005) to Joseph Farrell's belief in the Giza Death Star, a kind of pyramid-powered "phase conjugate howitzer" (2002, 2003, 2005). Hypotheses have also been proposed by more well-known alternative history theorists such as Graham Hancock, who argues for a technologically advanced civilization that existed long before current recorded history (1995; Hancock and Bauval, 1996; Hancock and Faiia, 1998), and Zecharia Sitchin (1976, 1980, 1985, 2007) and Erich von Däniken (1968, 1970, 1974, 2001), both of whom consider the pyramids—and a number of other ancient sites around the world—of extraterrestrial design and construction. Although he does not say it out loud, this is Jackson's theory as well, that human beings at the level of technological development enjoyed when the pyramids were built could not, in fact, have built them. Rather, they were built as landing pads for gigantic spacecraft: terrestrial stables for the chariots of the gods.

As he leaves the hotel, Jackson is a sorry sight, standing in the pouring rain, clutching his briefcase and a lone duffle bag. He has been evicted from his apartment, his academic grants have expired, and his career appears to be in tatters. However, he is offered an unexpected chance at redemption by Catherine Langford (Viveca Lindfors), the daughter of an archeologist who discovered a strange artifact on the Giza plateau in the late 1920s. Whisked away to a secret military installation, Stargate Command—which will become the "cosmic mountain" of the larger *Stargate* mythology—Jackson is asked to translate a line of hieroglyphs and perhaps prove his theories correct. Talking to himself, suddenly absorbed in this new puzzle, he works away at a blackboard, quickly crossing out words and changing translations.

JACKSON

```
Well, the translation of the inner track is
wrong. Must have used Budge. I don't know why
they keep reprinting his books . . . Who the
hell translated this? . . . This should read:
'A million years into the skies, Ra, Sun-god,
sealed and buried for all time'--it's not
'door to heaven'--it is . . . 'stargate.'
```

And so begins his adventure—and ours.

The basic plotline of the film and its two televisual offspring, *Stargate SG-1* and *Stargate: Atlantis*, is simple enough. Using an ancient device found in the sands of Egypt—the eponymous Stargate—a team of adventurers from Earth (SG-1) travel to distant points in the galaxy, battling evil aliens who have set themselves up as gods and freeing (or trying to free) the vast multitudes these creatures have enslaved. Many would say that there is not much more to it than that. The movie did a moderate box office business and was all but ignored by mainstream critics. The *Chicago Sun-Times*' Roger Ebert gave it one star and his review implies that he did that much grudgingly, suggesting that "the movie *Ed Wood,* about the worst director of all time, was made to prepare us for *Stargate*" (1994).

Stargate SG-1 and *Stargate: Atlantis,* on the other hand, the first of which picks up a year after the events in the feature film, went on to become two of the most popular science fiction series on American television, perhaps reminding us of what filmmaker and critic Adonis Kyrou wrote in *Le surréalisme au cinéma,* that we should "learn to look at 'bad' films. They are often sublime" (1963, 276). *Stargate: Universe,* the second sequel series, debuted in fall 2009. During its ten-season run, *SG-1* was nominated for eight Primetime Emmy awards and *Atlantis* for three, while both series were nominated for (and won) a host of specialized science fiction honors. Numerous "shared world" novels continue SG-1's adventures and a variety of Internet sites host *Stargate* fan fiction—new episodes into which enthusiasts often write themselves (McGrath-Kerr, 2004). Two made-for-TV movies, *Ark of Truth* and *Continuum,* rounded out the storylines of *Stargate SG-1,* and science fiction conventions eagerly seek to book regulars from both series for guest appearances. From action figures to board, video, and role-playing games (Kyer and Kyer, 2004), from artwork and memorabilia to episode guides (Storm, 2005) and critical analyses (Beeler and Dickson, 2006; Elrod and Conrad, 2004), the two television series clearly unlocked in legions of fans something the film could not: a sense of what media theorist Henry Jenkins calls "participatory culture" (2006; cf. Jenkins, 2008; Tabron, 2004).

Into what, though, are we invited to participate when the chevrons of the Stargate lock? And if, as literature scholar Frank McConnell (citing André Bazin) has argued, "film"—and we might now include television here—"is most correctly regarded as the realization of an aesthetic dream" (1975, 1), of what are we dreaming when confronted each week with the shimmering wavefront of the Stargate's stable wormhole?

True to its nature as action-adventure science fiction, many *SG-1* episodes are variations on such well-known themes as the "ticking time bomb" ("A Matter of Time"; "Singularity"), "run-and-gun" ("Enemies"; "Exodus"), or "escape the villain" ("The Serpent's Lair"; "The Tomb"), while others are simply played with a wonderful sense of self-deprecating fun ("200"; "The Other Guys"; "Window of Opportunity"; "Wormhole X-Treme!")—a particular requirement of series star and executive producer Richard Dean Anderson. Some are remakes of culturally popular storylines, such as the 2001 episode "Fail Safe," which adds *SG-1*'s interpretation to the prospect of a planet-killer asteroid, brought to the big screen three years earlier by Michael Bay (*Armageddon*) and Mimi Leder (*Deep Impact*). Although less obvious, perhaps, the 1976 film *Logan's Run* provides some of the generic background for voluntary population control in "Revisions." And, in the mid-series episode "Meridian," Brad Wright draws on a scene from Roland Joffé's *Fat Man and Little Boy* to write out one of the main characters on the SG-1 team. In the movie, Manhattan Project scientist Michael Merriman (John Cusack) saves his colleagues by separating two pieces of plutonium by hand, dying shortly afterward as a result of acute radiation poisoning. On *SG-1*, that scene is reprised when Daniel Jackson (Michael Shanks) similarly interrupts an experiment designed to make a bomb many hundreds of times more powerful than the ones produced at Los Alamos.

Like *Deep Space Nine*, however, over its ten-season career many of *Stargate SG-1*'s underpinning story arcs were laid down in terms of religion and power, and the series dealt with a number of issues central to questions of transcendence: the problem of false gods, be they the Goa'uld ("The First Commandment"; "Hathor"; "Seth"; "Metamorphosis") or the Ori ("Origin"; "Powers That Be"; "Crusade"); the possibility of alternate realities, whether dimensional ("Point of View"; "There but for the Grace of God"), temporal ("1969"; "2010"), or metaphysical ("Meridian"; "Threads"); and the question of power in whatever guise it appears ("Absolute Power"; "Emancipation"; "It's Good to be King").

For the most part, we are confronted once again with the problem of "false gods," initially in the form of the Goa'uld, which are malevolent, serpentine parasites that use other species as hosts and slaves. Later in the series, following the defeat of the Goa'uld, we are introduced to the Ori, a race of equally malevolent "Ascended Beings" who depend on the energy of worship to survive and who prosecute their cause in the form of a galactic crusade, a holy war of evangelism and forcible conversion. Although there are a few episodes that allude to the possibility of a "real God"—clearly, though nonspecifically modeled on the Christian god—most of *SG-1*'s religious and mythological subtext posits that the god-forms taken by the Goa'uld are meant to be viewed as false gods in the truest sense of the phrase. Among those used by the Goa'uld are: Anubis, Amaunet, Bastet, Hathor, Isis, Osiris, Ra, Sekhmet, Set, Thoth (Egyptian); Ares, Athena, Cronus (Greek); Morrigan (Celtic); Amaterasu (Shinto); Kali, Nirrti (Hindu); and Ba'al, Marduk, Moloch, and Tiamat (Ancient Near Eastern). In the episode "Demons," a Goa'uld does take the identity of Satan, but, sensitive to the dominant religious cultures of our time, nowhere do *SG-1*'s creators allow the Goa'uld to assume the identities of Yahweh, Jehovah, Jesus, or Allah. One can only imagine the popular outrage that would ensue. Even in "Demons," "Satan" is revealed later in the episode as Sokar, the Goa'uld version of one of the Egyptian gods of the underworld.

Although early in the pilot episode, "Children of the Gods," Jackson contends that the Goa'uld "borrowed the religion and culture of the ancient Egyptians . . . and used it to enslave them," it is important to note that *SG-1*'s larger narrative arc does not suggest that the Goa'uld are imposters or that they took on the identities of real gods in order to further their nefarious agenda. Rather, as the series progresses it consistently implies that the Goa'uld invented these god-forms. In the manner of von Däniken and Sitchin, the Goa'uld presence on Earth explains the origin of the gods and the religious structures that evolved to serve them. This subtle difference is understandable since, in the beginning, the Stargate team believed they were dealing with a single alien impersonating a particular deity. Onscreen, they were not yet aware of the extent to which the Goa'uld had influenced the development of religious culture and belief as a whole. Offscreen, series creators had no idea how popular the show would become and how extensively the mythology would need to evolve to carry a decade-long story.

Throughout the series, though they are always portrayed as arrogant and megalomaniacal, few of the Goa'uld seem to consider themselves gods in any ontological sense. Rather, they have intentionally extended their galactic influence on the basis of religion's power to motivate through hope and fear: ongoing hope for divine blessing and favor mingled with continual fear that the gods' blessing will be replaced by punishment. Similarly, in the final two seasons of the series, and demonstrating that even divine nature abhors a vacuum, the Ori step into the place left vacant once the Goa'uld are defeated and threaten to destroy—"to cleanse"—all those who will not accept the "teachings of Origin" and bow down before them as gods.

Seen thus, in *SG-1*'s universe most of humankind's religious history and evolution is predicated all but entirely on deception, conquest, and slavery, a seemingly endless succession of false deities that guide and terrorize humanity by turns. Reinforced throughout the series by many of the societies that still worship the Goa'uld—cultures that are often presented as stunted in their social evolution, superstitious and fearful of the unseen order, and content to live their lives under the dubious beneficence of their absentee gods—religious belief represents the infantilism of our race, a stage in development we are meant to outgrow. However, merely pointing out the origins of the various god-forms assumed by the Goa'uld, demonstrating that they are revealed as frauds, and perhaps assuming that this makes some kind of substantive comment on the nature of religion in late-modern society is the most superficial level of analysis (see, for example, Young, 2004).

As I noted in the previous chapter, and as such series as *Deep Space Nine*, *Babylon 5*, and *Battlestar Galactica* so amply demonstrate, if the history and sociology of religion teach us anything, it is that divinity is a function of ascription, not ontology—a product of the relationship between worshiper and worshipped, not an immutable aspect of being—and it is the nature of this bond that should be the proper object of analysis. Whether onscreen or off, arguing over whose god is "the true god" is often little more than a petty exercise in diminishing returns. Whether members of the SG-1 team believe in the reality of these gods or not, each time they step through the Stargate they continue the human quest for transcendence in two very particular ways: (a) exploring the boundaries that mark the transcendence of origins, and (b) affirming the importance we place on our sense of centrality in the quest for transcendence of those boundaries.

THE TRANSCENDENCE OF ORIGINS

We are fascinated by myths of origin. No matter how technologically advanced we become, no matter how far we travel from whatever we regard as our point of origin, where we are remains inevitably a function of where we're from. Who we are now—and, by implication, who we will be in the future—is intimately connected to who we believe we were in the beginning. Far more than stories passed along as the quaint trappings of outmoded superstition, the tales that mark our need to understand our origins transcend all attempts to establish boundaries around them. Despite considerable evidence to the contrary, for example, millions of devout Christians hold tight to their belief that Earth was created just a few thousand years ago—less than the blink of an eye in cosmic time. Far more than simply a myth of origin, as I note in chapter 3, this terracentric human exceptionalism anchors their place in God's universe. For them, origin is a necessary function of identity. Without a special creation, without a loving Creator who fashioned this planet for humans alone, an entire systematic theology threatens to unravel—a particular reality explored in the *SG-1* episode "New Ground," which is about a civilization at war over the social and theological implications of natural selection versus special creation. Yet, paradoxically, as the rise of fundamentalist Christianity in the late nineteenth and early twentieth centuries clearly demonstrates, the more our religious identities are challenged, the more firmly many of us seek to shore them up (see Marsden, 1991, 2006). There is something about our myths of origin that will not go quietly into the evolutionary night.

Unlike *Deep Space Nine* and *Babylon 5*, both of which are predicated on a galaxy populated by a wide variety of species, all of which evolved separate and distinct from each other and from humankind, *Stargate SG-1*'s main story arc posits a dispersal of human populations that were selected by the Goa'uld, taken from Earth and seeded among the stars to be the hosts, slaves, and worshipers of the different System Lords. To be sure, in addition to the Goa'uld, there are other alien races—the Unas, the Nox, the Ori, the Asgard, and the Ancients, who were the original builders of the Stargate system—but more often than not, the SG-1 team encounters cultural environments that seem remarkably familiar to us, though less technologically developed than we are and often branching off from clearly identifiable Earth societies. More than either *Deep Space Nine* or *Babylon 5*, this allows the series to explore myths of origin and, unburdened by *Star Trek*'s Prime Directive (which ostensibly forbids Starfleet interference in other cultures) to comment more directly on societies the writers deem either worthy as they are or in need of change.

In "Emancipation," for example, SG-1 encounters the Shavadai, a people descended from Mongols who were brought to another planet by the Goa'uld. True to their heritage, the Shavadai consider women property and either trade them for political stability or capture them as prizes in battles between warring clans. Since women have no rights, for a woman even to speak out of turn is a capital offense. Although not a fan favorite—many regard it as the first season's weakest episode, though admittedly, for many fans, much of this turns on the atrocious choice of costume for series regular Samantha Carter (Amanda Tapping)—it signals *SG-1*'s concern for the transcendence of origins. The message here is simple: women aren't chattel and your society must change to recognize that. In the episode "Spirits," on the other hand, among the Salish, who were taken from the Pacific Northwest thousands of years ago and deposited on the planet PXY-887, the spirits—particularly Ta'kaya, who appears as a wolf, and Xe'ls, a raven—function as protectors and guides. They are not Goa'uld, but members of another alien race who took the form of gods in order to protect and coexist peacefully with the transplanted humans. Even when they are revealed as imposters, the Salish do not reject them as other groups do the Goa'uld. Theirs is a harmonious existence, one the episode suggests should be maintained despite the evolution of the relationship between its human and nonhuman participants. Once again the message is clear: transcending one's origins does not necessarily mean abandoning one's beliefs.

In different ways, both episodes point to the principal mythology underpinning *Stargate SG-1* and *Stargate: Atlantis*: the ancient astronaut theory, the belief that the origins of civilization, if not of terrestrial life itself, lie in extraterrestrial intervention. The beings our ancestors worshiped as gods were, in fact, highly advanced alien races that chose to involve themselves in the affairs of our small, backwater planet for their own always mysterious, often malevolent purposes. In this, the power of cosmogonic mythology shows itself in two ways: the transcendent value of myths of origin, what I call here the von Däniken paradox, and the processes by which we transcend our myths of origin, which are explored most deeply through the story arcs of characters Daniel Jackson and Teal'c.

ANCIENT ASTRONAUTS AND THE VON DÄNIKEN PARADOX

In terms of *SG-1*'s initial narrative substrate, the logic of the ancient astronaut thesis is disarmingly simple: the Great Pyramids represent a feat of engineering far in excess of what the Egyptians of the Fourth and Fifth Dynasties—or even people today, for that matter—were capable. For writers such as Erich von Däniken and Zecharia Sitchin, mythology is the key to understanding. Instead of recounting fantastic stories of (now) unbelievable characters, ancient astronaut theorists contend that archeological and epigraphic records detail factual events, but render them according to the conceptual and imaginal limits of the day. That is, what we know as "civilization"—art, literature, architecture, mathematics, religion, and so forth—is largely the product of extraterrestrial visitation and intervention, much of which has been mythologized as the interaction between gods and humans. Buried in the middle of *Chariots of the Gods?*, his best-known work, von Däniken presses the theory's central claim:

> It is impossible and incredible that the chronicles of the Mahabharata, the Bible, the Epic of Gilgamesh, the texts of the Eskimos, the Red Indians, the Scandinavians, the Tibetans and many, many other sources should all tell the same stories of flying 'gods', strange heavenly vehicles and the frightful catastrophes connected with these apparitions, by chance and without any foundation . . . The almost uniform texts can only stem from facts, i.e. from prehistoric events. They related what was actually there to see. (von Däniken, 1968, 25)

Since *Chariots* first appeared in 1968, von Däniken's hypotheses have been ridiculed by a wide range of critics (Goran, 1978). Science fiction author L. Sprague de Camp charged that his "books are solid masses of misstatements, errors, and wild guesses presented as facts, unsupported by anything remotely resembling scientific data" (quoted in Frazier, 2001, 6). Only slightly more sanguine, Lutheran theologian Ted Peters suggests "that von Däniken's chariots and other UFO theologies offer us an ostensibly respectable way of talking about our deeper religious needs" (1977, 9), though he ultimately rejects the ancient astronaut theory because it does not fit with his conservative Christian theology. "The Hebrews did not mistakenly worship spacemen," Peters concludes. "They worshiped God. The Hebrews would never, knowingly, have worshiped spacelings" (1977, 173). His implicit psychologizing of the ancient astronaut thesis notwithstanding, the most obvious problem with Peters' counterargument turns on the word "knowingly." Von Däniken's theory posits that early contactees did not know they were dealing with extraterrestrials— "spacelings"—and that is the point implied throughout *Stargate SG-1*. Biblical literalist and young Earth creationist Clifford Wilson is similarly dismissive, arguing that "at times [von Däniken's] writing is ludicrous—with pathetically weak statements that surely cannot be taken seriously" (1972, 35; cf. Wilson, 1974). Like Peters, Wilson castigates von Däniken for his seeming inability to distinguish when the biblical record should be taken literally and when symbolically, but concludes his own rebuttal with a blatant appeal to fundamentalist Christian theology—von Däniken is wrong because Wilson's God is right—an explanatory ploy that is no less problematic than the ancient astronauts. "Although von Däniken has been largely discredited in the mainstream press," writes secular humanist Tim Callahan, "he continues to write and sell books read by the faithful" (2008, 37), and despite numerous attempts to limit the influence of his theory, according to the editors of *Skeptical Inquirer*, "von Däniken's conjecture lives on as fantasy fodder for numerous books and cable television documentaries on the unexplained" ("Ancient Effigies," 14; cf. Harrold and Eve, 1995). And, it seems, in enormously popular science fiction series.

Von Däniken, however, is not the only ancient astronaut theorist who reads sacred narratives as evidence of extraterrestrial paleocontact. The same year that *Chariots of the Gods?* appeared, Presbyterian minister Barry Downing published *The Bible and Flying Saucers*, contending among other things, that a UFO led the Hebrew people out of slavery in Egypt and that extraterrestrial intervention parted the Red Sea to facilitate their escape ([1968] 1997, 77–101). In his multivolume *Earth Chronicles*, Zecharia Sitchin, who is arguably the intellectual model for *SG-1*'s Daniel Jackson, considers the "sudden," "unexpected," and "inexplicable" emergence of civilization in the ancient Near East as evidence of extraterrestrial activity on Earth. Specifically, the Anunnaki—a race that Sitchin equates with the biblical *nephilim*, the "sons of God" who mated with the "daughters of men" in Genesis 6—came to Earth from a planet called Nibiru, which occupies such an eccentric elliptical orbit that it enters the inner solar system only every 3,600 years (1976, 1980, 1985). Robert Temple insists that the sacred narratives of the West African Dogon encode the story of extraterrestrial contact from the Sirius star system approximately five thousand years ago (1998). Raël, the founder of the Raelian religion, preaches that human beings were created in an extraterrestrial laboratory, then brought to Earth as part of a grand genetic experiment (1986, 1998). Although hardly a proponent of ancient astronauts, per se, even archrationalist Richard Dawkins is open to the idea of extraterrestrial intrusion into human evolution. Interviewed for Nathan Frankowski's documentary *Expelled: No Intelligence Allowed*, Dawkins told Ben Stein, "It could be that at some earlier time, somewhere in the universe, a civilization evolved—probably by some kind of Darwinian means—to a very, very high level of technology, and designed a form of life that they seeded onto, perhaps, this planet."

Thus, whereas the Fermi Paradox asks, "If there are so many aliens out there, where are they?" what I am calling the von Däniken paradox poses the question, "If we have so little evidence for them, why are these myths still so compelling for so many different kinds of people?"

Myth, as scholars have pointed out for decades, is not a synonym for fiction. Rather, it is a vehicle for explanation, a cache of symbols lodged in narrative that establishes a framework of cosmological significance for a particular group of people. They are stories that encode and, just as importantly, transmit cultural meaning and significance. As historian of religion Paul Brian Thomas points out, ancient astronaut theorists are deeply distrustful of dominant scholarship and propose a revisionist history that seeks to take myths of origin more seriously than they believe establishment archeologists do (2007). And, while few critics seem to recognize it, *Stargate SG-1* does just that as well, in the sense that myths of origin are not dismissed simply as fantasies or superstition, but understood as real cosmogonies that have been passed down from generation to generation among the people groups the team encounters. As even the most cursory look at history reveals, belief is real in its consequences, and this is the important point to remember. That the myths explored on *SG-1* have their origin in what the series establishes as false gods matters no more than the question of whether the Prophets or the Pah-wraiths are "real gods." To those who believe, the gods are real, and to suggest otherwise is to fall prey not only to the good, moral, and decent fallacy in the study of religion, but to a willful ignorance about the engines of significance in human history. Although he was writing about ghosts, and particularly the problems implicit in Tobe Hooper's 1982 film *Poltergeist*, Eugene Stewart's comment holds equally true for *Stargate SG-1*: "While bereft of fact, [it is] fraught with meaning" (1996, 23).

In terms of mythological understanding, and this is something skeptics of all stripes regularly fail to ask, the question is not how these various theories and hypotheses can be debunked, but why these myths of origin endure and, for our purposes, what that endurance in a long-running science fiction series like *Stargate SG-1* can tell us. Put simply, *SG-1* reinforces the transcendent value of cosmogonic myths. It highlights our collective need for myths of origin and questions the ability of technology, of science, and of modernity and postmodernity to corrode the power of those myths. Indeed, in science fiction, these myths are often reimagined, reinvigorated, and replayed.

TRANSCENDING ORIGINS

If the series itself demonstrates the transcendent value of myths of origin, Daniel Jackson and Teal'c are the two SG-1 team members who undergo the most radical development in terms of transcending their own myths of origin—one through death, the great transcendence, and the other through deicide, the murder of one's gods.

When actor Michael Shanks decided to leave the series in season five, instead of killing his character off—which would present significant narrative problems should Shanks decide to return—in the episode "Meridian," *SG-1* writers had Daniel Jackson evolve to a higher level of being, a state in which we exist as energy, not matter. Rather than die, with all the heaviness Western society invests death, Jackson follows the path of the Ancients and "ascends," moving on through the Stargate to the next stage of human existence. Death is denied its finality, not only in the context of the series but also in terms of Western culture's view of death as an enemy, a failure, or a punishment for transgressions only mythologically remembered. Rather than the traditional Christian view that humankind "is destined to die once, and after that to face judgment" (Hebrews 9:23), Jackson's great transcendence becomes a function of continuation, an ongoing affirmation of human significance in the cosmos.

In many ways, though almost inevitably mixed with new age notions of enlightenment and eternal progression, and although he ascends rather than descends, Jackson makes the classic hero's journey to the Underworld, what mythographer Joseph Campbell called "the spiritual deed, in which the hero learns to experience the supernormal range of human spiritual life and then comes back with a message" (Campbell, 1988, 123; cf. Campbell, 1968). As a being of light Jackson becomes—implicitly, at least—a light to others. In the episode "Abyss," Jack O'Neill (Richard Dean Anderson) has been captured by the Goa'uld Ba'al, who tortures, kills, and revives him again and again. For O'Neill, death holds no prospect of relief, only an endless cycle of pain and insanity. Jackson appears in his cell and offers O'Neill a sure way of escape, encouraging his friend to seek his own ascension. Although Jackson is able to effect change on the material plane—he could simply free O'Neill—he is forbidden to do so by the code of conduct established for all ascended beings.

In his classic essay, "Spirit, Light, and Seed," the eminent historian of religions Mircea Eliade writes that mystical light experiences—in which we might include Jackson's ascension—"bring a man out of his profane universe or historical situation, and project him into a universe different in quality, an entirely different world, transcendent and holy" (1971, 2). For Jackson, this is certainly the case. He has no idea what awaits him when he ascends, only that his quest for transcendence has entered a new stage. Eliade continues:

> The structure of this holy and transcendent Universe varies according to a man's culture and religion. Nevertheless they share this element in common: the Universe revealed through a meeting with the Light contrasts with the profane Universe— or transcends it by the fact that it is spiritual in essence, in other words only accessible to those for whom the Spirit exists. (Eliade, 1971, 2)

Eliade uses explicitly theological language here—indeed, a major criticism of his work has been that he used the history of religions to propagate a particular religious agenda—but his insights are particularly salient in terms of the quest for transcendence. Our understanding of "the Universe," by which I suggest Eliade means the unseen order, is culturally specific and always defined by such particulars as language, religion, education, and social position.

Although Daniel Jackson is a late-modern Western academic, an archeologist immersed not only in the myths of the past but in the rational and secular demands of the present, he is also open to the possibility that the material world does not exhaust reality and that what we discover about that world does not define the limits of what we can know or can become. Indeed, this is the function of his character throughout the series. If O'Neill is the soldier and protector, for whom all situations can be reduced to their tactical pragmatics, and Carter is the scientist, who sees the world in terms of problems to be solved, Jackson is the show's soul of wonder, as it were. He is the one who consistently tries to see beyond the limitations of the obvious and, through his ascension, transcends the boundaries that so much of late-modern rationalism insists mark the edge—and the end—of human experience. This sense of wonder has prepared him for the experience of ascension; he is ready to move on. He knows that the ascended Ancients are not gods any more than are the Goa'uld, and he knows that he will not become a god, but his openness to a world beyond his own has prepared him for the next stage in the journey. For Daniel Jackson, hope in the face of death is that death is not the end but merely one more boundary to be crossed.

For Teal'c, on the other hand, the possibility of transcendence is not a function of his own death, but that of his putative gods. He is a Jaffa, a member of the warrior race genetically manipulated by the Goa'uld to serve both as their military arm and as living incubators for their young. Like the Jem'Hadar's relationship with the Founders through Ketracel-white, the larval Goa'uld serve as a kind of symbiotic sacrament that circumscribes all of life for the Jaffa. Marked by ritual implantation once a Jaffa reaches puberty, the larva provides increased strength, longevity, and health for its host—the ongoing gifts of the god that is literally living within. A Jaffa's eventual and inevitable inability to carry a larval Goa'uld means the end of usefulness in the service of their gods—the end of life, purpose, and meaning.

Once the "First Prime of Apophis," the principal warrior in the service of a powerful System Lord, Teal'c has rejected the Goa'uld and is now considered a *shol'vah* by his people, a heretic, a traitor to the gods. Of all the SG-1 team, his journey is arguably the most significant. None of the others actually believe that the Goa'uld are gods. To O'Neill, they are "snakeheads" to be eradicated, to Carter an intriguing if deadly scientific puzzle, and to Jackson the vindication of his theories about extraterrestrial contact with Earth. To Teal'c, though, they are the only gods he has ever known, and when he rejects them as gods and fights against them, he commits not only heresy, but deicide.

In many ways, it is far easier to exchange gods—to set aside one pantheon for another, to convert between religious paths—than it is to cast aside one's beliefs entirely, to stand before one's gods, whose larval form has accompanied you day and night, strengthened you in battle and healed your injuries, lived always within you as a constant reminder of the relationship between the devotee and the divine, and to say, "I will worship you no more." In the series pilot, when Teal'c first turns on the Goa'uld, he expects nothing but an ignominious death, but at least he will die free, choosing to live no longer as a child of false gods. In the next episode, "The Enemy Within"—the title a significant, multiple entendre in the context of the series— when it becomes clear that American military leaders will not immediately trust him as a member of the SG-1 team, O'Neill reassures him: "Teal'c, I saw you stand up to a god. Refuse to kill, I saw you make that decision . . . In that moment I learned everything I needed to know to trust you."

Whereas for many, the quest for transcendence leads toward the divine, toward whatever gods populate the unseen order, Teal'c's quest for transcendence will not be complete until all the Goa'uld are dethroned or dead. He is the show's Promethean figure, stealing fire from the gods by exposing them for what they are. Their power as gods was rooted in their deception and once that has been unmasked, they are gods no more. More than simply a traitor and a heretic, however, a *shol'vah* who has traded one set of theological allegiances for another, he is a deicide, and when he kills the gods for himself he threatens to kill them for all.

In "The Serpent's Venom," while attempting to recruit other Jaffa to his "blasphemous rebellion," Teal'c is captured by Apophis (Peter Williams) and tortured in an effort to force him to renounce his heresy and proclaim the Goa'uld once again as gods. Appalled and in awe of his defiance, a young Jaffa named Rak'nor (Obi Ndefo) asks whether Teal'c does not fear the punishment of the gods, the possibility that his soul will be damned forever. Hanging in chains, his face beaten and bruised, barely able to speak through the blood in his mouth, Teal'c replies with his own version of Pascal's wager.

TEAL'C

I have seen the world from which they originated. I have stood beside the swamps from which they first arose. They are really flesh and blood, just like you or I.

RAK'NOR

Lies!

TEAL'C

Why would I lie, if there was a chance that they were gods? If I thought my soul would be forever punished, <u>why</u> would I lie? They have manipulated our bodies, so too are they manipulating our minds with false beliefs.

RAK'NOR

You believe this so strongly that you risk dying in sin?

For Teal'c there is no longer any chance that the Goa'uld are gods, so there is no wager. He has transcended the myths of origin that have kept his people enslaved and challenges others to do the same. The indecision on Rak'nor's face, however, marks the uncertainty that every Jaffa must face when the time comes to decide the fate of the gods. It is that terrible, yawning chasm that opens before us when the myths that anchor our very selves are cut loose, when we choose to leave behind the beliefs that have defined us and enter the undiscovered country that lies beyond the borders that have circumscribed our existence. Unlike the Vorta Weyoun, there is no Founder to offer comfort or blessing. For the Jaffa, there is only the dawning certainty of cruelty and deception at the hands of false gods and the possibility of freedom once those gods are dead.

THE CENTRALITY OF TRANSCENDENCE

We do not know where the human quest for transcendence began, or when. Theories abound, some more compelling than others, but certainty escapes us. As I pointed out in the previous chapter, many devout Christians believe that the impulse to worship was created in us by God, that the myths and rituals that surround our relationship with the divine are ontologically (and even biologically) inescapable. On the other hand, evolutionary anthropologists such as Scott Atran (2002) and Pascal Boyer (1994, 2001) argue that the development of a sense of cosmic meaning increased our potential for survival as a species, naturally selecting us over our evolutionary cousins who failed to make a similar leap. As we have seen, still others suggest that our predilection for a relationship with the unseen order—which is all but ubiquitous around the world and throughout history—is a function of extraterrestrial intervention and manipulation. Although, like so many popular science fiction series, it is easy to dismiss *SG-1* as little more than action-adventure laced with scientific improbability and narrative implausibility, it does offer us a series of stories replete with what Eliade calls "half-forgotten myths, decaying hierophanies, and secularised symbols" (1952, 18)—in particular, the encounter with the sacred, the place of the cosmic mountain, and the myth of centrality.

Encountering the Sacred at the Stargate

Named for the nineteenth-century anthropologist Pierre Paul Broca, "The Broca Divide" separates the planet designated P3X-797, which its inhabitants call Elora, into the Land of Light and the Land of the Dark. Descendants of the Minoans, Elorans who are "untouched" live in the Land of Light, believe themselves blessed by the gods, and regularly bring offerings in the temple built around the great ring of the Stargate. Once "touched" by what they consider the evil gods of the underworld, however, the Elorans devolve physically, mentally, and emotionally until they are banished to the Land of the Dark. To those who remain in the Land of Light, the banished are dead, remembered as they were and forgotten as they are. Rather than divine malevolence, however, Stargate Command's chief medical officer, Dr. Janet Frasier (Teryl Rothery), discovers that a "parasitical virus" is causing the condition by inhibiting the specific neurotransmitters responsible for language ability and higher reasoning, effectively shutting down "all but the most primitive parts of the brain." Instead of divine intervention, a simple antihistamine reverses the condition.

Considered from a mythological rather than a pharmacological perspective, "The Broca Divide" could as easily be titled "Eliade's Divide" since in many ways the Elorans are literally divided into the sacred and the profane, inhabitants of the light and the dark, those who remain blessed by the gods and those who have been "touched" by evil—cursed, in more traditional theological language. In *The Sacred and the Profane*, arguably the most accessible introduction to his thought, Eliade (1957) contends that the principal separation within all people groups is between the sacred and the profane, the world set apart for our relationship with the unseen order and the world of everyday life. Obviously, this is not a perfect analogy, but few are. By "profane," Eliade means the mundane, the ordinary, everything that occurs apart from the sacred, though this often is not how the concept is popularly understood today. According to Eliade, as an excerpt of the mundane, the sacred is always manifest in "hierophanies," in those times, places, things, and events that express at some concrete, historical moment the encounter between the seen and the unseen orders (1958, 1–33). Because these manifestations can take any form— once again the issue is ascription, not ontology—things have the meanings we give them, while nothing has meaning inherent in it. Whether we accept the hierophanies of others as reasonable expressions of the sacred is immaterial, a problem Eliade knew only too well. "What I propose is by no means always easy," he told his readers more than half a century ago in *Patterns in Comparative Religion*. "To the Western mind, which almost automatically relegates all ideas of the sacred, of religion, and even of magic to certain historical forms of Judeo-Christian religious life, alien hierophanies must appear largely as aberrations" (1958, 10–11). At the most basic level, this is precisely the issue with which *Stargate SG-1* deals throughout its ten-season run.

For the Elorans, as it is for so many societies we encounter in the series, the Stargate is the central point of hierophany. Far more than merely a large stone ring, it is the archetypal place of divine power, the expression of the sacred in their culture, and the point through which the world of the gods intersects with their own. Whether it is the product of "false gods" or not—created by the Ancients or appropriated by the Goa'uld—for those living in the Land of Light, the Stargate both establishes and symbolizes cosmos, order in the midst of chaos. It is the physical expression of their myth of origin, their connection to a transcendent order and the ongoing assurance of their place in it.

Even though the members of SG-1 tell the Elorans that there are no gods—though they themselves were originally mistaken for gods, since, perforce, only gods come through the Stargate—even when they demonstrate that there is no curse, only a "parasitical virus" that can be treated with (to us, at least) common antihistamines, there is no way to ensure that once the team steps back through the Stargate, the Eloran's old cosmology, which by this time is deeply embedded in their culture, will not reassert itself. As years go by, perhaps stories will be told of the strangers who came through the ring of the gods and cured the Touched, who brought the dead back to life, who reunited families and made the Eloran society whole once again. As more time passes, they too will be theologized, written into the sacred narratives, and possibly divinized because, after all, isn't that what gods do?

Professor Eliade Visits Stargate Command

If the Stargate is the primary locus of hierophany for societies such as the Elorans, what is Stargate Command (SGC), the military temple that guards it on Earth? In mythological terms, the enormous underground complex lying deep beneath Cheyenne Mountain—the real-life home of NORAD (North American Aerospace Defense Command)—is the *axis mundi*, the center of the world that anchors our perception of all other worlds and negotiates our communication with them. Once again, and bearing in mind that he is writing about so-called traditional societies, Eliade's insights help us see a different side to *Stargate SG-1* and the quest for transcendence it represents. For him, the "system of the world"—in this case, *SG-1*'s mythologically charged universe—has four principal, concentric elements:

> (a) a sacred place [that] constitutes a break in the homogeneity of space; (b) this break is symbolized by an opening by which passage from one cosmic region to another is made possible (from heaven to earth and vice versa; from earth to the underworld); (c) communication with heaven is expressed by one or another of certain images, all of which refer to the *axis mundi* . . . (d) around this cosmic axis lies the world (= our world), hence the axis is located "in the middle," and the "navel of the earth"; it is the Center of the World. (Eliade, 1957, 37)

Prior to the Stargate's discovery and Jackson's solution to the problem of interstellar navigation, humankind was planet-bound: limited to occasional excursions just beyond the wafer-thin layer of atmosphere in which our world is wrapped, our notions of transcendence circumscribed by the often petty bickering among, essentially, tribal religions. The Stargate changed all that in the most radical way possible. History, science, religion, cosmology—all of these are rewritten when the wormhole is engaged, and each time the wormhole opens, the homogeneity of our existence is challenged. For all the apparent differences between peoples and cultures on our planet, we are all human, and, as science fiction cinema from *The War of the Worlds* to *Independence Day* suggests, nothing makes that more obvious than the possibility of alien invasion. If the profane means the ordinary, the everyday, Stargate Command is the principal site for a "break in the homogeneity of space," the place from which we sight new horizons and realize new requirements in the quest for transcendence. No longer homogeneous, space is, indeed, frighteningly heterogeneous, populated by beings and forces we can scarcely imagine but with which we are now forced to deal. As the enigmatic Q (John de Lancie) demonstrates in *Star Trek: The Next Generation* ("Q Who?"), the universe is filled with wonders and terrors for which the pale differences of our planet have ill prepared us.

Just as more traditional cosmologies have envisioned passages to other worlds through a variety of openings—holes in the ground or caves behind waterfalls, disused wardrobes or secret pools in the forest (Lewis, 1950, 1955), the parting of the mists of Avalon (Bradley, 1982) or Harry Potter's Platform 9³/₄ (Rowling, 1997)—the Stargate is the literal gateway "from one cosmic region to another." But, like these other passageways, the Stargate is not for everyone; it is reserved, as it were, for those who have been called or initiated into its mysteries. Kept hidden hundreds of feet inside the cosmic mountain, it constitutes a crucial part of the esoteric knowledge that keeps the universe in balance, and its very existence is a secret available only to a few. Solving the problem of the gate address symbology—the means by which wormholes are created and destinations reached—Jackson is the Stargate's prophet, while Carter is the one who tends it as its priestess. O'Neill is the guardian of the cosmic mountain and Teal'c is SG-1's guide when they step through the gate. Although other societies on other worlds may use it as a commonplace means of transport, trade, or conquest, on Earth the Stargate is both the passage "from heaven to earth" and the symbol through which that passage is realized. Although the original film's Dr. Jackson translated the ancient text as "stargate," in mythological terms it is the "door to heaven."

Finally, as our presumptive homogeneity is fractured a bit more with each journey through the wormhole, Stargate Command becomes the Center of the World in defense of creation and order. In its war against the Goa'uld and the Ori—as well as a variety of other potential invaders—Stargate Command is the mythological center of order (cosmos) in the face of potential disorder (chaos). Besides the variety of ongoing extraterrestrial conflicts, a number of episodes recount attacks on Earth through the Stargate itself. In "Hathor," the eponymous Goa'uld seeks to control the men of Stargate Command with sexual pheromones, while in "Singularity," Nirrti sends an explosive Trojan horse through the gate in the form of a young girl. In "Foothold," aliens who are able to impersonate SGC personnel gain control of Stargate Command, while in "Redemption," the Goa'uld Anubis seeks to destroy Earth by means of the Stargate itself. In each case, our world stands on the brink of destruction and depends on those who inhabit the cosmic mountain to restore order.

The potential for chaos is inevitably met with the reestablishment of cosmos. As Eliade points out, "Any destruction of a city"—and here we may insert Stargate Command—"is equivalent to a retrogression to chaos. Any victory over the attackers reiterates the paradigmatic victory of the gods over the dragon (that is, over chaos)" (1957, 48). With the restoration of order comes the reiteration of meaning.

THE MYTHS OF CENTRALITY AND CONTINUITY

"No human being can exist for long," wrote psychologist Rollo May in *Power and Innocence*, "without some sense of his own significance" ([1972] 1998, 37). Although it may seem obvious, the myths of centrality and continuity are "central" to a number of religious traditions: the Israelites as God's "chosen people," the one before whom all other people groups in the Levant appear somehow rescindent, and the saved versus the damned, whether as a function of church sacrament or personal conversion. Indeed, from Psalm 8, which according to some versions tells how humankind was created just a little lower than God, to Hamlet's words to the hapless Rosenkrantz and Guildenstern, "Oh, what a piece of work is man . . . in action how like an angel, in apprehension how like a god" (act 2, scene 2), we constantly locate ourselves at the center of the universe. In many ways, the myth of centrality that is implicit in *Stargate SG-1* is the diametric opposite of the reverse zoom sequence that opens *Contact* and highlights our utter insignificance in the vastness of the cosmos. Many SETI scientists (as well as skeptics of the search for extraterrestrial intelligence) argue that alien visitation ranges from unlikely to impossible because Earth is too small and too out of the way, galactically speaking, to be of any interest. The ancient astronaut hypothesis on which *Stargate SG-1* rests, however, presupposes a significance that stands in direct counterpoint to these doubts. Two episodes in particular invoke the myth of centrality that underpins the series: "The Enemy Within" and "The Fifth Race."

After rejecting the Goa'uld in the series pilot, Teal'c arrives at Stargate Command to find that he has stepped into the center of the mythology that has shaped and guided Jaffa beliefs for thousands of years.

> TEAL'C
>
> There is a tale of a primitive world the
> Goa'uld discovered millennia ago. The
> Tau'ri. The First World where forms of this
> type first evolved. It is said the Goa'uld
> harvested among the primitives; some became
> Goa'uld hosts, others became Jaffa, the rest
> were taken as slaves and seeded among the
> stars to serve them. But that world has been
> lost for centuries.
>
> KENNEDY
>
> Teal'c, beings of this form evolved here on
> Earth.
>
> TEAL'C (astonished)
>
> This world . . . ?

When everyone in the room realizes that the human population of the galaxy—the transplanted slaves of the Goa'uld—began on Earth, and that it is from Earth that the Goa'uld's defeat must proceed, Teal'c intones the mythic significance of the entire series: "You are their greatest hope. And mine." Suddenly, the balance of the universe has swung and its center—its *axis mundi*—now rests firmly in Stargate Command.

More than simply the paleocontact progenitors of galactic slaves, however, on *Stargate SG-1* humans are also central to the development of a more harmonious galactic civilization. They are "the fifth race." While exploring a room on the planet designated P3R-272, bare except for columns of indecipherable hieroglyphs on the walls—writings Jackson hypothesizes were left by four great races that explored the galaxy millennia ago—O'Neill is inadvertently "uploaded" with a repository of Ancient knowledge. Indeed, their entire archive now resides in his human brain. Unequal to the challenge, he gradually loses the ability to communicate with his team, while at the same time designing and building equipment far in advance of human technology.

His final device generates sufficient power for the Stargate to dial eight symbols rather than the usual seven, something Carter believes allows a wormhole to be established not just between planets and stars, but across galaxies. O'Neill steps across the threshold and finds himself on the homeworld of the Asgard, one of the first four races. Building on the late-twentieth-century mythology of alien contact and abduction, science fiction fans will immediately recognize the Asgard as "grey aliens"—small, delicate beings with bulbous, tear-drop-shaped heads and huge, black eyes. In some science fiction narratives, such as *The X-Files* and *Communion*, the greys are malevolent invaders bent on conquest and colonization; for others, including *Stargate SG-1*, they are the benevolent interstellar visitors from *Close Encounters of the Third Kind*. After they have removed the Ancient knowledge from his brain, O'Neill learns that humans have been the subject of intense scrutiny for a long time. We are central to the shape of the universe.

                    ASGARD 1

    We have studied your race closely.

                    O'NEILL

    What did you learn?

                    ASGARD 2

    That your species has great potential.

                    ASGARD 1

    Understand this, there was once an alliance
    of four great races in the galaxy: the
    Asgard, the Nox, the Furlings, and the
    Ancients, the builders of the stargates . . .
    The alliance was built over many millennia.
    Your race has much to prove before we may
    interact on that level.

                    O'NEILL

    You folks should understand that we're out
    there . . . now. And we might not be ready

```
for a lot of this stuff, but we're doing the
best we can. We are a very curious race.
```

The two Asgard look at each other, enigmatic and inscrutable, communicating in a way O'Neill can only begin to understand. Slowly, one alien looks at the human and extends its hand in a gesture of friendship. O'Neill takes it in a moment that is distinctly reminiscent of Michelangelo's "Creation of Adam." As O'Neill stands, the Asgard tells him, "You have already taken the first steps toward becoming the fifth race." When he returns to Stargate Command, he tells his friends that, although he no longer possesses the knowledge of the Ancients, "you know that 'meaning of life' stuff? I think we're going to be alright."

"A myth," writes Eliade at the end of *Patterns in Comparative Religion*, "may degenerate into an epic legend, a ballad or a romance"—or, we might suggest, an action-adventure science fiction series. "For all this," he concludes, "it loses neither its essence nor its significance" (1958, 431). Myths of centrality and continuity anchor the hope that we matter in the grand context of some larger plan, that we are more than merely bit players stumbling about some insignificant corner on the universal stage. If through his ascension Daniel Jackson is *Stargate SG-1*'s microcosmic example of this, then humankind as the fifth great race in the galaxy is the macrocosm. Our centrality in the cosmos—the hope that our lives have meaning and purpose—is a mythic theme that is continued in the following chapter on *Babylon 5* and challenged subsequently aboard the *Battlestar Galactica*.

7

ALL ALONE IN THE NIGHT
Babylon 5

OUTTAKE: "THE PARLIAMENT OF DREAMS"

DELENN

Exactly what sort of demonstration does he
have planned?

IVANOVA

Unknown. He wouldn't even tell us. He just
said it would showcase Earth's dominant
belief system.

NA'TOTH (looking around)

I don't hear any drums.

VIR

Or bells.

LENNIER

Or chants. Are you sure that we've come to
the right place?

G'KAR

That's it, I'm leaving!

In an effort to increase understanding and promote peace, Babylon 5, the miles-long space station located in the Epsilon Eridani star system about ten light years from Earth, is hosting a convocation of religious faith—an interstellar version of the Parliament of the World's Religions held in Chicago (1893, 1993) and Melbourne, Australia (2009). All the races that live on the station have been invited to send delegates from their faith traditions, to demonstrate their various prayers and rituals, and, hopefully, to educate their fellow galactic citizens about their religious beliefs and practices. A splendid notion, in theory. The episode opens, however, with security chief Michael Garibaldi (Jerry Doyle) confiscating a large, ceremonial dagger from a Drazi pilgrim, who swears angrily that "the Maker of All Things will allow nothing to stand between me and the blade!" When Garibaldi does not relent, the Drazi moves on, clearly unhappy but willing to interpret the altercation as a test of his faith. As the camera pans around the public sections of the station, we see a variety of humans and nonhumans dressed in religious garb. In this episode, however, the principal demonstrations of faith are reserved for the Minbari and the Centauri, two of the major races aboard the station and key players in the *Babylon 5* saga.

Wearing a hooded robe made of white satin and surrounded by similarly attired acolytes, Delenn (Mira Furlan), the Minbari ambassador and a high-ranking member of her people's religious caste, leads what looks a bit like a Christian communion service commemorating the Last Supper between Jesus and his disciples. This ritual, though, is dedicated to the memory of Valen, the almost mythical founder of Minbari society and creator of their ruling body, the Grey Council. According to Minbari belief, it was Valen who joined them together as one people and forbade the Minbari to harm one another—a law that has stood for a thousand years in their society. Harp strings are plucked gently and the air is filled with the delicate tinkling of silver bells as Delenn's aide, Lennier (Bill Mumy), reverently offers her a crystal bowl filled with small, red fruit.

"Will you follow me into fire?" she asks, intoning Valen's enigmatic words from a millennium past. "Into storm? Into darkness? Into death?" As she speaks, Lennier passes among the people, offering each a piece of fruit from the bowl. Some refuse, others take but do not eat. A few taste the fruit warily.

DELENN

```
And the Nine said, 'Yes.' Then do this in
testimony to the one who will follow, who
will bring death couched in the promise of
new life, and renewal disguised as defeat.
From birth, through death and renewal. You
must put aside old things, old fears, old
lives. This is your death, the death of flesh,
the death of pain. The death of yesterday.
Taste of it and be not afraid. For I am with
you to the end of time.
```

Finishing the liturgy, Delenn looks intently at Commander Jeffrey Sinclair (Michael O'Hare), Babylon 5's first military governor, who hesitates, holding the fruit in his hand. "Taste of it," she repeats. When, finally, he eats, she pulls back her hood, satisfied. "And so," she says, concluding the ritual, "it begins." Like so many religious rituals, this one explicitly recalls the *Ur*-moment of meaning and purpose, the cosmogonic point of social origin that must be held in tension with the emergent and ongoing concerns of the present. Where we came from continues to shape who we are.

The solemnity, grace, and dignity of the Minbari ceremony, however, stand in marked contrast to the rude bacchanal that is the annual Centauri Festival of Life. Led by their ambassador, Londo Mollari (Peter Jurasik), the people prepare a magnificent feast to memorialize the Centauri victory over a rival species on their homeworld, the Xon—their *Ur*-moment as a people blessed by their gods. Laughter fills the air and lively baroque music plays in the background as beautiful Centauri women circulate among the tables, some dancing sensuously, others passing by with braziers of incense or trays laden with food and drink. It is an annual celebration of life and joy, the quasireligious backdrop to the basically hedonistic Centauri lifestyle.

As more drinks are served, Susan Ivanova (Claudia Christian), Sinclair's executive officer and second-in-command of the Earthforce contingent aboard Babylon 5—and the only non-Centauri who seems to be enjoying herself at the feast—asks about the variety of statues arranged on the large tables. "Ah," answers Mollari, laughing, "our household gods!" He leans in toward her and continues conspiratorially, "In a world where every day is a struggle for survival you need all the gods you can get." Raising his goblet in a traditional Centauri toast—"Val Too-oo!"—Mollari climbs drunkenly onto the table and grasps one of the small statues. "Here," he cries happily, "this is Venzann, god of food. And Li," picking up another, "goddess of passion." Mollari takes the gold figurine of a nude Centauri—clearly female, though displaying both sets of sex organs—and less than reverently kisses its buttocks. According to one fan Web site, the *Encyclopedia Xenobiologica*, Li was a real woman who lived during the Xon Wars and was "one of the first goddesses to enter the major pantheon," though "her advocation of passionate lovemaking, large families, and promiscuous behavior brought her scorn and derision during her lifetime" (Russo, 2004). Moving down the table, scattering food and drink, Mollari pushes another small statue toward his guests. Looking like a winged gargoyle, this is "Mogath, god of the underworld"—Mollari pauses for a moment, as if struggling to remember—"and protector of front doors." Suddenly overwhelmed by emotion and alcohol, he raises his hands in the air. "Gods by the bushel," he shouts, "gods by the pound! Gods for all occasions!" As the Centauri ambassador passes out on the table, his attaché, Vir Cotto (Stephen Furst), rises, announcing triumphantly, "He has become one with his inner self!"

In one of the many online discussion forums through which *Babylon 5* creator, executive producer, and principal writer J. Michael Straczynski generated interest in the series (Jenkins, 2006, 145–46; Lancaster, 2001, 1–33), fans wondered not only how religion would be handled aboard the station generally, but more specifically whether nonhuman religions would be presented as monolithic and whether there would be any significant representation of Earth religion. Although the issue of religious homogeneity is certainly a problem in science fiction at large—though, one could argue, as Jill Tarter does, that the only hope for a species to survive long enough to realize interstellar travel would be to develop "a universal religion with no deviations, no differentiations—absolutely global and compelling for all" (2000, 35)—there is at least some indication in later seasons of *Babylon 5*, particularly among the Narn and their ambassador, G'Kar (Andreas Katsulas), that nonhuman does not necessarily mean monolithic. In the early episodes, however—"The Parliament of Dreams" was the series' third episode—this is often the case, and as the epigraph above indicates, nonhumans on the show seem no less surprised than humans when the religions of others differ from their own. Mollari's seemingly outrageous behavior at the Centauri feast might offend some religious sensibilities, but even that must be seen both in the context of the series as a whole and wary of our penchant for the good, moral, and decent fallacy. What, then, as the representative of Earth, is Commander Sinclair to do? The key here is that each race has been invited to present its dominant religion, which does not necessarily mean its only one.

While his command staff and the station's diplomatic elite wait, wondering why they have been summoned to an apparently empty cargo bay, Sinclair appears and invites them into the next room, where he begins to introduce them to a group of humans standing in a long line.

> SINCLAIR
>
> This is Mr. Harris, he's an atheist. Father
> Cresanti, a Roman Catholic. Mr. Hayakawa,
> a Zen Buddhist. Mr. Rashid, a Muslim. Mr.
> Rosenthal, an Orthodox Jew. Running Elk, of
> the Oglala Sioux faith. Father Papapoulous, a
> Greek Orthodox. Ogigi-ko, of the Ibo tribe.
> Machukiak, a Yupik Eskimo. Sawa, of the
> Jivaro tribe. Isnakuma, a Bantu. Ms. Chang,
> a Taoist. Mr. Blacksmith, an aborigine. Ms.
> Yamamoto, a Shinto. Ms. Naijo, a Maori. Mr.
> Gold, a Hindu . . .

The nonhuman ambassadors quickly drop out of the frame as representatives of Earth's varied religions and religious cultures fill the screen, the camera pulling back along a line of men and women that does not end before the closing shot fades to black.

The message seems abundantly clear: the hope for the future lies not in dominance, but in an interdependence that recognizes the value of difference rather than the necessity of similarity. This recognition transcends the kind of exclusivist religious boundaries that have arguably perpetrated more misery in human history than any other single social or cultural division. Of course, there are times when religion is (and has been) a positive social force, when religious actors work for the good of all involved rather than according to their own narrowly defined theological or political self-interests, but the problem of interreligious conflict rarely has been far from the surface of human history.

THE RELIGIOUS CROSSROADS OF THE GALAXY

If Gene Roddenberry pitched the original *Star Trek* to the network executives at Paramount as a "Wagon Train to the stars"—a description that is arguably more apt for *Battlestar Galactica*—and *Stargate SG-1* can be understood as the mythic journey from the cosmic mountain to the heavens, *Babylon 5*, which is equally beloved by legions of fans (Lancaster, 2001), is a kind of Dodge City in space. Set in the mid-twenty-third century, like *Deep Space Nine* much of the action takes place on an enormous space station, the eponymous Babylon 5, a crossroads in the stars administered by a military governorship from Earth. As Sinclair explains over the opening credits of each first-season episode:

> SINCLAIR
>
> It was the dawn of the Third Age of mankind,
> ten years after the Earth-Minbari War. The
> Babylon Project was a dream given form. Its
> goal: to prevent another war by creating a
> place where humans and aliens could work out
> their differences peacefully. It's a port
> of call, home away from home for diplomats,
> hustlers, entrepreneurs and wanderers. Humans
> and aliens wrapped in 2,500,000 tons of
> spinning metal, all alone in the night.

In many ways the Babylon station is hope given form, the quest for transcendence pressing at the boundaries of conflict, both interpersonal and interstellar. And, as in the other series I discuss, different religious understandings—human and nonhuman—underpin significant parts of *Babylon 5*'s multiple story arcs. The series' second episode, for example, "Soul Hunter," concerns a race of mysterious beings who are drawn to the moment of death and whose purpose is to ensure that souls are preserved once death has occurred. Thought to be immortal, they believe that unless a soul is rescued at the moment of the great transcendence it dies with the body. Although the concept varies among the different faith traditions, as I point out in *Sacred Terror*, "the soul is an explicitly religious concept, one that makes little sense apart from the religious frameworks in which it comes embedded" (Cowan, 2008b, 6). Many religious believers consider it our most basic link to the unseen order. One of the first things we learn aboard Babylon 5 is that the concept of this link is limited neither to humans nor to the narrow theological visions that so often bound human understandings of the soul.

Unlike either *Star Trek: Deep Space Nine* or *Stargate SG-1*, both of which raise questions of belief in terms of the reality of the gods and the place of religion in the future, *Babylon 5*, which ran from 1994 to 1998, rarely questions either the rationality of religious belief or the irrationality implicit in the plethora of different, often competing religious beliefs. In a 1993 post to the online discussion forum alt.tv.babylon-5, Straczynski wrote to fans who were wondering just how the new series would tackle the thorny issue of religion on a science fiction television show.

> Let me just lay the foundation here for a moment in the area of religion and *Babylon 5*. I'm an atheist, that simple. But that's me. If you look at the long history of human society, religion— whether you describe that as organized, disorganized, or the various degrees of accepted superstition—has always been present. And it will be present 200 years from now. That may not thrill me, but when one is a writer, one must deal with realities, and that's one of them. To totally ignore that part of the human equation would be as false and wrong-headed as ignoring the fact that people get mad, or passionate, or strive for better lives.

As I pointed out in my discussion of *Deep Space Nine*, science fiction often appears less concerned with human religion than with nonhuman and, by and large, *Babylon 5* is no exception. Science fiction as a genre is, after all, beloved of its aliens and, like *Deep Space Nine*, the centralized location of *Babylon 5* allows for more detailed exploration of religious beliefs in nonhuman cultures. If nonhumans have developed an awareness of the unseen order, if this awareness has evolved into a religious system, what would that look like? How would it impact their relations with species other than their own? As Sinclair makes clear at the conclusion of "The Parliament of Dreams," the concept of dominance in religious belief is often entirely relative.

In "By Any Means Necessary," written by Katherine Drennan, we find the Narn ambassador, G'Kar, making his morning devotions during the Holy Days of G'Quan, the rough equivalent of Lent or Ramadan for those of his faith. Surrounded by candles and wearing a ritual robe, a brazier of incense smoking in front of him, and his sacred Scripture, *The Book of G'Quan*, open before him, he makes the ritual prayers.

G'KAR

    To you I give the grain, the light, and the
    sky. To you, a sacred heritage. To you, the
    land and sea.

As he begins a monophonic Narn chant, the doorbell chimes. His aide, Na'Toth (Julie Caitlin Brown), has arrived. "So spoke G'Quan at the dawn of all mornings," he concludes distractedly, closing the holy book. She reports that the crucial element for the culmination of the ritual period—a flower called the G'Quan Eth—has been lost in a shipping accident, setting up the B story for this episode. The only person on the station who has the plant is G'Kar's sworn enemy, the Centauri ambassador, Mollari, who will only sell it for an outrageous price. Later in the episode, desperate to obtain the ritual flower, G'Kar even considers killing Mollari. He sees *The Book of G'Quan* on the table and sits, touching his forehead and the book reverently. He is ashamed of himself.

G'KAR

    You're not a follower of G'Quan, are you,
    Na'Toth?

                    NA'TOTH

My father was a disciple of G'Lan. My mother
didn't believe in much of anything.

                    G'KAR

What do you believe in?

                    NA'TOTH

Myself, Ambassador.

                    G'KAR

Too easy an answer. We all believe in
something greater than ourselves.

Although throughout this episode we are subtly encouraged to think, "It's only a flower. How important could it possibly be?" this is, as G'Kar implies, too easy a question. Whether it is a flower, a piece of cloth, a small steel ring, or some other form of ritual object, material culture is not only reflective of one's religious belief and practice, but constitutive of it as well. Moreover, for members of a particular faith, though it may not be socially dominant and may even be proactively marginalized, the demands of that faith often dominate their personal horizons regardless of the derision such devotion provokes in others (cf. Cowan, 2008b, 147–51). What seems a trifle to many defines for some the very quest for the divine.

THE QUEST FOR THE DIVINE ABOARD BABYLON 5

The hopeful irony of *Babylon 5*—both the series and the station— lies in the first season's opening monologue. Sinclair may say that we are "all alone in the night," but the truth revealed throughout the series is that, however our varied agendas clash or correspond, we are all in this together—human and nonhuman alike. And, although Straczynski is an atheist, he has produced a chain of story arcs that demonstrates remarkable sensitivity to issues of religious belief and practice in all their problems and possibilities. Few *Babylon 5* episodes display the humanistic hubris of *Star Trek: The Next Generation*

or the a priori judgment on religious belief of *Stargate SG-1*, and even
when they do, other characters offer a cogent and often immediate
corrective.

In the first-season episode "Grail," when a religious seeker
named Aldous (David Warner) comes aboard the station, Delenn
insists that members of the command staff greet him with full diplomatic honors. Asked about the particular nature of his mission,
Aldous responds simply, "I am seeking the Sacred Vessel of Regeneration, known also as the Cup of the Goddess, or by its more common
name, the Holy Grail." Unable to find it on Earth, his religious order
has expanded their search out among the stars. "It has many names,"
he continues, "but only one promise: the regeneration and salvation
of humankind." However well they try to hide it, both Sinclair and
Garibaldi react to his story with mild amusement, while Delenn, vis-
ibly irritated by the human response, assures Aldous that he is "most
welcome" on Babylon 5. Later, though it is clear he didn't mean to
be deliberately rude, Sinclair tells Delenn that religious quests such
as these are "not often taken very seriously" among humans—not
incorrect, perhaps, but a bit puzzling for a race that overwhelmingly
believes in some kind of unseen order and trusts in some manner of
ultimate salvation. "How sad," the Minbari ambassador responds.

DELENN

> He is a holy man, a true seeker. Among my
> people, a true seeker is treated with the
> utmost reverence and respect. It doesn't
> matter that his grail may or may not exist.
> What matters is that he strives for the
> perfection of his soul and the salvation of
> his race. And that he has never wavered or
> lost faith.

For Delenn, clearly the character with whom we are meant to identify in this scene, Aldous emulates the quest for transcendence itself.
The state of the soul, the salvation of one's people—these are the
things we should value, for they are the hallmarks of the quest, the
common denominators of meaning and purpose. As Marcus Brody

(Denholm Elliott) says to the redoubtable Indiana Jones (Harrison Ford) in *The Last Crusade* (1989): "The search for the Holy Grail is the search for the divine in all of us."

Debating religion rather than dismissing it, many of *Babylon 5*'s story lines deal directly with Straczynski's conviction that, contrary to the predictions of critics ranging from Enlightenment philosophers to late-modern secular humanists, religious belief and practice—both the desire and the quest for transcendence—will not disappear soon or easily. It will retain its cultural valence, taking many forms aboard Babylon 5, including reconciliation, resistance, redemption, and revelation.

In "TKO," written by Lawrence Ditillio, two battles are fought—different in many ways, yet the same in others. The episode's A plot concerns a disgraced human boxer's desire to compete in a nonhuman mixed martial arts tournament, to demonstrate the faith in himself he thought he had lost—and, implicitly, to win back the trust of those he betrayed in the past. The much more poignant B plot explores the story of Susan Ivanova's estrangement from her father, Andrei, and her reconciliation with his memory in the months following his death. A Russian Jew, after her brother was killed in the Earth-Minbari War she joined Earthforce—over the passionate objections of her father, a scholar and Tolstoyan pacifist. Now her father has died, and, alienated from him for many years, Ivanova has not made the time to sit *shiva*, the seven-day period of mourning when a close relative has passed. Attempting to heal the rift, the family's rabbi, Yossel Koslov (Theodore Bikel), travels to Babylon 5—which he calls "*nes gadol*, a 'great miracle'"—to see Ivanova and, implicitly, to help her reconnect with her Jewish roots. When Ivanova reacts angrily to his interference, he replies with an unperturbed shrug, "I'm a rabbi. When I see a Jew denying one of our most basic traditions, I meddle."

As Koslov prepares to leave the station, his mission unfulfilled, Ivanova suddenly sees her father through the lens of her rabbi's counsel: that without forgiveness we cannot mourn, and without mourning we cannot let go of our pain. In the end, light years from Earth, though anything but alone in the night, she sits *shiva* and on the final evening of the ritual acts as a chorus for the show's audience on the importance of Jewish belief.

```
IVANOVA

Though it's traditional to recite the
mourning prayer in Hebrew, I would like
to read it in English tonight so that my
good friend, Jeffrey Sinclair, may share
it with us. 'Oh, God, full of compassion,
who dwellest on high, grant perfect rest
beneath the sheltering winds of thy divine
presence, among the holy pure who shine as
the brightness of the firmament, to Andrei,
my father, who has gone to his eternal home.
Amen.'
```

It is a moving final scene that betrays no hint of mockery or derision, no sense that in the twenty-third century and so far from Earth, the rituals that connect us to the transcendent have (or should have) lost any of their meaning or power. Rather, there is something warm and comforting about the reconciliation—both with family and tradition—that Ivanova realizes, a feeling that director John Flynn and cinematographer Fred Murphy reinforce through soft candlelight and the intimate framing of the final *shiva* scene. These believers are at peace with themselves and, for the moment, with their world.

Others, however, are not. Contrasting with the warmth and intimacy of Ivanova's *shiva* ceremony, many scenes in the episode "Believers" take place in the hard, sterile environment of the station's Medlab, its hospital facility, and highlight the offscreen problem of religious belief in deadly conflict with social mores. Tharg (Stephen Lee) and M'Ola (Tricia O'Neil), members of a race that calls itself the Children of the Egg, have brought their desperately ill son, Shon (Jonathan Charles Kaplan), to Babylon 5 in hopes of finding a cure. Although his condition is serious, Chief Medical Officer Stephen Franklin (Richard Biggs) is confident that a simple procedure will correct the problem and assure the boy a speedy, complete recovery. To Franklin's surprise, Shon's parents react with alarm at the prospect of surgery, no matter how minor. "Food animals are cut open," his mother explains to the doctor and his assistant, Dr. Hernandez (Silvana Gallardo). "They don't have a soul, so it's all right. But the Chosen of God may not be punctured."

Although it is clear that Shon's parents love him and are desperate to see him cured, they are also bound by the strictures of their beliefs, the very shape and texture of their worldview. To them, any violation of his body will allow his spirit to escape prematurely, leaving behind an empty shell that is open to invasion by demonic forces. "Without his spirit," Tharg declares bluntly, "he wouldn't be alive anyway." Realizing that they would rather allow their son to die than permit surgery, Hernandez demands, disgustedly, "What kind of a god do you worship?"

Tharg and M'Ola are presented alternately as loving parents frantic to save their son and as stern, unyielding fundamentalists who believe that they alone have access to the divine will. For instance, rather than watch the station's entertainment channels, which "demonstrate false belief systems," Shon "can study the [sacred] Scrolls if he gets bored" in Medlab. Rather than simply alien beliefs in a science fiction universe, however, these restrictions highlight numerous, very real offscreen conflicts. From Christian Scientists to Jehovah's Witnesses, and from nondenominational Pentecostals to Latter-day Saints, many religious people choose to place their faith in prayer rather than seek medical treatment. They trust in God rather than doctors—often placing themselves and their children in grave peril. In more than a few cases, children have died as a result, and in numerous others the state has intervened and terminated parental rights in the interest of a child's welfare (Peters, 2008).

Faced with what he considers nothing more than the superstitious intransigence of the parents, Franklin asks Sinclair to suspend their rights, allowing him to perform the surgery. When Tharg and M'Ola learn this, the panic in their eyes is obvious. For them, this is infinitely more than mere superstition and far more is at stake than their son's life. His immortal soul, his very being, is in jeopardy. To place the question in terms of false gods is, once again, to ask altogether the wrong question. Eventually, Sinclair supports the rights of the parents to determine the welfare of their child—both physical and spiritual. Echoing his father and immensely relieved, his mother says, "Without a spirit, it isn't life at all."

Refusing to abandon what he believes is his own calling, however, Franklin operates on Shon anyway. When the boy awakens, his parents react in fear and horror, pulling back from him and chanting what sound like prayers for protection. To them, he is no longer a "Child of the Egg"; he is no longer their son. That boy died on the operating table the moment Franklin made his first incision. Drawing a small knife, Tharg accuses Shon of being a demon, an animate body without a soul. "What unholiness spawned you?" he shouts, pulling his wife from the room. As Franklin cradles the understandably distraught boy, Shon begins to chant verses from their sacred scrolls, retreating into what little comfort they can offer. All he knows, though, is that his parents are gone, that he is gone, that his life may continue but his world is no more.

When Franklin next sees Shon, he is accompanied by his parents and dressed in the *lamuda*, the traveling robe for great journeys. Only too late does the doctor realize its implication. He races to the family's quarters to find that, according to the rituals and beliefs of their people, amidst candlelight and prayer, they have ended their son's life. They have exorcized the demon.

M'OLA

> Do not grieve. This was not our son. This was
> only a shell. There was nothing to do but end
> the pain of the shell.

Throughout the episode, it is easy to identify with Franklin, to condemn the parents as he does and dismiss them as narrow-minded fundamentalists who care more for their beliefs than for the life of their child. "May God save us from false religion," he spits at Sinclair, inviting our agreement. A worthy sentiment, perhaps, but writer David Gerrold refuses to make the choice that easy, either for the crew of Babylon 5 or for the audience.

SINCLAIR

> What makes a religion 'false'? If any
> religion is right, then maybe they all have
> to be right. Maybe God doesn't care how you
> say your prayers, just as long as you say
> them.

```
                    FRANKLIN

What if there's no God at all? . . .

                    SINCLAIR

Life has to be more than just a pulsebeat.
What we hold sacred gives our lives meaning.
What are we taking away from this child?
```

When Franklin first approaches Sinclair for permission to operate against the parents' wishes, he assumes that the station commander will be on his side, that it is a simply a matter of setting aside superstition in favor of saving a life. This is, though, one of the fallacies of limited alternatives into which discussion of contested religious belief often falls. Too often, we assume that protecting the right to freedom of religion means that we tacitly agree with the beliefs or practices in question. This is incorrect. Rather, Sinclair demonstrates that if we value freedom of religion, then that value is most severely tested when we are called to stand for the rights of people whose beliefs and practices we find incomprehensible, even repugnant. If we only support those beliefs with which we agree, then we don't value freedom of religion at all. It is a hard lesson and an often bitter truth.

If "TKO" demonstrates the beauty of reconciliation and "Believers" the polyvalent problem of religion and resistance, season three's "Passing through Gethsemane" shows us the difficult side of redemption, the demanding path to forgiveness in the face of great and terrible wrong. Brother Edward (Brad Dourif) is a Catholic monk who now lives on the station as part of a religious order dedicated to "learning all the names and faces of God from our nonhuman brothers" and sisters—a quest not unlike that undertaken by Tibetan monks in Arthur C. Clarke's famous 1953 short story, "The Nine Billion Names of God." Having learned a little of Minbari belief, he reveals to Delenn and Lennier the "defining moment" of his own faith, the "emotional core" of his Christianity, which is intimately caught up in the story of Christ's night alone in Gethsemane before his arrest, trial, and crucifixion (cf. Matt 26:35-37; Mark 14:31-33). He tells them how Christ could have avoided the soldiers, escaped the Roman dragnet for a few hours or days, and perhaps even allowed the cup of suffering to pass from him entirely—which is precisely the question explored in Martin Scorsese's *The Last Temptation of Christ* (1988; cf. Kazantzakis, 1960). "He knew what would happen," Edward continues, as the two Minbari listen, entranced, "but he chose to stay, to sacrifice himself, to atone for the sins of others. A very fragile human moment. And I've often thought about that night, and I honestly don't know if I would have had the courage to have stayed."

It is a gentle, intimate scene, an iconic representation of Babylon 5's raison d'être—two cultures sharing, learning, and perhaps finding a fragment of common ground on which to build a more promising future. But it is lodged in a much darker narrative. For a few days now, Brother Edward has been having disturbing hallucinations: words written in blood on the walls and visions of women murdered, each with a black rose stuffed in her mouth. The light and openness of Delenn's apartment contrast vividly with the tenebrous corridors of the station and reflect the growing darkness in Edward's mind as he searches for the cause of his distress. Kneeling in prayer in his own sparse quarters, a small crucifix on the wall above his bed, we have a feeling of Gethsemane closing in around him. He, too, senses the approach of unimaginable suffering.

Among the Earth colonies of the twenty-third century, capital punishment is a thing of the past. Rather than execution for capital crimes, convicted offenders undergo a telepathic "mind-wipe," a death of personality that removes all vestiges of the old persona and replaces it with one designed to serve the needs of the community harmed. They are never meant to encounter the family or friends of their victims, nor to remember anything of their crimes. Before his mind-wipe, Brother Edward was a serial killer who murdered at least nine women. Members of his victims' families have tracked him to Babylon 5 and used a Centauri telepath to break down the walls of the mind-wipe, allowing the full consciousness of his crimes to flood in upon him. From that moment, all his scenes are filmed in shadow and there is no clear light to follow. "How can I confess my sins to God," he demands of his superior, Brother Theo (Louis Turenne), "if I don't even know what they are? The mind forgets, but the stain remains with the soul." The structural support behind which he hides casts the shadow of a cross on his face. "If you ask God to forgive your sins," Theo pleads with him, "he knows what they are, even if you've forgotten. Leave it in his hands." But Edward cannot.

The families of his victims find him kneeling in prayer at a prie-dieu in a small chapel—a single spotlight illuminates him, a cross hangs on the wall behind. Among others, the scene replicates Heinrich Hoffman's now-iconic 1890 painting, "Christ in Gethsemane." Gregorian chanting plays in the background as they close in to exact their revenge. When Theo and the station personnel reach him, Edward has been crucified, hung up on scaffolding with chains, and beaten nearly to death. As they bring him down, he asks them to forgive his attackers for "what had to be done." "I always wanted to know if I would have the courage to stay at the Garden of Gethsemane. Now I know, Theo."

Dying, cradled gently in Brother Theo's arms, Edward's death is not unlike Weyoun's aboard the Federation runabout in *Deep Space Nine*'s "Treachery, Faith, and the Great River." "Theo," he croaks, his mouth swollen and choked with blood, "I'm afraid. Is there enough forgiveness for what I've done?" For such a man as he was, is the great transcendence a pit or a passageway? How many times must men and women throughout history have come to that same question: is the God he came to believe in so ardently still there? "Always, Edward," answers Theo, whose name means "God" in Latin and who refuses to call the dying monk by his pre–mind-wipe name. "Always."

BROTHER THEO

Through the mysteries of our redemption, may almighty God release you from all punishments in this life, and in the life to come. May he open to you the gates of Paradise, and welcome you to everlasting joy. Father, look with compassion on your servant, Edward, who has trusted in your promises. Welcome him into your kingdom in peace. By the authority which the Apostolic See has given me, I grant you full pardon and remission of all your sins.

(makes the sign of the cross)

```
In the name of the Father, and of the Son,
and of the Holy Spirit. Amen.
```

Amen. So be it. The seal of redemption and forgiveness is given as it has been in the Catholic Church for more than two millennia. And once again, just as with Weyoun and Odo, it matters little whether we believe in the Roman Catholic doctrine of salvation, if the remission of sins granted in the act of absolution carry any theological weight with us. In the moment of his transcendence, for Brother Edward it is enough.

Two points are worthy of mention here. First, while the symbolism in this episode is far more obvious and heavy-handed than in many others, it is also more ambiguous and resists any easy or definitive interpretation. We are certainly encouraged to see Edward as a Christ-figure, as someone who represents the sacrifice but not the person of Jesus (Malone, 1997), but the symbolism is muddied by the fact that he suffers for no crimes but his own—and those are particularly egregious. He passes through his own kind of Gethsemane, to be sure, but a fundamental tenet of Christian doctrine is that Christ led a sinless life—something Edward can hardly claim. Indeed, given the penchant of some film and television critics to see Christ-figures virtually everywhere (cf. Deacy, 2006; Kozlovic, 2004), it is altogether too easy and too trite to suggest him as a Christ-figure. Rather, perhaps he is the extreme representation of each of us, hiding our sins in secret, wondering whether the universe contains enough forgiveness for the wrongs we have visited on others. Rather than the central figure on Golgotha, he is one of the two criminals the gospel accounts allege were crucified on either side of Jesus. Although the crucifixion narratives do not agree on this point, and Christian theologians have argued its meaning and significance for centuries, according to Luke's gospel, one of the thieves recognized the just nature of his punishment and begged Christ "to remember me when you come into your kingdom" (23:42). Perhaps this is a more apt reading of Edward's character.

Second, the issue of redemption does not rest with the all-too-easy image of the repentant killer, conscious of his crimes, accepting of his punishment, and asking for forgiveness. In the episode's final scene, we learn that the enraged man who killed Brother Edward has been mind-wiped in punishment for his crime. He is now Brother Malcolm (Robert Keith), who, Brother Theo tells Babylon 5's new commander, John Sheridan (Bruce Boxleitner), "has just joined the order under most unusual circumstances" and is about to leave the station for his novitiate training. When the smiling young monk extends his hand in greeting, Sheridan recoils, but Theo intervenes. Looking sternly at the captain, he reminds him, "I believe you were saying that forgiveness is a hard thing, but something ever to be strived for, were you not, Captain?"

Finally, amidst reconciliation, resistance, and redemption, there is revelation. Among Babylon 5's diplomatic contingent, none is more enigmatic than the Vorlon ambassador, Kosh Naranek. Only very rarely, most prominently in the second-season finale "The Fall of Night," does Kosh appear without his massive "encounter suit," a self-contained environment that allegedly protects, but more effectively disguises him. A rare visitor to the station's ambassadorial council, when he does speak it is often in riddles reminiscent of Zen *koan.* In "Deathwalker," when Commander Sinclair complains that he doesn't understand what the Vorlon means, Kosh's mechanically reproduced voice intones, "Understanding is a three-edged sword." When the distraught Tharg and M'Ola seek his diplomatic intervention on behalf of their son, he tells them that "the avalanche has already started. It is too late for the pebbles to vote." Late in the second season, when an exasperated Commander Sheridan asks Kosh why he can't just show himself, the Vorlon replies that people are not ready, that he would be recognized. Since no one in living memory has ever seen a Vorlon, however, and no starship has ever returned from Vorlon space, who could possibly recognize him? Kosh replies simply, inscrutably, "Everyone."

Explaining the significance of the Vorlons during the late second-season episode, "In the Shadow of Z'Ha'Dum," Ambassador Delenn acts as a chorus both for Sheridan and for the audience. Of all the races in the galaxy, the Vorlons are the last of the First Ones, a group of races that walked among the stars like giants—"vast and timeless beings which predate humanity by billions of years" (Bassom, 1997, 74). Although their origins are lost in the nativity of time, for millennia they battled other beings known only as the Shadows—the first race in the universe, and ancient when even the First Ones were young. Like the monstrous cosmogony of the *Enuma Elish*, the Babylonian creation myth in which the younger gods led by Marduk slay the primordial dragon, Tiamat, the Shadows represent the dark, primeval chaos of the universe and the First Ones the bringers of light and cosmic order. Now, millennia later, chaos encroaches on cosmos and the old gods seek their return (cf. Cowan, 2008b, 75–84). The Shadows are moving once again, manipulating war among the younger races—principally the Centauri and the Narn—while Kosh stands alone, the last of the First Ones to remain in normal space and time.

By the end of the second season, the Centauri, their aggression facilitated by Londo Mollari's unwitting alliance with the Shadows, have invaded the Narn homeworld and Earth has signed an ill-advised nonaggression pact with the invaders. This dangerously destabilizes the fragile neutrality on which Babylon 5 is built and Sheridan moves to assert their independence of action in the face of Earth's self-serving political machinations. As he travels in a monorail along the ventral spine of the vast station, however, an assassin's bomb detonates, throwing him out of the car high above the ground. Panicked, Delenn turns to the Vorlon. "Kosh, you know what is at stake. If you're going to do anything, you must do it now."

A bright blue light forms within the Vorlon's encounter suit and its helmet slides back. As the station's rotating hull spins toward Sheridan at sixty miles per hour, its artificial gravity slowly pulling him out of weightlessness to his death, a being of light rises into the air on glowing wings. To Delenn and Lennier, he looks like a Minbari, to others, something else. As Kosh rises to catch him, Sheridan sees an angel, a human face on the being of light. Kosh does not smile per se, but wears an enigmatic, Mona Lisa–like expression as he takes Sheridan's hands and carries him safely to the ground. In the Vorlon, each race sees its own embodiment of the unseen order.

"It was G'Lan," declares a Narn, marveling at the experience. "I saw him with my own eyes. He swooped down as was told in the old stories."

"No, not G'Lan," replies a Drazi, though not antagonistically, "Droshalla—whose light fills the world." They turn to the Centauri diplomat. "And you, Ambassador Mollari, what did you see?"

"Nothing," Mollari answers sharply. "I saw nothing." The Centauri ambassador can spend his life drunkenly shouting, "Gods by the bushel, gods by the pound!" but the chaos with which he has aligned himself prevents him from seeing the personification of cosmos when it appears in front of him.

If they reveal nothing else, science fiction series such as *Deep Space Nine*, *Stargate SG-1*, *Babylon 5*, and, as we will see in the next chapter, *Battlestar Galactica*, teach us that when it comes to religion, to our understanding of the unseen order and the quest for transcendence it so often demands, perspective is everything. In a now-classic article on the nature of mystical experience, Steven Katz highlights the importance of perspective when the veil between the seen and the unseen orders is parted. Central to this is Katz's "single epistemological assumption": *"There are NO pure (i.e. unmediated) experiences"* (1978, 26; emphasis in original). Further, Katz argues that "the experience itself as well as the form in which it is reported is shaped by concepts which the mystic"—in this case, we can insert "the religious believer," whether human or not—"brings to, and which shape, his experience" (1978, 26). Put differently, when we are confronted with the transcendent, we interpret that experience through the various filters our culture has provided and that we have appropriated. Our social worlds shape our religious visions. When in the grip of a mystical experience, Catholics do not see the Hindu god Ganesh, just as Hindus do not envision Mary and the Holy Child. Each understands her experience, as it were, according to her own expectations. Thus, for the Narn, it is the "old stories" deeply embedded in his cultural consciousness and passed on across generations of his people that structure his experience of the Vorlon. To the Drazi, it is Droshalla, the being through which his people understand the embodiment of cosmos, the light that throws back the darkness. For the Minbari, it is the legendary figure Valerian. Once again, two points are important to note.

First, in the wake of Kosh's revelation, there is no obvious attempt to decide which is the correct interpretation of the experience, to assert whose vision is "real"—and, by extension, whose is not. Echoing Sinclair's introduction of Earth's religious adherents and presaging Brother Edward's encounter with the Minbari, each accepts the reality of the others' experiences. "It doesn't matter," replies the Narn amiably, despite the Drazi's vastly different perspective on who rescued Sheridan. "It was a good sign for the coming year." Implying the same basic premise with which Carl Sagan approaches the question of religion—that is, the "general problem with much of Western theology . . . is that the God portrayed is too small" (2006, 30)—Straczynski (who wrote the episode) none too subtly counters Jill Tarter's assertion that differentiated religious cultures must give way to some form of theological monolith if they are to survive. Since a universal religion is as unlikely as the disappearance of religion altogether, perhaps a more reasonable solution is admitting that at any time and any place, none of us has access to the entirety of truth, but that what we know of truth is always culturally conditioned and socially constructed (cf. Berger, 1967; Berger and Luckmann, 1966).

Second, however, notwithstanding the importance of the cultural mediation of religious experience, there is an implicit theological understanding at work in *Babylon 5*, one that draws on the same alien astronaut theory as *Stargate SG-1*, but which stands its meaning and significance on its head. Struggling to understand his own near-death experience, Sheridan learns more about the Vorlons.

SHERIDAN

Every race that was in the garden saw something different, yet the same. A being of light.

DELENN

Yes. Each according to his or her own type.

SHERIDAN

But it was Kosh, wasn't it? That's what he meant when he said if he left his encounter suit he'd be recognized by everybody.

DELENN

For millions of years, the Vorlons have visited other worlds, guided them--

SHERIDAN

Manipulated us? Programmed us so that when we saw them, we would react the right way?

DELENN

```
It is, as you say, a matter of perspective.
```

Rather than malevolently intervening in primitive societies as did the Goa'uld or the Ori, the Vorlons (and, by implication, others of the First Ones, such as Lorien [Wayne Alexander], who is introduced later in the series as the first of the First Ones) benevolently guided the development of the galaxy's younger races until they were ready to journey among the stars themselves. Reflecting once again the theories of Erich von Däniken and Zecharia Sitchin, *Babylon 5* suggests that the gods may be real, though they may not be who we have been taught to believe they are.

RELIGIOUS ACTORS
Transcending Space and Time

It is a common misconception that "religions" do things—that this religion practices this, while that religion does something else—but this is not properly the case. Religion is a concept, an imaginative placeholder that allows us to locate certain human actions and behaviors in their proper contexts. As Jonathan Z. Smith puts it, in a passage that never fails to annoy my students when they read it for the first time, "Religion is solely the creation of the scholar's study. It is created for the scholar's analytic purposes by his imaginative acts of comparison and generalization. Religion has no independent existence apart from the academy" (1982, xi). What Smith means by this is that the self-conscious ability to categorize human activity into such domains as "religious" and "nonreligious" is a relatively recent development and confined largely (though no longer exclusively) to the academy. His comment can be read in another way, however, suggesting that the analytic consideration of "religion" is only possible through the lens of "religious actors." That is, religion is not something that exists apart from the people that create it, and we can only discern what religion is when we understand what those people do in their ongoing acts of religious creation. There are, of course, religious institutions—individual congregations, for example, denominational aggregates, ecclesial and educational systems, and interreligious federations of one kind or another—but these exist only insofar as the people that constitute them continue their participation in them. Any number of ruined and abandoned religious sites around the world offer silent testimony to this basic reality.

Thus people do things, not religions, and though men and women act for a wide variety of reasons it is only through people that we understand what we mean by "religion." Similar to the ways in which we explored religion through various relationships on *Star Trek: Deep Space Nine*, I will conclude this chapter with a look at religion through a brief discussion of two particular characters: G'Kar and Delenn, who, respectively, illustrate the transcendence of self aboard Babylon 5 and the transcendence of being in the service of others.

G'KAR: THE TRANSCENDENCE OF SELF

When we first meet the Narn ambassador, G'Kar, played by veteran character actor Andreas Katsulis, he seems a bit of a fool, preparing a roast pig's head for dinner while singing a bawdy little ditty to himself. Indeed, in the establishing episodes of the series, both he and his archenemy, Londo Mollari, appear as little more than comic relief: insufferably pompous diplomats concerned more with their own petty intrigues and perceived slights than the welfare of their respective peoples or the maintenance of peace in the galaxy. As Mollari is drawn further and further into his unwitting alliance with the Shadows, however, and the Centauri once again devastate the Narn homeworld, G'Kar gradually realizes that there is more to life than mere survival. Like so many throughout history, his sense of meaning and purpose emerges only in the midst of profound crisis.

G'Kar's defining moment comes in "Dust to Dust," written by J. Michael Straczynski. Using "dust," an illegal and extremely powerful psychoactive drug that enhances telepathic powers, G'Kar enters Mollari's mind to uncover the origins of the plot against the Narn. As he mentally tortures the Centauri for information, though, he has a vision of his own father, a servant during the first Centauri occupation of Narn who was executed for some minor household mishap. During this experience, G'Kar learns that he can continue to lose himself in the all-consuming violence that war unfailingly begets, or he can choose a different path. It is not too late to change, to transcend the hatred that has defined him for so long and to recognize the interdependence of all life in the galaxy, the need we have one for the other, however much we seek to deny it. "We must realize we are not alone," his father tells him. "We rise and fall together."

Suddenly, his father disappears and G'Kar hears an altogether different voice, no longer wracked with pain, but grave and commanding. "You have the opportunity," it says, "here and now, to choose, to become something greater and nobler and more difficult than you have been before. The universe does not offer such chances often, G'Kar." "Why now?" the distraught Narn asks. "Why not earlier? All this time, where have you been?" The voice answers, "I have always been here." At that moment, a brilliant white light surrounds G'Kar and the luminous, angelic figure of his god G'Lan rises before him. Realizing the depths of his mistake and the wondrous opportunity he has been offered, G'Kar breaks down in tears. The camera pans up to reveal the Vorlon Kosh in his encounter suit turning away out of the frame.

Sentenced to several months in jail for his attack on Mollari, G'Kar uses the time to write *The Book of G'Kar*, the testimony of his mystical experience and his interpretation of it. Although he denied being either a religious leader or, worse, a religious icon, over the years *The Book of G'Kar*—which was published complete with the coffee stains provided by Garibaldi!—drew hundreds of thousands of Narns to G'Kar's way of thinking and elevated him to the status of a prophet both on his world and, paradoxically, on Centauri Prime.

Once again, without resorting to an evaluation of the ontological reality (or even reasonableness) of G'Kar's vision—after all, entheogens have been on the human religious menu for millennia—his experience does help us understand another model of religious formation: the revitalization movement. In a now-classic article published over half a century ago, anthropologist Anthony F. C. Wallace proposed that most (if not all) institutionalized religions are the social remnants of what he called the revitalization process, "visions of a new way of life by individuals under extreme stress" (1956, 268). Based on a psychological theory of deprivation and a crisis of needs management brought on by one or a number of cultural stressors—including "military defeat; political subordination; extreme pressure toward acculturation resulting in internal cultural conflict" (Wallace, 1956, 269)—Wallace argues that revitalization movements originate in the visionary experiences of these individuals. "With a few exceptions," he writes, "every religious revitalization movement with which I am acquainted has been originally conceived in one or several hallucinatory visions by a single individual. A supernatural being appears to the prophet-to-be, explains his own and his society's troubles as being entirely or partly a result of the violation of certain rules" (Wallace, 1956, 270)—in G'Kar's case, his ignorance of the interdependence of life in the galaxy. Through his writings and his personal example of suffering, G'Kar demonstrates that the quest for transcendence begins with the self. It falls to Delenn, however, to show how it continues in the transcendence of being.

DELENN: THE TRANSCENDENCE OF BEING

The Battle of the Line ended the devastating conflict between the Earth Alliance and the Minbari Federation. On Earth's planetary doorstep, twenty thousand ships fought in vain to defend the human homeworld against the vastly superior Minbari force. Yet, with victory clearly in sight, without explanation the Minbari surrendered what for them had been a holy war and withdrew to their own space. Only gradually, and often through Delenn, who is played marvelously by Croatian actor Mira Furlan, do we learn the reason for this and the implications it presents for the shape of the unseen order in the *Babylon 5* universe.

Before his own experience of "passing through Gethsemane," Brother Edward asks Delenn and Lennier about Minbari belief. "It is very hard to explain," she warns him. "We do not believe in any individual god or gods, but, rather, we believe that the soul is, um— what is a good term?—a non-localized phenomenon." Not surprisingly, the Catholic monk is a bit confused, and in the context of the series and its representation of the quest for transcendence, Delenn's explanation is crucial.

DELENN

```
We believe that the universe itself is
conscious in a way that we can never truly
understand. It is engaged in a search for
meaning. So it breaks itself apart, investing
its own consciousness in every form of life.
We are the universe, trying to understand
itself.
```

Although lodged in a science fiction series and placed in the mouth of an alien diplomat, Minbari cosmology—it cannot properly be called a theology—is not so unusual as we might think. Many readers might recognize in it an artistically licensed variation of Advaita Vedanta, a nondualistic form of Hinduism that was systematized twelve centuries ago by the Indian philosopher Sankara (788–820 CE). More recently, the concept of a universal consciousness, or, alternately, a conscious universe in which all sentient beings participate in one way or another, has been a popular part of new age belief since the publication of Fritjof Capra's *The Tao of Physics* in 1975 and Gary Zukav's *The Dancing Wu Li Masters* four years later. Since then, numerous other authors—both scientists and nonscientists—have explored similar terrain in a variety of ways (e.g., Goswami, Reed, and Goswami, 1993; Grof and Bennett, 1993; Talbot, 1991). One of the surprise, if somewhat controversial, hits of the 2004 art film season, *What the #$*! Do We (K)now!?*—produced and directed by three students at the gnostic Ramtha School of Enlightenment—brought new age metaphysics and quantum mechanics together in popular documentary format. For many years, University of Virginia Emeritus Professor of Physics Stanley Sobottka has offered "A Course in Consciousness," in which he explores many of these same ideas through the conceptual lenses of quantum physics and Advaita Vedanta. Although skeptics contest both this kind of interpretation of the scientific evidence and the use of physics as a framework for metaphysics (e.g., Stenger, 1997), Sobottka maintains that "from a sound, scientific point of view . . . it is Consciousness which manifests the world," a phenomenon that he concludes "must be nonlocal, universal Consciousness" (2009, 10)—put differently, "the universe, trying to understand itself."

In the ten years since the Minbari inexplicably halted their attack and surrendered to the Earth Alliance at the Battle of the Line, billions on both sides of the conflict have wondered why. The reason was known only to the nine members of the Minbari Grey Council and a few of their most trusted aides. In "Points of Departure," written by J. Michael Straczynski, we learn the secret.

Prior to the final assault on Earth, Delenn insisted that the Grey Council interrogate a human in order to understand more fully the race they were about to subjugate. For no readily apparent reason she

chose Jeffrey Sinclair, a lone fighter pilot battling an indefatigable
foe. During his interrogation, however, the Minbari learned something completely unexpected, "something terrible," as Lennier puts
it, something that changed the face of the conflict entirely.

LENNIER

It is our belief that every generation
of Minbari is reborn in each following
generation. Remove those souls, and the whole
suffers. We are diminished. Over the last
two thousand years, there have been fewer
Minbari born into each generation, and those
who are born do not seem equal to those who
came before. It is almost as if our greater
souls have been disappearing. At the Battle
of the Line, we discovered where our souls
were going. They were going to you. Minbari
souls are being reborn, in part or in full,
in human bodies.

As nonlocal and nondiscrete phenomena, for two millennia the Minbari and the human race have been inextricably linked in ways far
more profound than either ever imagined. To continue the war would
violate Valen's first commandment, the very foundation of Minbari
society—that no Minbari will harm another.

Delenn herself becomes the embodiment of this interconnected-
ness—and of the implicit interdependence of all sentient life in the
universe. Offering herself as a vessel of transcendence, she undergoes
a complex and painful metamorphosis and becomes the first Minbari-
human hybrid, a living bridge between both races that transcends the
boundaries and expectations of each. The quest for transcendence
often calls into question the nature of being, an explicit concern of
religious belief and practice for millennia. Throughout the series, but
especially through the Minbari and the Narn, aboard Babylon 5 we
learn that we are anything but "all alone in the night."

8

SO SAY WE ALL
Battlestar Galactica

OUTTAKE: "FLESH AND BONE"

LEOBEN

You believe in the gods, don't you? Lords
of Kobol and all that? . . . So you pray to
Artemis and Aphrodite?

KARA

Where's the warhead?

LEOBEN (smiling)

I was right. You see, our faiths are similar,
but I look to one God, not many.

KARA

I don't give a damn what you believe.

LEOBEN

To know the face of God is to know madness.

Somewhere, hidden aboard a ship in the ragged Colonial fleet, a
nuclear warhead counts down toward catastrophic dénouement.
All the survivors of the Twelve Colonies of Kobol live aboard a relative handful of starships, guarded by the massive, weary bulk of the

aging battlestar *Galactica*, and now at least one more ship faces imminent destruction. Planted by Leoben Conoy (Callum Keith Rennie),
one of the twelve extant human-model Cylons who only weeks before
engineered the almost total destruction of humankind. A race of
robots, the original Cylons were created by humans as servants, but
rebelled, waged war on their creators, and eventually evolved to emu-
late human physiognomy. The bomb is proof that even the vastness
of space offers no sanctuary, that the Cylons can now operate with
relative impunity within the fleet, and that their mission to exterminate humanity continues. The children have returned to destroy
their parents, and this time they have very nearly succeeded.

Caught stowing away aboard another ship, the *Gemenon Traveler*,
Leoben is interrogated—tortured, let's be clear—by Kara Thrace
(Katee Sackhoff), call-sign Starbuck, the fleet's lead pilot and one of
its many resident misfits. With thousands of lives at stake, like Jack
Bauer's use of torture throughout the television series *24*, her direct-
ness is presented as an asset and there is only one item on her agenda:
"Where's the warhead?" Leoben, on the other hand, whose various
lives—given the Cylon ability to download consciousness from one
body to the next—are intertwined with hers throughout the series,
seems interested only in talking theology and metaphysics. When
Kara first enters his holding cell, she finds him in prayer. "I don't
think the gods answer the prayers of toasters," she says derisively, sitting down at the table across from him. To her, the Cylon is nothing
but a machine, an appliance that has risen above its station. Taking
no offense, Leoben looks at her and responds simply, "God answers
everyone's prayers."

Premiering as a miniseries in 2003, Ronald D. Moore's reenvi-
sioned *Battlestar Galactica* (*BSG*) takes Glen Larson's original series
as an orienting "mythos" but departs from it in a number of significant ways (Moore, 2005). Gone are the campy costumes, Boxie and
his robot dog, the two-dimensional villains, and the swashbuckling
banter that marked the 1978 production. Moore, who cut his teeth
in a variety of production roles on *The Next Generation* and *Deep Space
Nine*, presents us with a vision so far removed from the optimism of
Star Trek that it seems part of another genre entirely. The new *BSG* is
dark, humorless, multifaceted, and, until season four, unrelenting in
its intensity. A number of commentators have suggested that Larson's

Latter-day Saint background heavily informed the earlier series, perhaps contributing to its more optimistic feel (cf. Porter, Lavery, and Robson, 2008; Wolfe, 2008). "Kobol," for example, is supposedly an anagram for "Kolob," a planet central to Latter-day Saint theology and eschatology. Although the new series makes no secret of its religious underpinnings, it resists simple associations with or allusions to offscreen beliefs and practices. Throughout the first three seasons at least, many episodes pose multivalent questions about religious belief, the reality of the divine, and the nature of the unseen order. "Flesh and Bone" is no exception. In the midst of the humans' desperate search for the nuclear warhead, ontology, epistemology, theology, morality, and intimacy circle each other like strange attractors in Leoben's cell.

ONTOLOGY: THE NATURE OF BEING

Consider first ontology, the conceptions we have of being and reality, the way we believe things are and, often, always have been. What we learn in the opening sequence of the *BSG* miniseries, however, as one of the beautiful Six models (Tricia Helfer) walks onto Armistice Station more than four decades after the first Human-Cylon War, is that things change. Ontologies alter. Realities shift. "Are you alive?" she asks the astonished human colonel, who has single-handedly staffed the station since he was a newly promoted lieutenant and who fully expected to retire never having seen an actual Cylon. "Yes," he responds, unsure what any of this means. The Six reaches toward his groin. "Prove it," she says, moments before the Cylons destroy both his shuttle and the entire outpost.

Things change, and for both races reality will never look the same again. Among other things, in the wake of the Cylons' sudden appearance after forty years of silence and their devastating surprise attack on the Twelve Colonies, there are now human-model Cylons, perfect in nearly every detail and created to be like humankind in almost every way. They are not androids, like *Star Trek*'s Lieutenant Commander Data, longing to be human in the face of impossible odds. Although routinely derided as "skin jobs," they are not the *Blade Runner* replicants fighting for a slim measure of longer life, nor commercial clones from *The Island*, suddenly self-aware and struggling for their rights as full human beings rather than walking organ banks. They are something else, though precisely *what* takes the entire series to explore—and even then is not entirely explained.

Throughout the interrogation, Kara's responses to Leoben reveal not only her abiding hatred for the Cylons but also the increasingly uncomfortable depth of ambiguity she feels toward them. As Leoben talks, questioning her more often than answering her questions, there is a sense that the boundaries of Being are slipping away, that the perceived differences between "us" and "them" that make war possible are fading. It is as if Turing were vying with Voight-Kampff once again, trying to find the heart of the machine. With the Cylon Raiders and the Centurions—the sleek alloy fighter craft and the chrome-metal foot soldiers—there is no need to invoke either test: clearly machines, they could no more pass for human than for polar bears. Leoben and his kind are vastly different. On the one hand, he remains a machine, a "toaster," and in Kara's eyes is worthy of no more respect and certainly no more civil rights than any other kitchen appliance. Unlike the various *Star Trek* franchises, which regularly invoke the "rights" of sentient beings of all kinds—whether orphaned through contact with the *Enterprise* ("Galaxy's Child," *TNG*) or created through the actions of her crew ("Evolution," *TNG*), in *Battlestar Galactica*'s early stages no such understanding extends to the Cylons. Indeed, as the perpetrator of another "enhanced interrogation" declares in the second part of "Resurrection Ship," "You can't rape a machine"—though by this point in the series it seems very clear both that you can and that some of the Cylons are far more humane than many of the humans.

On the other hand, faced with someone who under other circumstances could be a friend, a brother, even a lover, it is harder and harder for Kara to maintain the distinction between human and machine. Despite her taunts that Leoben is "just a bunch of circuits with a bad haircut," Kara knows that if "you cut him open, there's blood, guts, the whole thing." He is flesh and bone, but not, both less and more—and in that vanishing point of understanding reside the questions of ontology and transcendence for both species. Cylons are not human, but they challenge the boundaries of what it means to be human. Paradoxically, although in many ways they are immeasurably superior to humans—increased strength, speed, intelligence, and longevity through resurrection—it is their lack of completeness that drives them. Their own perceived deficiencies—love, intimacy, and their frustrated desire to procreate, deficits mirrored in many ways throughout the Colonial fleet—fuel the Cylon quest for transcendence. Whether from the Cylon or the human point of view, whenever we wonder "What are they?" we are forced to ask "What are we?"—both of which questions inevitably demand, "Really, how do you know?"

EPISTEMOLOGY: THE QUESTION OF KNOWING

How do we know? It's a reasonable question, one that constantly heckles us from the sidelines of our various quests for transcendence. So, Saul, how do you know it was really Jesus you heard on the road to Damascus? Mohammed, how do you know it was really the angel Gabriel who commanded you to read in the cave on Mount Hira? How do you know the Bible is the word of God, or the Qu'ran? How do you know? As Michael Kitz so trenchantly points out in *Contact*, how does Ellie Arroway know her cosmic journey in The Machine actually took place? How does Number Five know he's alive and not simply a malfunction, a random short circuit? How does Benjamin Sisko know that the Prophets are whom they claim to be and that he is far more than just the Federation commander of Deep Space Nine? And, more importantly, how do they convince others of what they know? Since we base our beliefs, our behavior, and our lives on what we think we know, what we know and how we know it are the central questions of epistemology.

In the colonial fleet, once the existence of the human-model Cylons is revealed, the problem of knowing comes in three principal forms. First, humans don't know who the Cylons are, which raises issues of confidence and betrayal. Few who have served in the military would rather face a traitor than an enemy. Trading on relationships of trust, often of the most intimate kind, traitors threaten the very essence of the social order—and on *Battlestar Galactica*, the very existence of humankind. With the appearance of the human-model Cylons, everyone in the fleet is forced to wonder, "Are you one? How do I know? I mean, I may not *like* you"—and, gods know, few people aboard *Galactica* truly like each other—"but are you like me?" Suspicion and mistrust become the order of the day and the traitor's mission is accomplished to precisely the degree that the social order falls apart. Once the notion of sleeper Cylons is introduced—Cylons who are unaware of their true nature—the hunt begins. As the seasons unfold and more masks are removed, audiences fill in their scorecards: Caprica/Six, check; Doral/Five (Matthew Bennett), check; Simon/Four (Rick Worthy), check; D'anna/Three (Lucy Lawless), check; Leoben/Two, check; Cavil/One (Dean Stockwell), check. And, since we know there are twelve (actually, thirteen), who are the remaining models, the so-called Final Five? Is Kara Thrace a Cylon—the poetic justice of which would be worthy of O. Henry, but heavy-handed, to say the least? Is the cowardly scientist, Gaius Baltar (James Callis) a Cylon, as it seems he so desperately hopes in "Taking a Break From All Your Worries"? Is Admiral Adama (Edward James Olmos) one? Or Laura Roslin (Mary McDonnell), president of the Twelve Colonies? Or Saul Tigh (Michael Hogan), Adama's best friend and the *Galactica*'s executive officer?

SPOILER SCORECARD: THE CYLON LINES

Cylon Line	*Character*	*Principal Models*
One	John Cavil	Brother Cavil
Two	Leoben Conoy	
Three	D'Anna Biers	
Four	Simon	
Five	Aaron Doral	
Six	Caprica	Shelley; Natalie; Gina
Seven	Daniel (non-operational)	
Eight	Sharon Valerii	Boomer; Athena
The Final Five	Galen Tyrol	
	Tory Foster	
	Saul Tigh	
	Samuel Anders	
	Ellen Tigh	

Second, since at least some of the Cylons—even members of the same model—don't know that they are Cylons, this invokes a profound existential crisis in all concerned. Humans wonder desperately if they are Cylons, while Cylons go through life believing themselves to be human. The panic that grips Boomer (Grace Park) in "Water" as she wrestles with the possibility that she may be a Cylon—as indeed we already know her to be from the opening credits of each episode—and the relief that washes over her when Baltar lies to her about her test results are almost palpable. His "Cylon Detection Test" proves that she is a Cylon, but often our understanding of reality is not a function of ontology or biology, but epistemology and social reinforcement. As long as Boomer "knows" she is not a Cylon, and those she trusts tell her she isn't, then she must be human—which only increases her anguish when she learns the truth in the episode "Downloaded." On the other hand, once you know you're a Cylon, whose side are you on? Season three's main story arc is the search for the so-called Final Five, four of whom—Galen Tyrol (Aaron Douglas), Saul Tigh, Sam Anders (Michael Trucco), and Tory Foster (Rekha Sharma)—wake up to their reality in the last moments of the season's two-part cliffhanger, "Crossroads," and spend much of season four trying desperately to understand what that means.

Third, even when both humans and Cylons find out the truth, they lie, which challenges the very foundations of knowing. When four of the Final Five learn the truth, one of their most obvious concerns is how to keep that knowledge to themselves, how to continue playing the role of human, in short, how to survive. The first time Baltar is asked to identify a Cylon, not only does his test turn out to be accurate, but he lies to Boomer—arguably to protect himself, but also out of a sense of concern for her. At some level, epistemology is a function of trust in the instruments of knowing, whether the physical senses through which we perceive the world, the diagnostic tests we develop to assess the reliability of our perceptions, or those around us on whose judgment we have come to rely. Once we know, the next logical question is: what does it all mean?

THEOLOGY: THE (UN)CERTAINTY OF BELIEF

"What is the most basic article of faith?" Leoben asks Kara, leaning forward in his shackles as she eats in front of him. "This is not all that we are." Not belief in God or gods; not the performance of specific rituals, nor assent to particular doctrines, nor the various and sundry sacred texts that crowd the shelves of religious thinking; not "the opium of the people," as Marx would say, nor Durkheim's often misunderstood notion of "society worshiping itself"—rather, simply, "this is not all we are." Here, Leoben echoes William James' concept of the "unseen order": that which is not us, but to which we are inexorably bound and in which we participate in ways we can barely begin to understand. "You see," he continues, "the difference between you and me is that I know what that means and you don't."

Unlike "Brother Cavil," the cynic priest who meets with Tyrol in *Galactica*'s brig in "Lay Down Your Burdens" and who is played with a sense of resigned disillusion by veteran character actor Dean Stockwell, Leoben points Kara toward something that exists well beyond the vague, utilitarian polytheism of the humans and Caprica/ Six's often blunt, unsophisticated monotheism. Although early on, some of Caprica/Six's dialogue sounds as though it was lifted straight from the talking points of Campus Crusade for Christ—"God has a plan for you, Gaius," she tells the archskeptic Baltar in the series pilot, "33"—it quickly becomes clear that *Battlestar Galactica* is anything but the simple "paganism versus fundamentalist Christianity" that some commentators contend. Indeed, in a *Beliefnet* interview at the end of the first season, Moore says that, while there are obvious parallels, the Cylons "aren't just really stalking horses for fundamentalist Christianity" (Moore, 2005). Rather, there are a variety of religious positions on both sides, human and Cylon, and neither can be reduced to the simple equation: this is that. This ambiguity is reflected most clearly in Leoben, whose various iterations range from skeptic to mystic, but all of which resist whatever easy categories religion is made to fit on *Battlestar Galactica*.

In the miniseries, the first Leoben we meet guides Adama through the service tunnels of the munitions depot at Ragnar Anchorage and muses on humanity's plight—which, at this point in the story, both seem to share. Like many civilizations that have risen and fallen in human history, he suggests that perhaps the destruction of the colonies was part of some divine master plan, that perhaps the chosen ones have fallen from favor and that the face of God's wrath should be seen reflected in the cold metal armor of the Cylon Centurions.

LEOBEN

Humanity is not a pretty race. I mean,
we're only one step away from beating each
other with clubs like savages fighting over
scraps of meat. Maybe the Cylons are God's
retribution for our many sins. What if God
decided he made a mistake and he decided to
give souls to another creature, like the
Cylons?

ADAMA

God didn't create the Cylons, Man did. And
I'm pretty sure we didn't include a soul in
the programming.

Whether included in the original programming or not, the question of the soul is one of the principal divisions separating human and Cylon. In "Flesh and Bone," now bruised and bleeding from hours of torture, Leoben pushes the boundaries of theological understanding even further. "I am more than you could ever imagine," he tells Kara. "I am God." Faced with what must seem the most ridiculous pronouncement in the history of her race, she bursts out laughing. "I am God!?!" she exclaims. "Wow! Nice to meet you!" At this point, it would be far too easy to make a "Christ before Pilate/Herod" analogy and, fortunately, the scene doesn't permit that (though Leoben does sound a bit like Obi-wan Kenobi).

LEOBEN

It's funny, isn't it? We're all God,
Starbuck, all of us. I see the love that
binds all living things together.

Rather than the skeptic, this is Leoben the mystic. Of course, we can choose to interpret the scene as though he is simply taunting Kara, throwing out an increasingly absurd set of theological non sequiturs in an effort to discomfit his interrogator and perhaps lessen the pain he knows must inevitably come. But nothing in the scene supports this. Indeed, nothing suggests but that Leoben expects to be taken seriously as Kara's derision quickly turns to hatred.

> KARA
>
> Love? You don't even know what the word means.

> LEOBEN
>
> I know that God loved you more than all other living creatures and that you repaid his divine love with sin, with hate, corruption, evil. So then he decided to create the Cylons.

> KARA
>
> The gods had nothing to do with it. We created you. It was a stupid, frakking decision and we paid for it. You slaughtered my entire civilization! That's a sin, that's evil, and you are evil.

MORALITY: THE PROBLEM OF ACTION

Bundled together, ontology, epistemology, and, in the context of religious belief, theology provide an organizing framework for social life and our place within it, what some sociologists call a *nomos* (Berger and Luckmann, 1966), others an *umwelt* (Goffman, 1971), and still others a "protective cocoon" (Giddens, 1991). Anthony Giddens describes Erving Goffman's *umwelt*, for example, as "a 'moving' world of normalcy which the individual takes around from situation to situation" (1991, 128). In other words, it tells us what is evil and what is not. It is the taken-for-granted nature of the world against which we measure the various threats we encounter, challenges that inevitably call into question whether we can (or should) trust our understanding of normalcy. That is, our notions of what we know, how we know these things, and what we believe they mean not only tell us what is, but also shape our understanding of what ought to be and inform our decisions about what ought to be done. In the context of the nuclear warhead hidden somewhere among all that remains of humanity, how far would you go in defense of your family, your race, your species? In one line of dialogue—"You slaughtered my entire civilization"—Kara calls into question the moral balance of genocide and torture. Although she contends that "the gods had nothing to do with it," a common enough position among those either unfamiliar with or willfully ignorant of religious history, the reality is that neither genocide nor torture is uncommon in human history and both have been carried out on the specific instructions of this or that god. Destruction in the name of religious belief, murder at the behest of one's gods—these are hardly new in human history.

Although, at the beginning, the series leaves no doubt that the Cylons sought the complete extermination of the human race, as the two species interact each becomes less monolithic, both within themselves and each to the other. Diversity emerges, unbidden and unwelcome, hopeful and terrifying in equal measure. In "Downloaded," one of the first episodes shown primarily from the Cylon point of view, we watch as Boomer struggles to come to terms with the reality that she is a Cylon—an Eight. Treated by the other Cylons as heroes of the initial attack on the human colonies, she and Caprica/Six begin to question the unquestionable: was genocide the only way? Killing one of the D'Annas at the end of the episode and letting Anders—at this point a leader in the tiny human resistance movement on the planet Caprica and unaware of his own Cylon nature—go free after his attack on a Cylon café, she tells Boomer, "Our people need a new beginning. A new way to live in God's love. Without hate. Without all the lies." In "A Measure of Salvation," on the other hand, the humans locate a derelict Cylon base ship, adrift, most of its crew already dead from lymphocytic encephalitis, the remaining few clinging desperately to life. When one of the Simons reveals that the virus could be transmitted through the Cylon resurrection process, reaching the entire civilization in a matter of hours or days, the humans too begin to think the unthinkable. In one stroke, they could erase the Cylon threat forever. "Genocide?" asks an astonished Helo (Tahmoh Penikett), who is by this time married to Sharon, another of the Eights, and father of a half-human, half-Cylon child. "So that's what we're about now?" "They're not human," answers Lee Adama (Jamie Bamber), reciting the human party line. "They were built, not born." Therefore, any moral proscription does not apply. "They're a race of people," Helo answers at the end of the scene. "Wiping them out with a biological weapon is a crime against—is a crime against humanity."

From the macrocosm to the microcosm, the question of torture lingers like a stench in Leoben's cell, the more so given that revelations about American torture of Iraqi prisoners at the infamous Abu Ghraib prison were emerging at the same time the series began (cf. Johnson-Lewis, 2008; Kind, 2008; Ott, 2008). "Torture," it seems, is a word we use with almost cavalier abandon, but which is notoriously hard to define precisely because, as researchers Richard Mollica and Yael Caspi-Yavin point out, relatively speaking "so few individuals have experienced torture" (1991, 581). Because so few will be called upon either to endure torture or to perpetrate it, the concept remains something of an abstraction, a roundtable discussion topic for ethicists, lawyers, and journalists. The "ticking bomb" scenario—the moral dilemma framing "Flesh and Bone"—asks simply: faced with the possibility of mass destruction, is the deliberate infliction of pain and suffering on another a lesser, and thus acceptable, evil? Many believe so. A recent survey conducted by the Pew Forum on Religion and Public Life reported that just over 50 percent of those who say they attend church "at least weekly" (and just over 60 percent of white evangelical Protestants) believe that the use of torture against suspected terrorists can be justified "in order to gain important information" (2009). Although the numerous assumptions underpinning the "ticking bomb" scenario have been challenged for decades (cf. Association for the Prevention of Torture, 2007), *Battlestar Galactica* introduces yet another assumption into the equation: Cylons are not human, therefore Cylons are not entitled to protection from torture. Even at this very early stage in the series, though, the ambiguity of that position is clear.

INTIMACY: THE MYSTERY OF PAIN

Finally, after a fashion, there is intimacy. For many people, intimacy implies tenderness, concern, and perhaps most importantly, reciprocity. There are the varieties of love between Tyrol and Boomer, Helo and Sharon, Kara and Sam, Adama and Roslin, Caprica/Six and Baltar, and even between Baltar and those who follow his putative new religious movement in seasons three and four. Although these vary widely—from the illicit to the pathological—the thought that there might be an intimacy to the torture relationship is not only alien, but highly repugnant. Not unlike the more well-known Stockholm Syndrome, through which hostages come to identify and even sympathize with their captors, there is an intimacy that develops between torturer and tortured—the intimacy of terror, pain, and subjugation (See Price, 2007a, 2007b, for example, on the CIA's Kubark Counterinsurgency Interrogation handbook, which for more than four decades defined "the agency's interrogation methods" [McCoy, 2006, 50]). Unlike in sexual subcultures of dominance and submission, however, in the torture chamber there is no safeword.

In *The Shoes of the Fisherman*, Michael Anderson's uneven film adaptation of Morris West's novel about the election of a Russian pope at the height of the Cold War, Piotr Ilyich Kamenev (Laurence Olivier) confronts Kiril Pavelovich Lakota (Anthony Quinn)—the torturer confronts the tortured—as Lakota is freed after decades in a Soviet gulag. It is a purely pragmatic decision on Kamenev's part. He is now the Soviet premier and Lakota is a Catholic priest, soon to be returned to the Vatican. In the dark Stalinist years immediately following World War II, Lakota was arrested and tortured by Kamenev in the infamous Lubyanka Prison.

KAMENEV

Think back to the Lubyanka. It was a kind of
mutual hell, wasn't it? I the tormentor, you
the tormented. The man in the mirror, the
man who looked into the mirror. In the end,
neither of us knew which was which, correct?

LAKOTA

Correct.

KAMENEV

I took you to pieces like a watch and put you
together again. It was a very . . . intimate
experience. I have never been able to forget
it.

Throughout this exchange, Lakota looks as we might imagine—unconvinced that Kamenev's experience in the Lubyanka was at all comparable to his own and unwilling to give in to Kamenev's implicit romanticization of it. It is in what the Soviet premier believes is the terrible intimacy of their relationship, however, that the torturer finds reason to release the tortured and to trust him in a way unfathomable to those who have never known the experience. "Wherever you are," he tells Lakota, "I will know there is one man who knows me as well as I know him."

On board the *Gemenon Traveler*, Kara has learned all she can—there is no bomb and there never was—and this Leoben is about to die, blown out of an airlock by Laura Roslin, former secretary of education, now president of all that survives of humanity. As they drag him to his fate, Roslin reiterates the situation simply and clearly. "He's a machine," she tells Kara. "And you don't keep a deadly machine around." "He's not afraid to die," Kara replies. "He's just afraid that his soul won't make it to God." After Leoben is "spaced"—a cruel way to die, as the series makes clear at numerous points—Kara returns to her quarters. Furtively, she goes through her locker, eventually removing a small cloth bundle. Inside, carefully protected and preserved, are two stylized statuettes—Artemis and Aphrodite, the goddesses of the hunt and of love, respectively. Holding them, looking at them softly, she prays.

KARA

```
Lords of Kobol, hear my prayer. I don't know
if he had a soul or not, but if he did, take
care of it.
```

The camera pulls back, showing her alone in the room she shares with other pilots. Her locker, the one place of relative privacy aboard the battlestar, has become a shrine, a small testimony to the transcendence of hatred and the resilience of hope.

"GOD HAS A PLAN FOR YOU, GAIUS"
The Religions of *Battlestar Galactica*

Although some devotees of the original series deride it as GINO ("Galactica In Name Only"; cf. Berger, 2008), Moore's reimagining of *Battlestar Galactica* has emerged as one of the most critically acclaimed science fiction series in recent memory. Before the end of the third season, before the Final Five were revealed or any of the serious questions answered, at least five volumes of criticism and commentary had appeared (Eberl, 2008; Hatch, 2006; Potter and Marshall, 2008; Porter, Lavery, and Robson, 2008; Steiff and Tamplin, 2008). Some critics analyze aspects of the series from philosophical perspectives as diverse as those of Aquinas, Nietzsche, Heidegger, and Sartre (Eberl and Vines, 2008; Sharp, 2008; Willems, 2008; Cuddy, 2008, respectively), while others address issues ranging from free will to alienation to gender identity (Johnson, 2008; Silvio and Johnston, 2008; Kungl, 2008, respectively). Not surprisingly, a number of writers discuss the series' religious dimensions, investigating among other things the place of prophecy in both Cylon and human religions (Marshall and Wheeland, 2008), the symbolic representation of Lilith and Eve in Caprica/Six and the two Eights, Boomer and Sharon (Rolufs, 2008), or *Battlestar Galactica*'s reflection of Zen Buddhism as an answer to the prospect of existential crisis (McRae, 2008).

Others, it seems to me, persist in posing entirely the wrong questions, questions that are either meaningless or unanswerable, both in the context of the series and of religious history and behavior. Noting the utilitarian ends to which both the Cylons and the humans put their respective religions, for example, Bryan McHenry asks, "Is the manipulation of religious beliefs ever justifiable?" (2008, 221)—and goes on to interpret Adama's original deception about knowing the way to Earth as a violation of the American Constitution. Although Ronald Moore admits that "the show is really supposed to be about our society and political structure," he cautions that relationships are not meant to be "as simple as the Cylons are Al Qaeda and Laura Roslin (the President) is George Bush" (Moore, 2005). One certainly hopes not, since the analogy makes very little sense in the context of the "war on terror" waged by the Bush White House since October

2001 and the American invasion of Iraq in 2003, which at this point has resulted either directly or indirectly in more than one hundred thousand civilian deaths. Indeed, though it shouldn't be necessary, it seems worth pointing out that the Twelve Colonies are not the United States and that the Cylon rout of humankind could arguably sanction any number of extraordinary measures. More importantly, however, the plain and simple fact is that, whether it seems justified or not, religious beliefs are manipulated regularly, often egregiously, to serve a wide variety of ends and agendas—not least by the Bush administration in the prosecution of its putative war on terror. Asking whether the manipulation of religion is warranted, legitimate, or ethically acceptable may be an interesting intellectual exercise, but the question relies on a naïve and simplistic understanding of religion and rings utterly hollow in the context of lived religious practice.

On the other hand, in his article "God Against the Gods," philosopher Taneli Kukkonen wonders, "Are the Cylons and Colonials both justified in their respective faiths? Or do religious believers on both sides merely impose meaning on an otherwise cold and uncaring universe?" (2008, 170). Kukkonen's implicit fallacy of limited alternatives notwithstanding, once again we are back to the problem of evaluation and adjudication: Is this a reasonable religion? Does it make sense? Indeed, as Kukkonen puts it, "Are there independent, rational criteria by which the merits of the two contending faiths can be assessed"? (2008, 170). Although we have encountered this kind of presumed analysis before—particularly in the dismissal of religion in such series as *Deep Space Nine* and *Babylon 5*—put simply, "No, there aren't," and for two very particular reasons. First, religion as a social and a human (or, perhaps, Cylon) phenomenon is neither rational nor irrational. It is both, and both rationality and irrationality depend on situation and perspective. What seems eminently reasonable to some—from simple belief in a nonempirical entity to the willingness either to kill or to die at the behest of that entity, or from prayer in the face of personal crisis to belief in the efficacy of that prayer—is for others profoundly irrational. More importantly, while Kukkonen wants to stand on the platform of "independent, rational criteria," he both introduces and concludes his argument in explicitly theological ways—rational from a certain perspective, perhaps, but hardly independent. According to him, "the Cylon God's plan seems cruel and inscrutable if it includes the Cylons' attempt to eradicate humanity" (2008, 169). But inscrutable to whom, and according to what criteria? Is this any more cruel than the commands of the Hebrew God to eradicate various Canaanite tribes when the newly designated chosen people escaped from Egypt and made their way into the promised land? Falling completely into the trap of the good, moral, and decent fallacy, Kukkonen seems to forget that what is one group's sacred story is another's hidden history of genocide. Quoting the fourth-century rhetorician and statesman Themistius, however, Kukkonen concludes that "whether one believes in one God or many, it would seem obvious that our lot in communicating with the divine and with each other is to listen rather than to proclaim, to consent rather than to coerce" (2008, 178). Once again, it is entirely unclear what makes this "obvious," how it is the product of "independent, rational criteria," or how it amounts to anything more than vague sermonizing and the imposition of Kukkonen's own normative theology.

Second, there are not "two contending faiths" in *Battlestar Galactica*, and to suggest that there are seriously diminishes the potential richness of the series. Put differently, I begin many of the various religious studies courses I teach with some version of the statement, "There is no such thing as 'Christianity,'" a comment that never fails to draw the ire of at least one student in the class. "Of course," I respond to their almost inevitable indignation, "there's no such thing as Buddhism either, or Judaism, or Islam, or Hinduism." By this point, many students are wondering if they've enrolled in the wrong course, but the point is this: there *is* no one thing that we can definitively call "Christianity"; there are only various and sundry Christianities, religious traditions that can vary dramatically depending where in the world one looks and when, and which are often as different from each other as they are from other religions. Roman Catholicism in the twenty-first century, for example, seems an entirely different religion from that of the fifteenth century. And, in many ways, it is. In the same way, though, there is no such thing as *the* human religion in the Colonial fleet clustered around *Galactica*, just as there is no such thing as *the* Cylon religion, resurrection hub or not. There are only the *religions* of *Battlestar Galactica*, and as we have seen in each of the other series we have considered, they reveal themselves most clearly through the people in whom they are embodied.

Embracing a basic polytheism, the human religion is founded on elements of Greek and Roman mythologies. Just as they do in real-life religions, subtle but significant differences emerge in the Colonial fleet. The Sagittarons, for example, come from one of the poorest of the Colonies and have adapted the basic framework of Colonial religion to suit themselves and their circumstance. Like many historical rural human cultures, they are devoutly religious but practice a blend of folk tradition and Colonial religion that many others condemn as superstition. They abjure modern medicine as an abomination before the gods, relying instead on faith and herbal remedies, a practice that leads to marginalization and stigmatization just as surely onscreen as it does off ("The Woman King"). The Gemenese, on the other hand, who inhabited another of the poorer Colonial planets, are portrayed as religious fundamentalists, believers in the literal truth of the sacred texts ("Fragged"), in a strict moral code ("The Captain's Hand"), and in the fulfillment of prophecy in Laura Roslin, the "dying leader" who will lead the people to salvation. Caprica, on the other hand, the wealthiest of the Colonies, is the center of Colonial government, and, according to Baltar, is "the seat of politics, culture, art, science, learning" ("Dirty Hands"). Notably, though, it is not the center of Colonial religion, and those who are presented as Capricans (either by birth or by choice) are often most resistant to religious interpretations of either political or military matters. These religious generalizations in the series also reflect certain offscreen realities and perceptions that have been deeply ingrained in us for more than a century. Rural areas have long been considered the prime breeding ground for religious fundamentalism and backward folk traditions. Urban areas, by comparison, while more overtly secular, have often been seen as the source of emergent monotheistic challenges to the dominant religion.

It is important to reiterate, though, that this is not a matter of simple equation, of this equals that: the Sagittarons stand for Jehovah's Witnesses or Christian Scientists; the Gemenese are Southern Baptists; the Capricans are secular Manhattanites. Because if they are, if that's all we're meant to see in the series, then it fails what I call the "So what?" test. Let's say the Cylons are supposed to represent fundamentalist Christians or radical Islamists; once we've said that, so what? How much more have we learned than that? It is precisely this kind of superficial equation, however, that leads so often to the dismissal of religion in science fiction, as though there is nothing more to learn. Rather, through the different religions of *Battlestar Galactica* we can see a far more nuanced vision of the complex relationships between belief, hope, circumstance, and the quest for transcendence. And once again, these visions are revealed in the people through whom the various relationships are realized. In this case, these relationships are seen in two humans—Laura Roslin and Gaius Baltar—and in two Cylons, John Cavil and D'Anna Biers.

SIGNS AS PORTENTS

                    ROSLIN

    It's real. The Scriptures, the myths, the
    prophecies, they're all real.

                    ELOSHA

    So say we all.

What constitutes "the sacred"? What makes something "holy"? Is it the word of God (or the gods), an imperious "thus sayeth the Lord" that commands thus and so? Is it the touch and the vision of a prophet or a seer that give meaning to the vagaries of life and place them (and us) in cosmic context? Is it a personal gnosis, an inner knowledge or intuition, that paints the ordinary in extraordinary colors, sanctifying the mundane—a book, a statuette, a painting, an arrow—and rendering it, in Eliade's word, a hierophany? Certainly all these have been part of the religious process historically, and we see them all in *Battlestar Galactica*, but in many ways they are second-order experiences. The first-order experience of the sacred resides, strangely enough, in agreement—that is, in the consensus that groups of believers share or come to share about the nature of reality and their place in it. We agree that this book or that is the word of God and read from it as though God speaks to us through it. We agree that this site or that is a holy place and approach it with awe and reverence. We agree that these rituals or those are meaningful in the way we understand "our supreme good" and through them seek to "harmoniously adjust ourselves" to the unseen order they help us negotiate (cf. James, [1902] 1999, 61). As scholars of religion have pointed out for nearly a century now, nothing is inherently sacred, but becomes so only as agreement about its sacrality emerges among those to whom it is meaningful. This is the "So say we all" with which the priestess Elosha (Lorena Gale) responds to Laura Roslin and with which the Colonial survivors begin their search for Earth. For those who remain, this is the agreement that brings meaning out of chaos and forges a sacred hope from the raw iron of despair.

Despite her apparent lack of religious faith, when she learns the extent of her cancer Roslin does what so many do when faced with their own mortality: she seeks the comfort and counsel of a religious professional. In "The Hand of God," she tells Elosha about the hallucinations she has been experiencing—specifically, snakes on her presidential podium—symptoms she attributes to the drugs that keep the cancer in check. Although the symbolism could be read in any number of ways, Elosha's response is, to say the least, unexpected.

ELOSHA

You're kidding me, right? You read Pythia and now you're having me on.

ROSLIN

No. Who is Pythia?

ELOSHA

One of the oracles in the sacred scrolls. three thousand six hundred years ago, Pythia wrote about the exile and the rebirth of the human race: 'And the Lords anointed a leader to guide the caravan of the heavens to their new homeland and unto the leader they gave a vision of serpents, numbering two and ten, as a sign of things to come.'

ROSLIN

Pythia wrote that?

ELOSHA

```
She also wrote that the leader suffered a
wasting disease and would not live to enter
the new land. But you're not dying . . . are
you?
```

The audience knows, of course, that Roslin is dying of the quint-essential late-modern "wasting disease," and here we see the power of agreement in the construction of the sacred. If Elosha, the one person in the fleet Roslin believes would know the religious texts of their people, were to have told her that the snakes were a product of the cancer treatment and perhaps represent her fears of betrayal by those who surround the presidential podium, then this thread in the storyline would have ended. The sacred would be stillborn. For the priestess, however, Roslin is a revelation: everything to which she has committed her life as a religious leader, but in which for all practical purposes she has ceased to believe, is real. Interpreting Roslin's experience as a fulfillment of prophecy creates the bond of sacrality between them. Reading the signs as portents, they agree on the nature of the sacred, and in that agreement one finds faith while the other finds it again.

For Roslin, hope suddenly resides in the religious artifacts of her people's faith—the sacred scrolls, the prophecies of Pythia, the Arrow of Apollo, the Temple of Athena, the Eye of Jupiter. These are no longer dusty books, ancient weapons, and long-forgotten places of worship. They are hierophanies, repositories of transcendence. They have become material markers of the grand design into which she weaves herself a central role: the dying leader who will lead the lost tribe to Earth. Like *Deep Space Nine*'s Gul Dukat and Kai Winn searching the *Kosst Amojen* for knowledge of the Pah-wraiths, Elosha and Roslin form the self-reinforcing core of a revitalized Colonial religion. Indeed, for them, these various artifacts are not adjunct to this re(new)ed faith, they are constitutive of it. Without them— the scrolls to guide, the arrow to point, the eye to mark—there is no faith, there is no hope, there is no possibility of transcendence. Although by the fourth season, Elosha will be dead, Earth is found to to be a burned-out wasteland, and the prophecies of Pythia prove to be all but worthless ("Sometimes a Great Notion"), for now, hope is alive. "It's real," Roslin says, amazed. "They're all real."

FEAR AND RELIGION

                    CAVIL

    Do you know how useless prayer is? Chanting
    and singing and mucking about with old half-
    remembered lines of bad poetry. And you know
    what it gets you? Exactly nothing.

                    TYROL

    Are you sure you're a priest?

                    CAVIL

    I've been preaching longer than you've been
    sucking down oxygen. And in that time, I've
    learned enough to know that the gods don't
    answer prayers. We're here on our own.

If Elosha is the professional religious who rediscovers faith and hope in the midst of crisis, John Cavil, the Cylon model one, is the believer permanently lost in the cynicism of unbelief. His name, "cavil," means to jeer at, to find petty fault with anything and everything, and indeed, when he walks into a room, hope inevitably leaves. Throughout the series, Cavil is one of the principal touchstones of fear: fear that the gods are there but indifferent, fear as an instrument of the gods wielded against the unrighteous, and fear that the gods are there and anything but indifferent.

We first meet "Brother" Cavil in *Galactica*'s brig as he is "counseling" Chief Tyrol, who has been arrested for beating one of his deck-hands while in the grips of a recurring suicidal nightmare. Raised on the religiously conservative colony of Gemenon, the son of a priest and an oracle, Tyrol tells Cavil, "I pray to the gods every night, but I don't think they listen to me." In the bit of dialogue quoted above, it is important to note that Cavil does not tell him that the gods don't exist or that they never existed. He tells him that faith placed in them is at best naïve, at worst a lie. Very often, what we fear most is not the absence of the gods, but their apathy. We are afraid that they are there, somewhere, but that they just don't care. Somehow, it's easier to imagine a universe without the gods than ones unconcerned with human (or Cylon) affairs. Their indifference becomes the measure of our insignificance, of the cardinal reality that "we're here on our own."

Later in the series, on New Caprica at the beginning of season three, a group of Cylons, including two of the Cavil models, meets with the puppet president, Baltar, to discuss the growing problem of human resistance to their "occupation." Caprica/Six and Boomer, the two hailed as heroes of the original Cylon attack on the Colonies, are searching for a way that both species can learn to live in peace. Ever the cynical pragmatist, however, Cavil reiterates their original mission.

> CAVIL (A)
>
> Let's review why we're here, shall we? Uh, we're supposed to bring the word of 'God' to the people, right?
>
> CAVIL (B)
>
> To save humanity from damnation by bringing the love of 'God' to these poor, benighted people.
>
> CAPRICA
>
> We're here because a majority of the Cylon felt that the slaughter of Mankind had been a mistake.
>
> BOOMER
>
> We're here to find a new way to live in peace, as God wants us to live.
>
> CAVIL (B)
>
> And it's been a fun ride, so far. But I want to clarify our objectives. If we're bringing the word of 'God,' then it follows that we

```
should employ any means necessary to do so,
any means.

                    CAVIL (A)

Yes, fear is a key article of faith as I
understand it. So perhaps it's time to
instill a little more fear into the people's
hearts and minds.
```

"Fear is a key article of faith" is a concept that would appall many believers who hold to theological notions of a God whose "perfect love casts out fear" (1 John 4:18). What may seem a throwaway line in this extended bit of dialogue, however, highlights the reality that fear, dread, terror, and anxiety have been integral components of human religious consciousness for many thousands of years (Cowan, 2008b; Hankiss, 2001). Fear, opined the Roman novelist Petronius, brought the primal gods into being. "Religious dread," wrote Rudolf Otto in his classic study, *The Idea of the Holy*, is a more developed experience of "'something uncanny,' 'eerie,' or 'weird'" that, "emerging in the mind of primeval man, forms the starting-point for the entire religious development in history" (Otto [1923] 1950, 14). According to various sages in the Hebrew Scriptures, "fear of the Lord" is, among other things, "the beginning of wisdom" (Psalm 111:10; Proverbs 9:10), "a fountain of life" (Proverbs 14:27), and the one thing that helps us "avoid evil" (Proverbs 16:6). Although any number of Christian preachers have tried to soften the plain sense of these texts by construing fear in terms of awe and reverence, many of the Hebrew God's actions as recorded in Scripture clearly suggest other, far darker interpretations. For centuries, fear has been a tool of evangelism, especially when either death or eternal punishment (or occasionally both) are offered as alternatives to conversion. It has been a means of preventing defection, especially when we're told, "If you leave us, God won't love you anymore." It has been used to forestall questions about the nature of faith, especially when those questions are far more dangerous than the presence of either non-believers or defectors. And it has been perhaps the principal means of quelling religious dissent, especially when one's most basic beliefs are challenged.

"That's enough!" Cavil shouts at Natalie, another of the Sixes, in the fourth-season episode "Six of One." "Don't you realize what you're doing? You're openly discussing the Final Five! That's forbidden! You're toying with our survival." For him, any investigation into the mysteries of the Final Five Cylons is sacrilege—the hubris of transgression, not the quest for transcendence—and it places them all at risk. However jaded or cynical Cavil may have become, like religious zealots throughout human history, he will do whatever it takes to preserve the presumed orthodoxy of his beliefs. Fear still runs the show. In season three, he "boxes" the consciousness of the entire Three line; that is, he takes her entire model offline because D'Anna will not give up her search for the Final Five. For Cavil, it was D'Anna's "messianic quest for secrets better left alone" that led to civil war among the Cylons. When the Raiders refuse to attack the Colonial Fleet, believing the Final Five to be somewhere aboard the remaining human starships, Cavil orders them lobotomized, arguing that they are "simple machines." As the civil war intensifies, Cavil commands his ships to attack the basestars held by those he now considers heretics, destroying his own people far from the reach of the nearest resurrection ship. This time when they die, they die. When Boomer, who to this point has sided with him, objects, his complete lack of hope reemerges.

CAVIL

They can trust their God to watch over their immortal souls.

BOOMER

What about ours?

CAVIL

We're machines, dear, remember? We don't have souls.

Or do they?—the possibility of which is Cavil's greatest fear.

HERESY AND TRANSCENDENCE

```
            D'ANNA (to CENTURION)

    After you execute this command, you'll delete
    the order from your logs, then override the
    corresponding memory locations. Execute.
```

Sometimes, the quest for transcendence catches us by surprise.

In the episode "Hero," in the harsh glare of a Cylon detention cell, one of the Threes torments a human pilot who was captured during a secret mission into Cylon space a year before the attack on the Colonies. For some reason, the Three looks ragged, her face haggard, her hair disheveled. "Are you trying to stave off getting old?" she asks, as the man does pushups. "Doesn't seem like such a tragedy to me, given the alternatives. You know what I'm saying?" She runs a pipe along the metal bars of his cage, taunting him. "Do I look that bad? You know what I think? I think you're afraid." Enraged, the pilot leaps from the floor and smashes the heel of his palm into her nose. With a single grunt, she drops, her septum driven deep into her brain, her eyes open, wide and staring. Dead. Surprised.

In a flashback a few scenes later, D'Anna is walking through a restricted area aboard *Galactica*, shadowed by security personnel. Running from them, she reaches a hatch marked "End of Line" and turns, her face bathed in a brilliant white light. "Fire," she says, calmly. As she dies, though, the scene cuts to the bed she now shares with Caprica/Six and Baltar aboard a Cylon basestar. D'Anna awakens and looks around, wondering, confused, as though trying to make sense of an experience beyond her imagining. "More nightmares?" asks Caprica. "Dreams," D'Anna replies. "Something different this time, though. I think God's trying to tell me something." Her recurring death continues to haunt her resurrected life.

Away from the others, D'Anna gives her final orders to a Centurion. Impassive, its glowing red eye slowly traversing its visor, it gives no indication of concern, no hint of potential disobedience. She closes her eyes and whispers, "Execute." A single gunshot echoes down the corridor and she drops to the floor, shot through the head. Immediately, she finds herself in the visionary Caprica opera house, the setting throughout the series that indicates the luminal presence of the

Final Five. Moving across the stage toward the figures robed in white, she sees a number of her deaths—on the basestar, on New Caprica, a moment ago. Just as she is about to touch one of the Five, however, she snaps awake in a resurrection tank, surrounded by an Eight, a Five, Caprica/Six, and another Three. As her line-sister looks intently into her eyes, D'Anna whispers from the viscous fluid of the tank, "There's something beautiful, miraculous between life and death."

For D'Anna, and implicitly for both Cylons and humans, hope is found in what lies between lives, in what the bardo, the state between life and death and life, can tell her about the nature of reality and the reality of God. "This is my destiny," she tells Cavil a few episodes later in "Rapture," "to see what lies between life and death." She is willing to endure the shattering experience of death and the shock of resurrection in order to fathom the secrets of their origins, of the Final Five, and, ultimately, of God. Although suicide is considered a sin among Cylons, she walks the path heretics have trod throughout religious history, challenging the dominance of orthodoxy, picking the lock on the holy of holies, daring to seek the unseen order for herself.

Even her hope, though, ends in despair. In the fourth season, on the ravaged Earth, D'Anna decides to step off the wheel of death and rebirth, to escape samsara and choose her own special kind of enlightenment. The resurrection hub is gone and she will not participate in it once it is rebuilt. For her, by this time, hope resides in release, not in another resurrection, not in the faces of the Final Five on the opera stage between life and death.

OPPORTUNISM AND CHOICE

```
            BALTAR (to CENTURION)

I can see a real hierarchy around here. And I
have to tell you, you're on the lower end of
the scale, my friend. Yes, you are. Which is
odd when you think about the Cylon God . . .
They told you about God, didn't they? . . .
Well, he's your God as well. And God doesn't
want any of his creations to be . . . slaves.
Not that you're a slave . . . exactly.
```

In a series that is so relentless in its intensity and offers so few moments of real humor, the image of Baltar preaching to a battered and dented Cylon Centurion stands out, and no discussion of the religions of *Battlestar Galactica* would be complete without some consideration of the religions of Gaius Baltar—a topic that could easily consume an entire chapter. We meet him first as the quintessential rationalist, the hedonistic scientist interested only in his intellect, his sense of self-importance, and his libido. Rescued at the last minute in the aftermath of the initial attack, much of what we learn about Baltar comes through his internal dialogues with the original Six who seduced him on the planet Caprica and used him to breach the human security grid.

Few episodes better illustrate the speed with which Baltar can shift allegiances than "Six Degrees of Separation." Trying to perfect a Cylon detection test, Baltar taunts his inner Six (who is known among *Battlestar Galactica* fans variously as "Head Six," "Virtual Six," and "Fugue Six"). Looking through his microscope, he doesn't see the hand of God in a Cylon cell. Suddenly, he finds himself in one of the many hallucinatory dialogues set in his palatial oceanfront home on Caprica. "It's important you form a personal relationship with God," the Six tells him. "Only you can give yourself over to His divine love . . . I'm trying to save your immortal soul, Gaius."

BALTAR

> But what you're doing, darling, is boring me
> to death with your superstitious drivel, your
> metaphysical nonsense, which to be fair to
> you, actually appeals to the half-educated
> dullards that make up most of human society,
> but which I hasten to add no rational,
> intelligent, free-thinking human being truly
> believes.

Later in the episode, Baltar is arrested for treason after another of the Six models implicates him in the initial Cylon attack on the Colonies. Kneeling beside his cot in *Galactica*'s brig, the unwitting traitor prays.

BALTAR

```
Dear God, and I now acknowledge that you are
the one true God, deliver me from this evil
and I will devote the rest of what is left
of my wretched life to doing good, to, uh,
to carrying out your divine will. It's what
I want to do . . . to carry out your divine
will.
```

It is important to note here that though this is very early in the series, he does not pray to the Colonial gods but to what he has been told is the Cylon God. That is, in the contest of divinity, he turns to the deity that appears to have the stronger hand. This may seem venally pragmatic—a gross caricature of Pascal's famous wager—but it is consistent with much of what we know about the nature of religious conversion and practice. That is, while fear may be his principal motivation, Baltar remains a rationalist. He makes a rational choice based on his available options and his assessment of their relative pros and cons. Indeed, throughout the series we see him as the embodiment of what many sociologists of religion call the rational choice model of religious practice. Although it has been subject to significant criticism and is clearly not without its flaws (cf. Young, 1997), rational choice theory posits that people will make religious decisions, engage in religious behavior, and even switch religious allegiance in much the same way that they make economic decisions: they seek to maximize their benefits and minimize their costs. Miracle stories aside, there is considerable historical evidence that conversions or shifts in divine adherence occurred not because people suddenly believed in different theologies or cosmologies, but because one god or pantheon was demonstrated to be clearly superior to another (see, for example, Fletcher, 1997; Stark, 1996).

Potential messiahs abound in *Battlestar Galactica*—Laura Roslin, Kara Thrace, D'Anna Biers, even Leoben Conoy. But none is so striking as Gaius Baltar and what the online Battlestar Wiki labels "The Cult of Baltar" that emerges at the beginning of season four. During his trial for treason, Baltar writes his memoir, *My Triumphs, My Mistakes*. A class analysis of the Twelve Colonies that is smuggled out and reprinted throughout the fleet *samizdat*-style, it clearly strikes a chord among the increasingly desperate human population. Released following his acquittal but still uncertain about his safety, he is whisked away to a commune that has emerged devoted both to him and to his "teachings." A number of beautiful young men and women (mostly the latter) lounge about on blankets and pillows. Rather than a refuge in a dry stowage, however, it resembles a seraglio or harem, and Moore refers to it as "Baltar's Lair." Wrapped in a blanket, his long hair and beard rather heavy-handedly intended to represent Jesus (the episode is entitled "He That Believeth in Me"), he takes in the scene as followers he never knew he had rise to greet him, yet are unable to meet his eyes. Dominating the space is an altar dedicated to Baltar, while floating in the background are ethereal Anglo-Saxon lyrics series composer Bear McCreary wrote specifically for the scene (2008).

> We gadriaþ in nihtscuan
> (We gather in shadow,)
> Neoðan þin gledstede,
> (Beneath your altar,)
> þin liċfæst in blode ond lieġe.
> (Your image in blood and flame.)
> Nu þin ġebann, æþreddaþ us
> (By your command, deliver us)
> To þæm anliċum æltæwan gastcyninge
> (Unto the One True God)
> Gaius Baltar, ure dryhtweorþ nergend
> (Gaius Baltar, our divine savior)
> Nu ond æfre to alder.
> (Now and for eternity.)
> Swa we ġehwilc ġehalsiaþ.
> (So say we all.)

"Right," says Baltar, appalled and astonished in roughly equal measure, though neither of these stop him from taking advantage of the situation as the "cult of Baltar" story arc unwinds.

It is easy to read in this the resonance of numerous pop culture stereotypes about new religions and new religious leaders. Once again, though, writing Baltar off as just another pathological cult leader would be overly simplistic. Rather, with an emotional "So say we all," we are back to the issue of agreement and the sacred. The relationship between a religious leader and a devotee is rarely as uncomplicated as the user and the used. New religious conversion is a complex interplay of social, situational, and cognitive variables, some of which we glimpse in two particular scenes from this episode.

As the de facto leader of the group warns Baltar not to move about the battlestar, he recognizes her as the mother of a child in *Galactica*'s sick bay. She is especially flattered when he tells her that he is praying for her son, though she does not seem to miss the sarcastic roll of his eyes. As they leave, his inner Six reappears, wondering at his "long face."

BALTAR

```
Oh, gee, I don't know, from president of the
Colonies to this. King of fools. Probably
best to be hated by everyone than loved by
this lot. Doomed to live out the rest of my
life in this loony bin.
```

He drops to his knees beside the altar, clearly despondent, as his inner Six tries to give him some perspective on the situation. He lifts his clasped hands and she takes them in hers, comforting him. "I need some encouragement," he says, "a ray of hope about the future. An inkling—" When the camera repositions, the inner Six is gone and we take in the scene from the perspective of one of his followers, Tracey (Leela Savasta), who sees a man kneeling in prayer, his eyes closed and his face upturned, listening intently for the voice of God. "That is so beautiful," she says, kneeling in front of him.

BALTAR

```
Hello? Sorry, what?
```

TRACEY

```
The way you were praying . . . Not some
hollow ritual . . . It's as if the Gods are
right here beside you . . . When I pray to
the Gods, I feel empty.
```

                    BALTAR

Do you? That's a shame, isn't it?
  (INNER SIX reappears, watching)

                   INNER SIX

Her gods are false. Tell her.

                    BALTAR

Well, if you feel empty when you pray to Zeus
or Poseidon or Aphrodite, it's because it
is empty. It's a totally empty experience.
They're . . .
  (TRACEY touches his face)
They're not real. They've been promulgated by
. . .
  (TRACEY unbuttons his shirt)
A ruling elite, uh, to stop you from learning
the truth.

                    TRACEY

And what truth is that?

                    BALTAR

Um, that's a very good question . . .
  (to INNER SIX)
What is the--the--

                   INNER SIX

There's only one God.

                    BALTAR

There is only one God. In a nutshell, that's
the truth.

Tracey opens her own shirt and places his hands on her breasts. "Do
you feel God's presence?" she asks. "You know what?" he responds.
"I think I do." "So do I," she tells him, as the scene closes with a shot
of the altar dedicated to Baltar.

As Ronald Moore points out in his podcast commentary on this episode, those who have chosen to follow Baltar are living in desperate circumstances. They have spent four years running from the Cylons, and at this point there appears to be no end in sight. Their dreams of a fresh start on New Caprica were dashed in a brutal Cylon occupation. Earth seems an ever-more-distant hope. In the face of this, one can only imagine how many prayers have been offered to the Colonial gods and still the Cylon basestars jump in, still the Raiders attack. Perhaps the gods do not hear; perhaps, as the Cylons believe and as Baltar preaches (however self-servingly), there is only one true God.

The leader of the group, Jeanne (Keegan Connor Tracy), reappears with her son, Derrick. Suffering from viral encephalitis, he is clearly worse and she does not want him to die in sick bay. Though it seems a sham to watch, Baltar prays for the boy.

BALTAR

```
Please, God. I'm only asking you this one
last time. Don't let this child die. Has he
sinned against you? He can't have sinned
against you. He's not even had a life
yet . . . How can you take him and let me
live? After all I've done. Really, if you
want someone to suffer, take me. We both know
I deserve it . . .
   (weeping)
I have been selfish and weak. I have failed
so many people. And I have killed. I'm not
asking for your forgiveness. I'm just asking
that you spare the life of this innocent
child. Don't take him. Take me. Take me, take
me please.
```

He gets his chance at self-sacrifice a few minutes later when he and another of his followers are attacked by a vengeful mob who remember Baltar's service to the Cylons on New Caprica. They escape and return to his "lair," where a miracle apparently has occurred.

Derrick's fever has broken and his color has returned. He is healed. Even though Baltar told the people gathered around the deathly ill boy that there were no drugs that could touch the virus and that the child's own immune system would have to suffice, and even though there is no reason to think that this is anything other than a coincidence, for the followers of the "cult of Baltar" it is more evidence of his unique place in the divine plan of salvation. It is the "So say we all" that creates and reinforces the charismatic bond.

WHAT THE FRAK . . . ?

Like many series that develop a devoted fan base, opinions vary widely on the quality of *Battlestar Galactica*'s final season and the various storyline resolutions—or lack thereof. Reading the series through the lens of his Christian theology, for example, Gabriel McKee, author of *The Gospel According to Science Fiction* (2007), suggests that "mystical questions received mystical answers" (2009). Thus, "Baltar's story is an extended take on the Parable of the Lost Sheep" and Laura Roslin's "role, as expected, was that of Moses, leading a nation through the wilderness only to die on the threshold of the promised land" (McKee, 2009). Like the one-to-one comparisons I touch on in the next chapter, however, these kind of pat theological equations leave many viewers frustrated. They are too simplistic, too easy, too mundane. If, as writer Benjamin Plotinsky contends, "the whole series is a retelling of the biblical book of Exodus" (2009), then where, precisely, is the mystery?

For fans like these, the "mystical answers" that McKee wrote of come in a series of annoying "What the frak?" episodes with no real resolution at all. They feel that *Battlestar Galactica*'s creators stretched a three-season story arc into a four-season series, padding many of the final episodes with irrelevant and maudlin backstory while refusing to answer any of the series' lingering, more substantial questions. That is, do we really need to know that Kara nearly slept with Lee Adama while her fiancé (Lee's brother) lay drunk on the sofa beside them, or that Laura Roslin had a one-night stand with a former student? A host of questions remain either unanswered or explained by a series of clumsy *dei ex machina*. Simply disappearing before Lee's eyes in "Daybreak, Part 2," was Kara Thrace an angel after all, as Baltar intimates in one of the penultimate scenes? Humans and Cylons together find Earth—though not the Earth of the Thirteenth Colony—as it was 150,000 years ago, and the only known hybrid child, Hera, becomes our mitochondrial Eve. For fans such as these, God may have had a plan, but Ronald Moore was making it up as he went along.

Wherever one falls on this continuum of fan satisfaction, no one contests that from the opening scenes of the miniseries to the two-part finale, "Daybreak," *Battlestar Galactica* raises a host of issues—indeed, far too many for consideration in one brief chapter. From the transcendent value of a homeland in a time of desperation and diaspora to the transcendent value of myths of origin lost and regained; from the problem of self-aware technology that challenges the nature of reality for all concerned to the question of a guiding power behind the scenes of apocalypse and millennium; from the risk that humans are not necessarily the favored of the gods to the certainty that the Cylons are more than even they imagined or hoped they could be—*Battlestar Galactica* demonstrates what religious people, professional or otherwise, have often discovered: it is easy to ask questions about the unseen order, to believe that God has a plan, but it is far more difficult to provide satisfactory answers to the multiple contingencies that obscure the clear outline of that plan. In the end, perhaps we are left with the mystery of the unseen order. As Baltar pleads with Cavil to understand in "Daybreak, Part 2," "Whether we want to call that 'God,' or 'the gods' or some sublime inspiration, or a divine force that we cannot know or understand, that doesn't matter. It doesn't matter. It's here. It exists. And our two destinies are entwined in its force." Ever true to his nature, unable to transcend his programming, Cavil wants assurances. "How do I know this 'force' has our best interests in mind? How do you know 'God' is on your side, doctor?"

BALTAR

```
I don't. God's not on any one side. God's a
force of nature, beyond good and evil. Good
and evil, we created those. Want to break
the cycle? Break the cycle of birth, death,
rebirth, destruction, escape, death. Well,
that's in our hands--in our hands only. It
```

```
requires a leap of faith. It requires that we
give in to hope, not fear.
```

In many ways, with some questions answered and others left hang-ing, this brings us back to "Flesh and Bone," to the holding cell aboard the *Gemenon Traveler* where a human tortures a Cylon, and the machine responds, "This is not all we are."

So say we all.

9

THE TRUTH IS OUT THERE
Transcendence and the Neverending Quest

OUTTAKES: *THE MATRIX*

APOC

Morpheus is right. He's got to be the One.

. . .

ORACLE

I'd say the bad news is, you're not the One.

. . .

NEO

Morpheus, I know you won't believe me but the Oracle told me I'm not the One.

MORPHEUS

It doesn't matter if I don't believe you. What matters is that you don't believe her.

. . .

TRINITY

Morpheus is right, you know. It doesn't matter what he believes or even what the Oracle believes. What matters is what you believe.

It's hard to know what Frederik Pohl, the venerable science fiction author, three-time Hugo and six-time Nebula Award winner, would make of *The Matrix*, Andy and Larry Wachowski's visionary film about a computer-generated environment and humanity's place as a renewable energy source within it. Nearly ninety now, Pohl blogs regularly but only rarely mentions movies or television. Like so many science fiction authors whose work has been optioned for film and then either languished at a studio or vanished down the memory-hole when funding disappeared (Pohl, 2009), he is somewhat less than sanguine about the value of science fiction film and, by extension, television. "Film does not offer a hospitable venue for intellectual discussion," Pohl wrote in the *Skeptical Inquirer* three years before *The Matrix* hit theaters in 1999, "because that is the nature of film: movies wonderfully stimulate the senses and excite the emotions, but of rational intellectual content there is seldom very much" (1996, 26). With all due respect to Pohl, even if there are not that many films (or television shows) that contain much "rational intellectual content," this does not mean that they cannot be sites for serious "intellectual discussion." Once again, we should always bear in mind Ado Kyrou's maxim that we "learn to look at 'bad' films. They are often sublime" (1963, 276). While *The Matrix: Reloaded* and *The Matrix: Revolutions* come close to defining the reason not to make sequels, *The Matrix* is a very good film and, like *Blade Runner* before it and *Battlestar Galactica* after, has generated something of a cottage industry in philosophical discussion and criticism (see, for example, Grau, 2005; Irwin, 2002, 2005; Kapell and Doty, 2004; Yeffeth, 2003).

What is the Matrix, the virtual reality at the heart of the story, and what does it mean to live there? What does "reality" even mean in that context, or "freedom"? Are we already in the Matrix or something frighteningly similar, as transhumanist philosopher Nick Bostrom suggests (2003b)? If so, is any sense of self-determination we enjoy merely the grandest illusion of all? Is Neo the One, and what does *that* mean? Is he the Christ who saves us, a Buddha who points the way to salvation, an adept who masters the arcana of reality, or something else altogether? These are just some of the questions writers have grappled with in the decade since the film's release.

For all its action, intrigue, and dazzling special effects, however, and for all the commentary it has generated, I suggest that *The*

Matrix is essentially *tabula rasa*, a blank slate. A visual feast in many ways, it is also an empty canvas on which viewers inevitably paint their own understandings of reality, their own perceptions of the quest for transcendence. Contrary to outdated media theories that posit the audience as a collection of passive receivers and filmmakers as the ultimate arbiters of cinematic meaning, *The Matrix* is one of the best science fiction examples of the fact that what we take away from a film or television experience is inevitably a function of what we bring to it. Movies, as director Joe Dante says, are like Rorschach tests; "there is what you mean when you make them, and then there's what people get out of them. And sometimes those two things are not always the same" (1995). This is never more true than when we attempt to understand a film such as *The Matrix* in terms of the varied human quests for transcendence.

"*The Matrix* resounds with the elements of Jewish and Christian apocalyptic thought," writes Paul Fontana, a New Testament student at the Harvard Divinity School, "specifically, hope for messianic deliverance, restoration and establishment of the Kingdom of God" (2002, 160, 161). Indeed, Fontana asserts confidently that "anyone with a religious background"—by which we must assume he means either Jewish or Christian—"can notice some of the more obvious Biblical parallels in *The Matrix*" (2002, 160). There is no guarantee of this, however, as Stephen Prothero's findings on the appalling lack of religious literacy in America make clear (2007), but others concur, including fellow Christian Mark Stucky, who sees the first film as the "Gospel of Neo" and the two sequels—*Reloaded* and *Revolutions*—as the "Acts" and the "Apocalypse According to St. Neo" respectively (2005, par. 5). "Although various other allusions exist," Stucky opines, "a major mythological motif in the film and its two sequels consists of blatant and vital references to Christ" (2005, par. 3). Lest anyone think that *The Matrix* is little more than Christian missiology in black leather and bullet-time, however, there are a number of other interpretive options.

Acknowledging the film's "messianic motifs," Buddhologist Paul Ford points out that "the Buddhist parallels in *The Matrix* are numerous" (2002, 137). "The Matrix itself is analogous to *samsara*, the illusory world that is not the reality it appears to be" (Ford, 2002, 137); discipline and control à la Buddha's Noble Eightfold Path allow Neo to enter the Matrix as a bodhisattva; and the different characters' actions demonstrate the balancing effects of karma. Moreover, at the conclusion, "no longer constrained by fear, doubt, or ignorance, Neo, like a Buddha, has transcended all dualities, even the ultimate duality of life and death" (Ford, 2002, 140; cf. Brannigan, 2002). On the other hand, Muslim philosopher Idris Hamid discusses "the Cosmological Journey of Neo" as "an Islamic *Matrix*" (2005), while Anna Lännström writes about *"The Matrix* and Vedanta: Journeying from the Unreal to the Real"* (2005). Matt Lawrence offers a Taoist interpretation of the films (2004), and Frances Flannery-Daily and Rachel Wagner see in them an unmistakable Gnostic allegory (2001). Reading the films through the Advaitic teachings of the Indian guru Ramana Maharshi, Pradheep Chhalliyil interprets *The Matrix* trilogy as an elaborate tale of Self-realization (2004). *The Matrix* has even found its way into new religious consciousness, and in the years immediately following the trilogy's release, I received regular emails inviting me to join Matrixism, "the Path of the One," an online religion that, among other things, makes psychedelics a sacrament, equates pornography with prostitution, and locates the origins of its beliefs nearly a century ago in the public speeches of 'Abdu'l-Bahá, son of the founder of the Bahá'i faith ("Matrixism," n.d.; cf. Morehead, forthcoming).

Morpheus is right, you know. What matters *is* what you believe. In this brief last chapter, I will look once again at some of the ways believers have colonized popular science fiction, planting theological flags and staking claim to other worlds in the name of their own particular god.

THEOLOGIZING A GALAXY FAR, FAR AWAY

In George Pal's production of *The War of the Worlds* we see the Protestantization of H. G. Wells' overtly antireligious novel. On the other hand, although Christian references were subliminal at best when *The Day the Earth Stood Still* was released in 1951, since the late 1970s it has been almost impossible to find a critic who does not confidently (and in my view mistakenly) read Robert Wise's classic first-contact film as an overt Christian allegory (Cowan, 2009). A generation later, media studies scholar Read Mercer Schuchardt boldly declares *The Matrix* "a parable of the original Judeo-Christian worldview of entrapment in a world gone wrong . . . a new testament for a new millennium" (2002, 5). In each case, the relationship between the onscreen product and the offscreen stock of cultural knowledge on which audiences draw to make sense of their cinematic experience has produced a theological hybrid, a social construction that has less to do with onscreen action and dialogue than with offscreen quests for transcendence and meaning. All three of these films notwithstanding, the science fiction series that has been most heavily pressed into theological service is *Star Wars*.

Star Wars is told in two chronologically inverted trilogies—the stories of Anakin Skywalker and the origin of Darth Vader (Ep. I–III), released between 1999 and 2005, and the stories of Luke Skywalker and Darth Vader's redemption (Ep. IV–VI), released between 1977 and 1983. The films combine a number of well-known mythic motifs: the hero's quest and the lover's sacrifice, the temptation of evil and the promise of redemption, and the will to power and power of the unseen order—all served up with memorable characters, action, adventure, and such special effects "as dreams are made on." Since *Star Wars* is arguably the most popular science fiction series in cinema history, I am not going to discuss it as I have other films and television series in this book, if for no other reason than that so many others have done so it seems there is little left to say about the films themselves (cf. Decker and Eberl, 2005; Galipeau, 2001; Hanson and Kay, 2002; Henderson, 1997; Silvio and Vinci, 2007; Wetmore, 2005). Instead, this section points out some of the ways religious believers have incorporated the films into their own belief systems, essentially mapping their own particular quest for transcendence onto a more general cinematic product. Although Jesuit film critic Richard Blake insists that movies "must not and cannot be baptized and then coerced into ecclesial servitude" (1991, 289), this is precisely what has happened with *Star Wars*, and fans have seen a variety of religious paths reflected in Lucas' vision. *The Tao of "Star Wars,"* for example, reads the films through the lens of Lao Tzu's venerable *Tao te Ching* (Porter, 2003), and Matthew Bortolin's *The Dharma of "Star Wars"* discusses "The Jedi Art of Mindfulness" and "Darth Vader's Karma" (2005). These, however, are not the most common interpretations.

I saw *Star Wars*—what is known to the current generation of fans as *Episode IV: A New Hope*—when it was first released in 1977. Indeed,

I was so entranced, I saw it over and over, often at consecutive show-
ings when I should have been back in my dorm room studying. A
few months later, I found a small booklet on the paperback rack at
a local convenience store entitled "The Truth Behind the Force." I
don't have it anymore, but I remember it as a conservative Christian tract arguing on the one hand that the impersonal Force of the
film—the "energy field created by all living things [that] surrounds us
and penetrates us . . . [that] binds the galaxy together," as Obi-Wan
(Alec Guinness) tells young Luke—was an agency for evil because it
implicitly denied the personal relationship with God through Jesus
that is the benchmark of salvation for tens of millions of Christians.
On the other hand, the pamphlet offered an understanding of the
"real power" of the Force through just such a relationship. Less than
a year after its release, and decades before the six-episode chapter
play would finally play out, Christian evangelists were already seeking to colonize George Lucas' galaxy far, far away.

Rather than warn believers about the dangers of Lucas' mythic
vision, however, many of the Christian *Star Wars* books that have
appeared since then use the films to illustrate—and not infrequently
rhapsodize—aspects of their own religious tradition. Onscreen
action is meant to lead unerringly and inevitably to the deepening
of offscreen faith. Thus, Dick Staub writes of *The Christian Wisdom
of the Jedi Masters* (2005) while Russell Dalton takes readers on *Faith
Journeys through Fantasy Lands: A Christian Dialogue with "Harry Potter," "Star Wars," and "The Lord of the Rings"* (2003), and David Wilkinson shares with them *The Power of the Force* (2000). In *Finding God
in a Galaxy Far, Far Away* (2005), Baptist pastor Timothy Paul Jones
reads his way through the saga in a series of folksy homilies leavened
with anecdotal personal disclosure and a liberal sprinkling of biblical
quotes and citations. Playing off epigraphs included in each chapter—
one a quote from a *Star Wars* episode, the other a quotation from the
Bible—with "Spiritual Exercises for the Serious Padawan," he constantly admonishes his readers to "Be Mindful of the True Force."
Sometimes, though, his exegesis seems a bit strained. In "Afraid, Are
You?" for example, Jones quotes the Jedi Master Yoda from *Episode
III: Revenge of the Sith*—"Train yourself to let go of everything you
fear to lose"—and correlates this with God's words to the people of
Israel, "Do not be afraid, for I am with you" (Isaiah 43:5). This is not

the most useful parallel, however, since one could easily argue that Yoda's advice to Anakin (Hayden Christensen) is more directly in line with the well-known Zen story about the general's favorite tea cup and the value of nonattachment. The issue, though, is not the question of which is the more apt analogy, but what the use of the analogy can tell us about the relationship between religion and popular film. Similarly, in *Star Wars™ Jesus*, Caleb Grimes works his way through all six films, aligning passages and images from each with selected biblical texts designed to elucidate his Christian interpretation. Thus, one chapter begins with Obi-Wan Kenobi's last words to Darth Vader as they battle in the first Death Star's docking bay: "If you strike me down, I shall become more powerful than you can possibly imagine." To this, Grimes adds, Yoda-style, "The power paradox of Christ, this is"—plus an assortment of obligatory supporting verses from the New Testament (2007, 69). (All this said, for a fascinating debate arguing that *Star Wars* has no redeemable spiritual or religious significance whatsoever, see Brin and Stover, 2006, esp. 97–134.)

Unlike many of his more enthusiastic coreligionists, however, in *The Gospel According to "Star Wars,"* systematic theologian John McDowell wrestles with whether a Christian reading of these films is appropriate at all, especially for believers who are "worried that *Star Wars* is occultic, perhaps we could say 'sinematic'" (2007, xvii). For McDowell, the issue is moral and spiritual compatibility: can Christians safely watch *Star Wars*, or must it remain a guilty pleasure dutifully confessed on Sunday? Although there are more than a few believers who believe Lucas' films are thinly veiled occultism (e.g., Montenegro, 2002; Walker, 1999), McDowell ultimately concludes that they can be turned to worthwhile Christian advantage. As a point of movie trivia, however, what McDowell may not know is that the original *Star Wars* owes its existence at least partially to *The Omen*, Richard Donner's 1976 horror film that gave a cash-strapped Twentieth Century Fox enough money for Lucas to finish the saga's first installment (Zacky, 2001; Cowan, 2008b, 191–99). That is, but for the cinematic mainstreaming of the Antichrist, Luke Skywalker might never have seen the big screen. In each case, though, the authors read the films in terms of their own particular theological perspectives, seemingly unaware of the larger issues of cultural hegemony these interpretations reveal.

In his classic and controversial text *Orientalism*, literary critic Edward Said interprets Antonio Gramsci's seminal concept of "hegemony" to mean that in nontotalitarian societies "certain cultural forms predominate over others, just as certain ideas are more influential than others" (1978, 7). Hegemony is most deeply rooted when those dominant cultural forms become the lenses through which even people who do not participate directly in them view the world, and it becomes most insidious when we no longer recognize that the lenses exist at all. In terms of religion in the West, of course, this dominance means Christianity—whether one is a Christian or not. Deployed as a regular part of the general stock of cultural knowledge, these ideas become the common sense of culture, the local currency of interpretation, not because they are necessarily reasonable, correct, or germane in any particular instance, but because they are socially and culturally ascendant.

In North America, Christian interpretations can be successfully overlaid on any number of cultural products, and according to whatever theological or hermeneutic frameworks the interpreters choose, for two principal reasons. First, the Christian story, at least as it is nominally understood in the West, is ubiquitous enough so that explaining its broad outlines is largely unnecessary; those familiar with it will pick up the cues and fill in the blanks as needed. This is clearly illustrated in the interpretive sediment laid down around *The Day the Earth Stood Still*, as critics and commentators gradually read more and more of the Christian story into a first-contact film (Cowan, 2009). Second, elements of that Christian story are broad enough in the context of ordinary human experience—release from oppression, the nobility of self-sacrifice, a "Golden Rule" of ethical behavior—that *not* to find something to interpret in this fashion would be surprising. Creatively misreading Said, as I have written elsewhere (Cowan, 2009, par. 35), "if *orientalism* renders the different exotic and thereby exerts control over it, *occidentalism* renders the exotic familiar, enclosing it in non-contested interpretive spaces, bounding out competing interpretations, and exercising similar control."

In terms of the cultural hegemony of Christianity, the most obvious way this kind of occidentalism occurs is through precisely the interpretive similitude we see here: some product or element of popular culture is read as reflecting or approximating some aspect of the gospel or the larger biblical story. Whether its creators intended the reference or not, the product is theologized—colonized in the service of a particular religious understanding. Thus, Thomas Bertonneau and Kim Paffenroth can proclaim of *Dr. Who* that "many of the Doctor's nemeses bear a strong resemblance to the competitors of Christianity in Paul's day," that "television's most famous science-fiction series, *Star Trek*, consistently portrays broad Christian ethics," that in *The Twilight Zone* the "depiction of evil is predominantly and unmistakably Christian," and that by investigating *The X-Files* we are taken into "a world deeply imbued with the imagery and urgency of Christian apocalyptic" (2006, 26, 27). Thus, a very conservative Presbyterian minister can recast Terence Fisher, one of Hammer Studio's most prolific horror directors during the 1950s and 1960s, as a closet Christian evangelist. By "baptizing" Fisher and his work, he can indulge a passion for pop cultural products that many of his parishioners might find problematic at best, blasphemous at worst (Leggett, 2002). Thus, film studies scholar Anton Kozlovic can develop a set of twenty-five putative "Structural Characteristics of the Cinematic Christ-Figure" (2004), including that such a figure is simple and poor; that he is almost always male; that he is accompanied by twelve associates, including "a sexually associated woman" (par. 41); that at some point he strikes "a cruciform pose" (par. 53); and that he is "frequently depicted with blue eyes" (par. 65). That superficial similarity in no way indicates coordinate relationship, causal connection, or subtextual significance seems to have completely escaped Kozlovic's notice (Deacy, 2006). Put differently, not everyone who throws out their arms is a Christ-figure, bent knee or no. I am not suggesting that those who want to interpret Neo, Klaatu, and Luke Skywalker as Christ-figures and their respective films as gospel allegories are not free to do so. They paid their money and they're entitled to their interpretation. Like the interpretive sedimentation that has built up around *Star Wars*, however, this process bounds out other, often more plausible readings. It maps the cinematic territory in terms of one particular quest for transcendence, one particular vision of hope, and frequently forecloses other options.

THE QUEST FOR TRANSCENDENCE
AND THE IMAGINATION OF HOPE

Whether implicit or explicit, every science fiction story, novel, film, or television show begins with two words: What if? What if we could travel faster than light and explore the stars? What if we could achieve immortality through cloning, transhuman augmentation, or computer uploading? What if the machine-beings we create seek their own evolution? What if those we have dominated in whatever fashion suddenly return the favor?

"Millennialism," writes Catherine Wessinger, "is an expression of the human hope for the achievement of permanent well-being, in other words, salvation" (2000b, 6). Though she is careful to point out that millennialism comes in different forms, some progressive, others catastrophic (Wessinger, 2000a, 16–17), this is one way of conceptualizing what I have been calling the quest for transcendence. While the landscape of pop cultural eschatology does reveal some pockets of hope for a brighter future, some occasional dreams of "permanent well-being," more often than not those dreams come wrapped in a wide range of nightmares. For every paradise envisioned by *Star Trek*, there are a multitude of postapocalyptic wastelands; for every putative savior from the stars—from Klaatu in *The Day the Earth Stood Still* to the hopefully beneficent occupants of the mothership in *Close Encounters of the Third Kind*—there are any number of invaders from outer (or inner) space.

Admittedly, in this volume, I have only scratched the surface of what science fiction offers in terms of the human (and, perhaps, non-human) quest for transcendence, and a multitude of other examples wait to be explored. There are, for example, the different visions of transcendence in Fritz Lang's monumental *Metropolis* and William Menzies' art deco vision of *Things to Come*, his adaptation of H. G. Wells' novel *The Shape of Things to Come* ([1933] 2005). From the wasteland, whether industrial or post-war, to utopia, whether a worker's paradise or the soaring towers of a reborn civilization, the decline of society in each of these films is eerily prescient of the rise of Soviet communism under Stalin and of the Second World War. Though many British audiences laughed openly in 1936 when *Things to Come* showed bombs falling on London, less than five years after its release the Luftwaffe brought the nightmare to life and any sense of naïve security vanished. How is hope realized from the ashes of despair? How do we grasp millennium from apocalypse?

Sometimes we don't, and new hopes evolve to replace (or to repeat) the old.

In *The Planet of the Apes*, for example, and its four cinematic sequels, we find an extended exercise in the social construction of hope lost and regained, of the quest for transcendence sacrificed over and over on the altar of hubris (cf. Greene, 1996; Russo and Landsman, 2001). When Taylor (Charlton Heston) and his fellow astronauts return to Earth two thousand years into the future, simian scientists find in them the key to life, proof that apes evolved from a lower species—humanity. More importantly, though, "if he is a missing link," says the chimpanzee-scientist Cornelius (Roddy McDowell), "it means the Sacred Scrolls aren't worth their parchment." For other apes, however, the first article of faith is clear and simple: "The Almighty created the ape in his own image; that He gave him a soul and a mind; that He set him apart from the beasts of the jungle, and made him the lord of the planet." The very thought that there might be a relationship or a connection between apes and humans is tantamount to heresy. The social analogy here is hard to miss: hope for one group means the ruin of hope for another.

In the first sequel, *Beneath the Planet of the Apes*, hiding from a holy war waged to exterminate humanity for the good of all apes, a group of human telepaths live underground, worshiping an atomic bomb two millennia old. A poignant comment on the principles of Cold War détente and the doctrine of mutually assured destruction, the humans see the bomb as "God's instrument on Earth," "a Holy Weapon of Peace." As Mendez (Paul Richards), the leader of the survivors, intones:

MENDEZ

```
For it is written that, in the First Year of
the Bomb, the Blessing of the Holy Fallout
descended from above and my people built a
new city in the blackened bowels of the old.
Blessed be the Bomb Everlasting, to whom
```

```
alone we may reveal our inmost truth, and
whom we shall serve all our days in peace.
```

Sometimes we do grasp millennium, though new and unfamiliar saviors often must take the stage to bring that hope to life.

Between 1918 and 1920, a pandemic H1N1 influenza infected five hundred million people, roughly one-third of the world's population. Between fifty and one hundred million died. From the SARS outbreak in 2002 to global fears of further H1N1 pandemics in 2007 ("bird flu") and 2009 ("swine flu"), the prospect of a biomedical apocalypse has loomed large on the cultural horizon for nearly a century. Since the turn of the millennium, we have also seen in science fiction film a new kind of savior, a beautiful, violent, female antihero who walks the path of transcendence aggressively and often reluctantly (cf. Inness, 2004). A number of these films hinge on dystopic plague narratives. In *Ultraviolet*, Violet Song jat Sharrif (Milla Jovovich) is "born into a world you may not understand," one in which the population is consumed by germophobia while a "hemoglophagic virus" has divided the population into uninfected humans and vampire-like creatures with increased strength but a dramatically decreased lifespan. The *Resident Evil* trilogy pits a genetically enhanced Alice (also Milla Jovovich) against a spreading plague of zombism, the product of secret medical experiments by a powerful transnational biomedical company. An expert in martial arts and all manner of weaponry, she is eventually called to lead the surviving humans across the desert to a promised land free of disease. A third plague story that has seen a variety of pop cultural iterations is *Æon Flux*, originally produced as a series of MTV shorts, then rewritten for the big screen in 2005. Early in the twenty-first century, the "industrial disease" wiped out 99 percent of the world's population and the remaining few million now live in the walled city of Bregna, the last city on Earth. Ostensibly, Bregna is a paradise, but others see it as a gilded cage, and a resistance movement has risen to challenge the biomedical empire that controls it. Æon Flux (Charlize Theron) is that movement's top operative, the unlikely instrument of transcendence. From the Marvel Comics character *Elektra* (Jennifer Garner), who dies and is resurrected as the world's deadliest assassin, to the elegant *Lara Croft* (Angelina Jolie), the video-game *Tomb Raider* come to the big screen to save the world not once but twice, salvation and transcendence are found in improbable places and unlikely persons—but they are found.

On the maiden voyage of *The Next Generation*'s *Enterprise-D*, Q, the mysterious, ostensibly omnipotent being who remains one of the favorite characters in the *Star Trek* universe, transported Captain Picard and his crew light years beyond their original mission in "Encounter at Farpoint" and placed them on trial for what he considered the crimes of humanity—our presence in the universe as "a dangerous, savage, child-race." The Q Continuum believed our quest for transcendence should be foreclosed, that any hope we might have of becoming more than we are was barren from the beginning. Taken to the Asgard homeworld in "The Fifth Race," on the other hand, *Stargate SG-1*'s Jack O'Neill learns that we "have great potential," but that "we have much to prove" to the older races in the galaxy. "We might not be ready for a lot of this stuff," O'Neill replies, "but we're doing the best we can. We are a very curious race." "You're an interesting species," the extraterrestrial tells Ellie Arroway during her moment of contact, "an interesting mix. Capable of such exquisite dreams; such horrifying nightmares." "The unknown future rolls toward us," says Sarah at the close of *Terminator 2: Judgment Day*. "I face it for the first time with a sense of hope, because if a machine, a Terminator, can learn the value of human life, maybe we can too." And, coming full circle in the series, in "All Good Things . . . ," the final episode of *The Next Generation*'s seven-season mission, Picard is brought back to Q's court, where the ultimate point of the quest for transcendence is revealed.

Q

```
You just don't get it, do you, Jean-Luc? The
trial never ends. We wanted to see if you
had the ability to expand your mind and your
horizons, and for one brief moment you did.

          PICARD

When I realized the paradox.
```

Q

> Exactly. For that one fraction of a
> second, you were open to options you had
> never considered. That is the exploration
> that awaits you, not mapping stars and
> studying nebulae, but charting the unknown
> possibilities of existence.

Whether we find it in serial pulps, comic books and graphic novels, big screen blockbusters, direct-to-DVD movies, or television series, science fiction reveals a number of foundational beliefs that inform and shape our different quests for transcendence. First, as O'Neill says, human beings are *curious*. We are not satisfied with the shadows dancing on the walls of Plato's cave, and our varied quests for transcendence are often the direct result of being told, as Q says to Picard in the *TNG* pilot, "Go back or you will certainly die!" Second, human life is *fragile*. We are vulnerable and, as individuals, remarkably easy to kill. We often depend on our science, our weaponry, and not infrequently our gods, to survive in the most rudimentary situations. But, paradoxically, it is that very fragility that gives meaning to our lives. It is the possibility that we can be lost in an instant that forces us to press against whatever boundaries we encounter. Third, human technology is *fickle*. It is a double-edged sword and, although often useful for cutting down those who threaten our survival, it can just as quickly turn into that which threatens our survival. Fourth, the human spirit is *strong*; according to many of the narratives we have considered, it is all but indomitable. Although at times the nightmares seem more popular, even more plausible, they do hold dreams within them—our fundamental belief in the possibilities of the future.

FILMOGRAPHY

CINEMA

Title	Year	Director
2001: A Space Odyssey	1968	Stanley Kubrick
2010: The Year We Make Contact	1984	Peter Hyams
Æon Flux	2005	Karyn Kusama
A.I.: Artificial Intelligence	2001	Steven Spielberg
Alien	1979	Ridley Scott
Aliens	1986	James Cameron
Apocalypse	1998	Peter Gerretsen
II: Revelation	1999	André van Heerden
III: Tribulation	2000	André van Heerden
IV: Judgment	2001	André van Heerden
Armageddon	1998	Michael Bay
Atomic Brain, The	1964	Joseph V. Mascelli
Bad Boys	1995	Michael Bay
Battle for the Planet of the Apes	1973	J. Lee Thompson
Beneath the Planet of the Apes	1970	Ted Post
Blade Runner	1982	Ridley Scott
Blue Thunder	1983	John Badham
Brain That Wouldn't Die, The	1962	Joseph Green
Brother from Another Planet, The	1984	John Sayles
Close Encounters of the Third Kind	1977	Steven Spielberg
Cocoon	1985	Ron Howard
Colossus: The Forbin Project	1970	Joseph Sargent

CINEMA *(cont.)*

TITLE	YEAR	DIRECTOR
Communion	1989	Philippe Mora
Conquest of the Planet of the Apes	1972	J. Lee Thompson
Contact	1997	Robert Zemeckis
Day of the Triffids, The	1962	Steve Sekely
Day the Earth Stood Still, The	1951	Robert Wise
Deep Impact	1998	Mimi Leder
Elektra	2005	Rob Bowman
Escape from L.A.	1996	John Carpenter
Escape from the Planet of the Apes	1971	Don Taylor
E.T.: The Extra-Terrestrial	1982	Steven Spielberg
Expelled: No Intelligence Allowed	2008	Nathan Frankowski
Fat Man and Little Boy	1989	Roland Joffé
Fire in the Sky	1993	Robert Lieberman
Forbidden Planet	1956	Fred M. Wilcox
Galaxy Quest	1999	Dean Parisot
Gattaca	1997	Andrew Niccol
I, Robot	2004	Alex Proyas
Independence Day	1996	Roland Emmerich
Indiana Jones and the Last Crusade	1989	Steven Spielberg
Invasion of the Body Snatchers	1956	Don Siegel
Island, The	2005	Michael Bay
It! The Terror from Beyond Space	1958	Edward Cahn
Jaws	1975	Steven Spielberg
Johnny Mnemonic	1995	Robert Longo
Jurassic Park	1993	Steven Spielberg
Land Before Time, The	1988	Don Bluth
Lara Croft: Tomb Raider	2001	Simon West
Last Temptation of Christ, The	1988	Martin Scorsese
Lawnmower Man	1992	Brett Leonard
Logan's Run	1976	Michael Anderson
Lost in Space	1998	Stephen Hopkins
Mars Attacks!	1996	Tim Burton
Mary Shelley's Frankenstein	1994	Kenneth Branagh
Matrix, The	1999	Andy & Larry Wachowski
Matrix, The: Reloaded	2003	Andy & Larry Wachowski

TITLE	YEAR	DIRECTOR
Matrix, The: Revolutions	2003	Andy & Larry Wachowski
Men in Black	1997	Barry Sonnenfeld
Metropolis	1927	Fritz Lang
Mists of Avalon, The	2001	Uli Edel
Mummy, The	1932	Karl Freund
Omega Man, The	1971	Boris Sagal
Omen, The	1976	Richard Donner
Plan 9 from Outer Space	1959	Ed D. Wood Jr.
Planet of the Apes	1968	Franklin J. Schaffner
Poltergeist	1982	Tobe Hooper
Resident Evil	2002	Paul W. S. Anderson
Resident Evil: Apocalypse	2004	Alexander Witt
Resident Evil: Extinction	2008	Russell Mulcahy
Robocop	1987	Paul Verhoeven
Samson and Delilah	1949	Cecil B. DeMille
Saturn 3	1980	Stanley Donen
Shoes of the Fisherman, The	1968	Michael Anderson
Short Circuit	1986	John Badham
Star Trek: First Contact	1996	Jonathan Frakes
Star Wars		
I: The Phantom Menace	1999	George Lucas
II: Attack of the Clones	2002	George Lucas
III: Revenge of the Sith	2005	George Lucas
IV: A New Hope	1977	George Lucas
V: The Empire Strikes Back	1980	Irvin Kershner
VI: Return of the Jedi	1983	Richard Marquand
Stargate	1994	Roland Emmerich
Starman	1984	John Carpenter
Stepford Wives, The	1975	Bryan Forbes
Terminator, The	1984	James Cameron
Terminator 2: Judgment Day	1991	James Cameron
Them!	1954	Gordon Douglas
Things to Come	1936	William Cameron Menzies
Total Recall	1990	Paul Verhoeven
Ultraviolet	2006	Kurt Wimmer
Voyage dans la lune, Le	1902	Georges Méliès

CINEMA *(cont.)*

TITLE	YEAR	DIRECTOR
Wall Street	1987	Oliver Stone
War of the Worlds, The	1953	Byron Haskin
War of the Worlds, The	2005	Timothy Hines
War of the Worlds, The	2005	David Michael Latt
War of the Worlds, The	2005	Steven Spielberg
WarGames	1983	John Badham
Westworld	1973	Michael Crichton
What the #$! Do We (K)now!?*	2004	William Arntz, Betsy Chasse, & Mark Vicente
When Worlds Collide	1951	Rudolph Maté

TELEVISION

TITLE	DATES	EPISODE	DIRECTOR
24	2001–		
Babylon 5	1994–1998		
"Believers"	1994	S.1, Ep.10	Richard Compton
"By Any Means Necessary"	1994	S.1, Ep.12	Jim Johnston
"Deathwalker"	1994	S.1, Ep.9	Bruce Seth Green
"Dust to Dust"	1996	S.3, Ep.6	David J. Eagle
"Fall of Night, The"	1995	S.2, Ep.22	Janet Greek
"Grail"	1994	S.1, Ep.15	Richard Compton
"In the Shadow of Z'Ha'Dum"	1995	S.2, Ep.16	David J. Eagle
"Parliament of Dreams, The"	1994	S.1, Ep.5	Jim Johnston
"Passing through Gethsemane"	1995	S.3, Ep.4	Adam Nimoy
"Points of Departure"	1994	S.2, Ep.1	Janet Greek
"TKO"	1994	S.1, Ep.14	John C. Flinn III
Battlestar Galactica	1978–1979		
Battlestar Galactica	2003	Miniseries	Michael Rymer
Battlestar Galactica	2004–2009		
"33"	2004	S.1, Ep.1	Michael Rymer
"Captain's Hand, The"	2006	S.2, Ep.17	S. Mimica-Gezzan

Title	Dates	Episode	Director
"Crossroads, Part 1"	2007	S.3, Ep.19	Michael Rymer
"Crossroads, Part 2"	2007	S.3. Ep.20	Michael Rymer
"Daybreak, Part 1"	2009	S.4, Ep.19	Michael Rymer
"Daybreak, Part 2"	2009	S.4, Ep.20	Michael Rymer
"Dirty Hands"	2007	S.3, Ep.16	Wayne Rose
"Downloaded"	2006	S.2, Ep.18	Jeff Woolnough
"Flesh and Bone"	2004	S.1, Ep.8	Brad Turner
"Fragged"	2005	S.2, Ep.3	S. Mimica-Gezzan
"Hand of God, The"	2005	S.1, Ep.10	Jeff Woolnough
"Hero"	2006	S.3, Ep.8	Michael Rymer
"Home, Pt. 1"	2005	S.2, Ep.6	S. Mimica-Gezzan
"Hub, The"	2008	S.4, Ep.9	Paul A. Edwards
"Kobol's Last Gleaming, Pt. 1"	2005	S.1, Ep.12	Michael Rymer
"Lay Down Your Burdens, Pt. 1"	2006	S.2, Ep.19	Michael Rymer
"Occupation"	2006	S.3, Ep.1	S. Mimica-Gezzan
"Rapture"	2007	S.3, Ep.12	Michael Rymer
"Resurrection Ship, Part 2"	2006	S.2, Ep.12	Michael Rymer
"Six Degrees of Separation"	2004	S.1, Ep.7	Robert M. Young
"Six of One"	2008	S.4, Ep.2	Anthony Hemingway
"Taking a Break From All Your Worries"	2007	S.3, Ep.13	Edward Jas. Olmos
"Ties That Bind, The"	2008	S.4, Ep.3	Michael Nankin
"Water"	2004	S.1, Ep.2	Marita Grabiak
"Woman King, The"	2007	S.3, Ep.14	Michael Rymer

Bionic Woman, The　　1976–1978
CSI: Crime Scene Investigation　　2000–
CSI: Miami　　2002–
Earth: Final Conflict　　1997–2002
Enterprise　　2001–2005
Invasion　　2005
Logan's Run　　1977–1978
Lost in Space　　1965–1968
Roswell　　1999–2002
Six Million Dollar Man, The　　1974–1978

TELEVISION *(cont.)*

TITLE	DATES	EPISODE	DIRECTOR
Star Trek	1966–1969		
"Amok Time"	1967	S.2, Ep.1	Joseph Pevney
"Apple, The"	1967	S.2, Ep.5	Joseph Pevney
"Man Trap, The"	1966	S.1, Ep.1	Marc Daniels
"Who Mourns for Adonais?"	1967	S.2, Ep.2	Marc Daniels
Star Trek: Deep Space Nine	1993–1999		
"Assignment, The"	1996	S.5, Ep.5	Allan Kroeker
"Blood Oath"	1994	S.2, Ep.19	Winrich Kolbe
"Body Parts"	1996	S.4, Ep.24	Avery Brooks
"Changing Face of Evil, The"	1999	S.7, Ep.20	Michael Vejar
"Covenant"	1998	S.7, Ep.9	John T. Kretchmer
"Destiny"	1995	S.3, Ep.15	Les Landau
"Duet"	1993	S.1, Ep.18	James L. Conway
"Emissary"	1993	S.1, Ep.1	David Carson
"Emperor's New Cloak, The"	1999	S.7, Ep.12	LeVar Burton
"Ferengi Love Songs"	1997	S.5, Ep.20	René Auberjonois
"Hard Time"	1996	S.4, Ep.18	Alexander Singer
"Heart of Stone"	1995	S.3, Ep.14	Alexander Singer
"Hippocratic Oath"	1995	S.4, Ep.3	René Auberjonois
"In the Hands of the Prophets"	1993	S.1, Ep.19	David Livingston
"Let He Who Is Without Sin . . ."	1996	S.5, Ep.7	René Auberjonois
"Little Green Men"	1995	S.4, Ep.7	James L. Conway
"Nagus, The"	1993	S.1, Ep.10	David Livingston
"Penumbra"	1999	S.7, Ep.17	Stephen L. Posey
"Prophet Motive"	1995	S.3, Ep.16	René Auberjonois
"Reckoning, The"	1998	S.6, Ep.21	Jesús S. Treviño
"Rules of Acquisition"	1993	S.2, Ep.7	David Livingston
"Resurrection"	1997	S.6, Ep.8	LeVar Burton
"Ship, The"	1996	S.5, Ep.2	Kim Friedman
"Sons of Mogh"	1996	S.4, Ep.14	David Livingston
"Strange Bedfellows"	1999	S.7, Ep.19	René Auberjonois
"Sword of Kahless"	1995	S.4, Ep.8	LeVar Burton
"Tears of the Prophets"	1998	S.6, Ep.26	Allan Kroeker
"'Til Death Do Us Part"	1999	S.7, Ep.18	Winrich Kolbe

TITLE	DATES	EPISODE	DIRECTOR
"Treachery, Faith, and the Great River"	1998	S.7, Ep.6	Stephen L. Posey
"What You Leave Behind"	1999	S.7, Ep.25	Allan Kroeker
"When It Rains . . . "	1999	S.7, Ep.21	Michael Dorn
"You Are Cordially Invited"	1997	S.6, Ep.7	David Livingston
Star Trek: The Next Generation	1987–1994		
"All Good Things . . . "	1994	S.7, Ep.25	Winrich Kolbe
"Devil's Due"	1991	S.4, Ep.13	Tom Benko
"Elementary, Dear Data"	1988	S.2, Ep.3	Rob Bowman
"Evolution"	1989	S.3, Ep.1	Winrich Kolbe
"Galaxy's Child"	1991	S.4, Ep.16	Winrich Kolbe
"In Theory"	1991	S.4, Ep.25	Patrick Stewart
"Justice"	1987	S.1, Ep.7	James L. Conway
"Outrageous Okona, The"	1988	S.2, Ep.4	Robert Becker
"Q Who?"	1989	S.2, Ep.16	Rob Bowman
"Rightful Heir"	1993	S.6, Ep.23	Winrich Kolbe
"Ship in a Bottle"	1993	S.6, Ep.12	Alexander Singer
Star Trek: Voyager	1995–2001		
"Barge of the Dead"	1999	S.6, Ep.3	Mike Vejar
"False Profits"	1996	S.3, Ep.5	Cliff Bole
"Live Fast and Prosper"	2000	S.6, Ep.21	LeVar Burton
"Muse"	2000	S.6, Ep.22	Mike Vejar
Stargate: Ark of Truth	2008		Robert C. Cooper
Stargate: Atlantis	2004–2009		
Stargate: Continuum	2008		Martin Wood
Stargate SG-1	1997–2007		
"200"	2006	S.10, Ep.6	Martin Wood
"1969"	1999	S.2, Ep.21	Charles Correll
"2010"	2001	S.4, Ep.16	Andy Mikita
"Absolute Power"	2001	S.4, Ep.17	Peter DeLuise
"Abyss"	2002	S.6, Ep.6	Martin Wood
"Bloodlines"	1997	S.1, Ep.11	Mario Azzopardi
"Broca Divide, The"	1997	S.1, Ep.4	William Gereghty
"Children of the Gods"	1997	S.1, Ep.1	Mario Azzopardi
"Crusade"	2006	S.9, Ep.19	Robert C. Cooper

TELEVISION *(cont.)*

TITLE	DATES	EPISODE	DIRECTOR
"Demons"	1999	S.3, Ep.8	Peter DeLuise
"Emancipation"	1997	S.1, Ep.3	Jeff Wolnough
"Enemy Within, The"	1997	S.1, Ep.2	Dennis Berry
"Fail Safe"	2001	S.5, Ep.17	Andy Mikita
"Fifth Race, The"	1999	S.2, Ep.15	David Warry-Smith
"First Commandment, The"	1997	S.1, Ep.5	Dennis Berry
"Foothold"	1999	S.3, Ep.14	Andy Mikita
"Hathor"	1997	S.1, Ep.13	Brad Turner
"It's Good to be King"	2005	S.8, Ep.13	William Gereghty
"Matter of Time, A"	1999	S.2, Ep.16	Martin Wood
"Meridian"	2002	S.5, Ep.21	William Waring
"Metamorphosis"	2003	S.6, Ep.16	Peter DeLuise
"New Ground"	2000	S.3, Ep.19	Chris McMullin
"Origin"	2005	S.9, Ep.3	Brad Turner
"Other Guys, The"	2002	S.6, Ep.8	Martin Wood
"Past and Present"	1999	S.3, Ep.11	William Gereghty
"Point of View"	1999	S.3, Ep.6	Peter DeLuise
"Powers That Be"	2005	S.9, Ep.5	William Waring
"Redemption: Part 1"	2002	S.6, Ep.1	Martin Wood
"Redemption: Part 2"	2002	S.6, Ep.2	Martin Wood
"Revisions"	2003	S.7, Ep.5	Martin Wood
"Serpent's Lair, The"	1998	S.2, Ep.1	Jonathan Glassner
"Serpent's Venom, The"	2000	S.4, Ep.14	Martin Wood
"Seth"	1999	S.3, Ep.2	Bill Corcoran
"Singularity"	1997	S.1, Ep.14	Mario Azzopardi
"Spirits"	1998	S.2, Ep.13	Martin Wood
"There but for the Grace of God"	1998	S.1, Ep.19	David Warry-Smith
"Threads"	2005	S.8, Ep.18	Andy Mikita
"Tomb, The"	2001	S.5, Ep.8	Peter DeLuise
"Window of Opportunity"	2000	S.4, Ep.6	Peter DeLuise
"Wormhole X-Treme!"	2001	S.5, Ep.12	Peter DeLuise
Threshold	2005		
UFO	1970		

TITLE	DATES	EPISODE	DIRECTOR
V	1983		Kenneth Johnson
War of the Worlds: The Second Invasion	1988–1990		
"Eye for an Eye"	1988	S.1, Ep.5	Mark Sobel
"Good Samaritan, The"	1988	S.1, Ep.9	Paul Tucker
"Last Supper, The"	1989	S.1, Ep.18	George McCowan
"Thy Kingdom Come"	1988	S.1, Ep.3	Winrich Kolbe
X-Files, The	1993–2002		
"Biogenesis"	1999	S.6, Ep.22	Rob Bowman
"Hollywood A.D."	2000	S.7, Ep.19	David Duchovny
"Host, The"	1994	S.2, Ep.2	Daniel Sackheim
"Je Souhaite"	2000	S.7, Ep.21	Vince Gilligan
"Kill Switch"	1998	S.5, Ep.11	Rob Bowman
"Provenance"	2002	S.9, Ep.9	Kim Manners
"Providence"	2002	S.9, Ep.10	Chris Carter
"Sixth Extinction, The"	1999	S.7, Ep.1	Kim Manners
"Terms of Endearment"	1999	S.6, Ep.7	Rob Bowman

BIBLIOGRAPHY

Achenbach, Joel. (1999). *Captured by Aliens: The Search for Life and Truth in a Very Large Universe*. New York: Simon & Schuster.

Aldiss, Brian. (2005). "Introduction." In *The War of the Worlds*, by H. G. Wells. Edited by Patrick Parrinder. New York: Penguin.

Alexander, Victoria. (1994). "The Alexander Religious Crisis Survey: The Impact of UFOs and Their Occupants on Religion." The Bigelow Foundation. Available online at http://www.nidsci.org/articles/alexander/survey_religion.html.

Alnor, William M. (1998). *UFO Cults and the New Millennium*. Grand Rapids: Baker.

Amarasingam, Amarnath. (2008). "Transcending Technology: Looking at Futurology as a New Religious Movement." *Journal of Contemporary Religion* 23 (1): 1–16.

"Ancient Effigies." (1998). *Skeptical Inquirer* 22 (6): 13–14.

Anderson, Susan Leigh. (2008). "Asimov's 'Three Laws of Robotics' and Machine Metaethics." *AI and Society* 22: 477–93.

Asa, Robert. (1999). "Classic *Star Trek* and the Death of God: A Case Study of 'Who Mourns for Adonais?'" In Porter and McLaren, *"Star Trek" and Sacred Ground*, 33–60.

Asimov, Isaac. ([1940] 1977). "Robbie." In *I, Robot*, 1–27. New York: Bantam.

Association for the Prevention of Torture. (2007). *Defusing the Ticking Bomb Scenario: Why We Must Say No to Torture, Always*. Geneva, Switzerland: Association for the Prevention of Torture.

Atran, Scott. (2002). *In Gods We Trust: The Evolutionary Landscape of Religion*. Oxford: Oxford University Press.

Atwood, Margaret. (1985). *The Handmaid's Tale*. Toronto: McClelland & Stewart.

Bainbridge, William Sims. (2003a). "Massive Questionnaires for Personality Capture." *Social Science Computer Review* 21 (3): 267–80.

———. (2003b). "Religious Opposition to Cloning." *Journal of Evolution and Technology* 13 (2). Available online at http://www.jetpress.org/volume13/bainbridge.html.

———. (2005). "The Transhuman Heresy." *Journal of Evolution and Technology* 14 (2): 91–100.

———. (2006). "Cyberimmortality: Science, Religion, and the Battle to Save Our Souls." *The Futurist* 40 (2): 25–29.

Bainbridge, William Sims, and Rodney Stark. (1979). "Cult Formation: Three Compatible Models." *Sociological Analysis* 40 (4): 283–95.

Baines, John, and Jaromir Malek. (2000). *Cultural Atlas of Ancient Egypt*. New York: Facts on File.

Balch, Robert W. (1995). "Waiting for the Ships: Disillusionment and the Revitalization of Faith in Bo and Peep's UFO Cult." In *The Gods Have Landed: New Religions From Other Worlds*, edited by James R. Lewis, 137–66. Albany: State University of New York Press.

Balch, Robert W., and David Taylor. (1977). "Seekers and Saucers: The Role of the Cultic Milieu in Joining a UFO Cult." *American Behavioral Scientist* 20 (6): 837–60.

Barnhart, Joe. (1988). "Faith Healers in a Naturalistic Context." *The Humanist* 48 (5): 5–7, 36.

Barr, Marleen. (1997). "Metahuman 'Kipple' Or, Do Male Movie Makers Dream of Electric Women?: Speciesism and Sexism in *Blade Runner*." In Kerman, *Retrofitting "Blade Runner,"* 25–31.

Barrett, Justin L., and Frank C. Keil. (1996). "Conceptualizing a Nonnatural Entity: Anthropomorphism in God Concepts." *Cognitive Psychology* 31: 219–47.

Bassom, David. (1997). *The A–Z Guide to "Babylon 5."* New York: Dell.

Beeler, Stan, and Lisa Dickson, eds. (2006). *Reading "Stargate SG-1."* New York: I. B. Taurus.

Bellah, Robert N. (1969). "Transcendence in Contemporary Piety." In *Transcendence*, edited by Herbert W. Richardson and Donald R. Cutler, 85–97. Boston: Beacon.

Berger, Peter L. (1967). *The Sacred Canopy: Elements of a Sociological Theory of Religion*. New York: Anchor.

Berger, Peter L., and Thomas Luckmann. (1966). *The Social Construction of Reality: A Treatise on the Sociology of Knowledge*. Harmondsworth, UK: Penguin.

Berger, Richard. (2008). "GINO or Dialogic: What Does 'Re-Imagined' Really Mean?" In Steiff and Tamplin, *"Battlestar Galactica" and Philosophy*, 317–28.

Berlitz, Charles, and William Moore. (1980). *The Roswell Incident*. New York: Grossett & Dunlap.

Bertonneau, Thomas, and Kim Paffenroth. (2006). *The Truth Is Out There: Christian Faith and the Classics of TV Science Fiction*. Grand Rapids: Brazos.

Binder, Eando [Earl and Otto Binder]. (1940a). "Adam Link Fights a War." *Amazing Stories* (December).

———. (1940b). "Adam Link in Business." *Amazing Stories* (January).

———. (1940c). "Adam Link, Robot Detective." *Amazing Stories* (May).

———. (1942). "Adam Link Saves the World." *Amazing Stories* (April).

Biskind, Peter. (1983). *Seeing is Believing: How Hollywood Taught Us to Stop Worrying and Love the Fifties*. New York: Owl Books.

Blake, Richard A. (1991). *Screening America: Reflections on Five Classic Films*. New York: Paulist.

Bonting, Sjoerd L. (2003). "Theological Implications of Possible Extraterrestrial Life." *Zygon* 38 (3): 587–602.

Bortolin, Matthew. (2005). *The Dharma of "Star Wars."* Somerville, Mass.: Wisdom Publications.

Bostrom, Nick. (2003a). "Are We Living in a Computer Simulation?" *Philosophical Quarterly* 53 (211): 243–55.

———. (2003b). "Are We Living in *The Matrix*? The Simulation Argument." In Yeffeth, *Taking the Red Pill*, 233–41.

———. (2003c). "The Transhumanist FAQ: A General Introduction, Version 2.1." Available online at http://humanityplus.org/learn/philosophy/faq.html.

———. (2005). "A History of Transhumanist Thought." *Journal of Evolution and Technology* 14 (1): 1–25.

Boyer, Pascal. (1994). *The Naturalness of Religious Ideas: A Cognitive Theory of Religion*. Berkeley: University of California Press.

———. (2001). *Religion Explained: The Evolutionary Origins of Religious Thought*. New York: Basic Books.

Boyer, Paul S. (1992). *When Time Shall Be No More: Prophecy Belief in Modern American Culture*. Cambridge, Mass.: Belknap.

Bradley, Marion Zimmer. (1982). *The Mists of Avalon*. New York: Alfred A. Knopf.

Brannigan, Michael. (2002). "There Is No Spoon: A Buddhist Mirror." In Irwin, *"The Matrix" and Philosophy*, 101–10.

Brin, David, and Matthew Woodring Stover, eds. (2006). *"Star Wars" on Trial: Science Fiction and Fantasy Writers Debate the Most Popular Science Fiction Films of All Time*. Dallas, Tex.: BenBella Books.

Brooke, John Hedley. (2005). "Visions of Perfectibility." *Journal of Evolution and Technology* 14 (2): 1–12.

Brooker, Will, ed. (2005). *The "Blade Runner" Experience: The Legacy of a Science Fiction Classic*. London: Wallflower.

Brooks, Rodney. (2001). "Steps Toward Living Machines." In Gomi, *Evolutionary Robotics*, 72–93.

Brown, Bridget. (2007). *They Know Us Better Than We Know Ourselves: The History and Politics of Alien Abduction*. New York: New York University Press.

Bryan, C. D. B. (1995). *Close Encounters of the Fourth Kind: Alien Abduction, UFOs, and the Conference at M.I.T.* New York: Alfred A. Knopf.

Byrge, Duane. (1997). "'Contact.'" *Hollywood Reporter* (July 7).

Callahan, Tim. (2008). "A New Mythology: Ancient Astronauts, Lost Civilizations, and the New Age Paradigm." *Skeptic* 13 (4): 32–41.

Campbell, Joseph. (1968). *The Hero with a Thousand Faces*. 2nd ed. Princeton: Princeton University Press.

———. (1988). *The Power of Myth*. With Bill Moyers. Edited by Betty Sue Flowers. New York: Doubleday.

Cantril, Hadley. (1940). *The Invasion from Mars: A Study in the Psychology of Panic, with the Complete Script of the Famous Orson Welles Broadcast*. With Hazel Gaudet and Herta Herzog. Princeton: Princeton University Press.

Capra, Fritjof. (1975). *The Tao of Physics: An Exploration of the Parallels Between Modern Physics and Eastern Mysticism*. Boulder, Colo.: Shambhala.

Carper, Steve. (1997). "Subverting the Disaffected City: Cityscape in *Blade Runner*." In Kerman, *Retrofitting "Blade Runner,"* 185–95.

Chhalliyil, Pradheep. (2004). *Journey to the Source: Decoding "Matrix" Trilogy*. Fairfield, Iowa: Sakthi Books.

Chidester, David. (1990). *Patterns of Transcendence: Religion, Death, and Dying*. Belmont, Calif.: Wadsworth.

Chryssides, George D. (2003). "Scientific Creationism: A Study of the Raëlian Church." In Partridge, *UFO Religions*, 45–61.

Clarke, Arthur C. (1953). "The Nine Billion Names of God." In *Star Science Fiction Stories*, edited by Frederik Pohl, 195–202. New York: Ballantine.

———. (1968). *2001: A Space Odyssey*. New York: ROC Books.

———. (1982). *2010: Odyssey Two*. New York: Ballantine.

Clarke, Roger. (1993). "Asimov's Laws of Robotics: Implications for Information Technology, Part 1." *Computer* 26 (12): 53–61.

———. (1994). "Asimov's Laws of Robotics: Implications for Information Technology, Part 2." *Computer* 27 (1): 57–66.

Collodi, Carlo. ([1883] 1986). *The Adventures of Pinocchio*. Translated by Nicolas J. Perella. Berkeley: University of California Press.

Cook, Emily Williams, Bruce Greyson, and Ian Stevenson. (1998). "Do Any Near-Death Experiences Provide Evidence for the Survival of Human Personality after Death? Relevant Features and Illustrative Case Reports." *Journal of Scientific Exploration* 12 (3): 377–406.

Cook, Ryan J. (2003). "News Media and the Religious Use of UFOs: The Case of Chen Tao—True Way." In Lewis, *Encyclopedic Sourcebook*, 301–20.

Cornils, Ingo. (2003). "The Martians Are Coming! War, Peace, Love, and Scientific Progress in H. G. Wells' *The War of the Worlds* and Kurt Laßwitz's *Auf zwei Planeten*." *Comparative Literature* 55 (1): 24–41.

Corso, Philip J. (1997). *The Day After Roswell*. With William J. Birnes. New York: Pocket.

Cowan, Douglas E. (2003). *Bearing False Witness? An Introduction to the Christian Countercult*. Westport, Conn.: Praeger.

———. (2008a). "Pulp Evangelism: Structure and Voice in Christian Apocalyptic Fiction." In *Festschrift for Irving R. Hexham*, edited by Ulrich van der Heyden and Andreas Feldtkeller, 31–42. Berlin: Berlin Society for Missionary History.

———. (2008b). *Sacred Terror: Religion and Horror on the Silver Screen*. Waco, Tex.: Baylor University Press.

———. (2009). "Seeing the Saviour in the Stars: Religion, Conformity, and *The Day the Earth Stood Still*." *Journal of Religion and Popular Culture* 21 (Spring). Available online at http://www.usask.ca/relst/jrpc/art21(1)-EarthStoodStill.html.

———. (Forthcoming). "Dreams Wrapped in Nightmares: Millennium, Apocalypse, and American Popular Culture." In *The Oxford Handbook of Millennialism*, edited by Catherine Wessinger. Oxford: Oxford University Press.

Cowan, Douglas E., and David G. Bromley. (2008). *Cults and New Religions: A Brief History*. London: Blackwell.

Crowe, Michael J. (1986). *The Extraterrestrial Life Debate, 1750–1900: The Idea of a Plurality of Worlds from Kant to Lowell*. Cambridge: Cambridge University Press.

———. (1997). "A History of the Extraterrestrial Life Debate." *Zygon* 32 (2): 147–62.

Cuddy, Luke. (2008). "The Avatar and the Ego: Reconciling Ourselves with Videogames." In Steiff and Tamplin, *"Battlestar Galactica" and Philosophy*, 29–38.

Dalton, Russell W. (2003). *Faith Journeys through Fantasy Lands: A Christian Dialogue with "Harry Potter," "Star Wars," and "The Lord of the Rings."* Minneapolis: Augsburg.

Dante, Joe. (1995). Interview in "Making the Earth Stand Still." *The Day the Earth Stood Still*. Directed by Robert Wise. Produced by Julian Blaustein. Twentieth Century Fox Studio Classics DVD. Beverly Hills, Calif.: Twentieth Century Fox Home Entertainment.

———. (2005). "Commentary." In *The War of the Worlds* (1953). Directed by

Byron Haskin. Produced by George Pal. Collector's Edition DVD. Hollywood, Calif.: Paramount Pictures.

Darlington, David. (1997). *Area 51: The Dreamland Chronicles*. New York: Owl Books.

Davies, Paul. (2003). "E.T. and God." *Atlantic Monthly* (September): 112–16, 118.

Deacy, Christopher. (2006). "Reflections on the Uncritical Appropriation of Cinematic Christ-Figures: Holy Other or Wholly Inadequate?" *Journal of Religion and Popular Culture* 13. Available online at http://www.usask.ca/relst/jrpc/art13-reflectcinematicchrist.html.

Decker, Kevin S., and Jason T. Eberl, eds. (2005). *"Star Wars" and Philosophy: More Powerful Than You Can Possibly Imagine*. Peru, Ill.: Open Court.

Dennett, Daniel C. (1991). *Consciousness Explained*. Boston: Little, Brown.

———. (1996). *Kinds of Minds: Toward an Understanding of Consciousness*. New York: Basic Books.

———. (2005). *Sweet Dreams: Philosophical Obstacles to a Science of Consciousness*. Cambridge, Mass.: MIT Press.

Denzler, Brenda. (2001). *The Lure of the Edge: Scientific Passions, Religious Beliefs, and the Pursuit of UFOs*. Berkeley: University of California Press.

Desser, David. (1997). "Race, Space, and Class: The Politics of the SF Film from *Metropolis* to *Blade Runner*." In Kerman, *Retrofitting "Blade Runner,"* 110–23.

Diamond, Sara. (1990). *Spiritual Warfare: The Politics of the Christian Right*. Montréal: Black Rose.

Dick, Philip K. (1968). *Do Androids Dream of Electric Sheep?* New York: Ballantine.

Dick, Steven J. (1982). *Plurality of Worlds: The Origins of the Extraterrestrial Life Debate from Democritus to Kant*. Cambridge: Cambridge University Press.

Disch, Thomas M. (1998). *The Dreams Our Stuff Is Made Of: How Science Fiction Conquered the World*. New York: Touchstone.

Downing, Barry H. ([1968] 1997). *The Bible and Flying Saucers*. New York: Marlowe.

Dunn, Christopher. (1998). *The Giza Power Plant: Technologies of Ancient Egypt*. Rochester, Vt.: Bear.

———. (2005). "Return to the Giza Power Plant." In Kenyon, *Forbidden History*, 229–35.

Durkheim, Émile. ([1895] 1982). *The Rules of Sociological Method*. Edited by Steven Lukes. Translated by W. D. Halls. New York: Free Press.

———. ([1912] 1995). *The Elementary Forms of Religious Life*. Translated by Karen E. Fields. New York: Free Press.

Eberl, Jason T., ed. (2008). *"Battlestar Galactica" and Philosophy: Knowledge Here Begins Out There*. Oxford: Blackwell.

Eberl, Jason T., and Jennifer A. Vines. (2008). "'I Am an Instrument of God': Religious Belief, Atheism, and Meaning." In Eberl, *"Battlestar Galactica" and Philosophy*, 155–68.

Ebert, Roger. (1994). "Stargate." (October 28). Available online at http://www.rogerebert.com.

———. (1997). "Sky's the limit for 'Contact.'" *Chicago Sun-Times* (July 11): Movies, 29.

Eliade, Mircea. (1952). *Images and Symbols: Studies in Religious Symbolism*. Translated by Philip Mairet. Princeton: Princeton University Press.

———. (1957). *The Sacred and the Profane: The Nature of Religion*. Translated by Willard R. Trask. New York: Harper & Row.

———. (1958). *Patterns in Comparative Religion*. Translated by Rosemary Sheed. Lincoln: University of Nebraska Press.

———. (1971). "Spirit, Light, and Seed." *History of Religions* 11 (1): 1–30.

Elrod, P. N., and Roxanne Conrad, eds. (2004). *Stepping Through the Stargate: Science, Archeology, and the Military in "Stargate SG-1."* Dallas, Tex.: BenBella Books.

Farrell, Joseph P. (2002). *The Giza Death Star*. Kempton, Ill.: Adventures Unlimited.

———. (2003). *The Giza Death Star Deployed: The Physics and Engineering of the Great Pyramid*. Kempton, Ill.: Adventures Unlimited.

———. (2005). *The Giza Death Star Destroyed: The Ancient War for Future Science*. Kempton, Ill.: Adventures Unlimited.

Ferguson, Marilyn. (1980). *The Aquarian Conspiracy: Personal and Social Transformation in the 1980s*. Los Angeles: J. P. Tarcher.

Festinger, Leon, Henry W. Riecken, and Stanley Schachter. (1956). *When Prophecy Fails*. Minneapolis: University of Minnesota Press.

Flannery-Daily, Frances, and Rachel Wagner. (2001). "Wake up! Gnosticism and Buddhism in *The Matrix*." *Journal of Religion and Film* 5 (2). Available online at http://www.unomaha.edu/jrf/gnostic.htm.

Flesher, Paul V. M., and Robert Torry. (2007). *Film & Religion: An Introduction*. Nashville: Abingdon.

Fletcher, Richard A. (1997). *The Barbarian Conversion: From Paganism to Christianity*. Berkeley: University of California Press.

Foerst, Anne. (1998a). "Cog, A Humanoid Robot, and the Question of the Image of God." *Zygon* 33 (1): 91–111.

———. (1998b). "Embodied AI, Creation, and Cog." *Zygon* 33 (3): 455–61.

———. (2004). *God in the Machine: What Robots Teach Us About Humanity and God*. New York: Penguin.

Fontana, Paul. (2002). "Finding God in *The Matrix*." In Yeffeth, *Taking the Red Pill*, 159–84.

Ford, James L. (2003). "Buddhism, Mythology, and *The Matrix*." In Yeffeth, *Taking the Red Pill*, 125–44.

Frazier, Kendrick. (2001). "L. Sprague de Camp: Erudite Writer on Archeology, Ancient Engineering, and Pseudoscience (and Science Fiction Too)" [obituary]. *Skeptical Inquirer* 25 (2): 6–7.

Freud, Sigmund. ([1927] 1961). *The Future of an Illusion*. Translated and edited by James Strachey. New York: W. W. Norton.

———. ([1930] 1961). *Civilization and Its Discontents*. Translated and edited by James Strachey. New York: W. W. Norton.

Friedman, Stanton T. (1996). *Top Secret/MAJIC*. New York: Marlowe.

———. (2008). *Flying Saucers and Science: A Scientist Investigates the Mysteries of UFOs: Interstellar Travel, Crashes, and Government Cover-Ups*. Franklin Lakes, N.J.: New Page Books.

Frykholm, Amy Johnson. (2004). *Rapture Culture: "Left Behind" in Evangelical America*. Oxford: Oxford University Press.

Fuller, Robert C. (1995). *Naming the Antichrist: The History of an American Obsession*. Oxford: Oxford University Press.

Gabriel, Theodore. (2003). "The United Nuwaubian Nation of Moors." In Partridge, *UFO Religions*, 149–61.

Galipeau, Steven A. (2001). *The Journey of Luke Skywalker: An Analysis of Modern Myth and Symbol*. Peru, Ill.: Open Court.

Gardner, Martin. (1998). "What's Going On At Temple University?" *Skeptical Inquirer* 22 (5): 14–17.

Garrett, William R. (1974). "Troublesome Transcendence: The Supernatural in the Scientific Study of Religion." *Sociological Analysis* 35 (3): 167–80.

Geraci, Robert M. (2007). "Robots and the Sacred in Science and Science Fiction: Theological Implications of Artificial Intelligence." *Zygon* 42 (4): 961–80.

———. (2008). "Apocalyptic AI: Religion and the Promise of Artificial Intelligence." *Journal of the American Academy of Religion* 76 (1): 138–66.

Geraghty, Lincoln. (2003). "Homosocial Desire on the Final Frontier: Kinship, the American Romance, and *Deep Space Nine*'s 'Erotic Triangles.'" *Journal of Popular Culture* 36 (3): 441–65.

Gerhart, Mary, and Allan Melvin Russell. (1998). "Cog Is To Us As We Are To God: A Response to Anne Foerst." *Zygon* 33 (2): 263–69.

Gibson, William. (1984). *Neuromancer*. New York: Ace Books.

Giddens, Anthony. (1991). *Modernity and Self-Identity: Self and Society in the Late Modern Age*. Stanford, Calif.: Stanford University Press.

Gilmer, James Edward. (2002). *Chariots of Gods or Demons: The Incredible Truth About UFOs and Extraterrestrials*. Bloomington, Ind.: AuthorHouse.

Goetz, William R. (1997). *UFOs: Friend, Foe, or Fantasy? A Biblical Perspective on the Phenomenon of the Century*. Camp Hill, Pa.: Horizon.

Goffman, Erving. (1971). *Relations in Public: Microstudies of the Public Order*. New York: Basic Books.

Gomi, Takashi, ed. (2001). *Evolutionary Robotics: From Intelligent Robotics to Artificial Life*. Berlin: Springer-Verlag.

Good, Timothy. (1993). *Alien Contact: Top-Secret UFO Files Revealed*. New York: William Morrow.

———. (1996). *Beyond Top Secret: The Worldwide UFO Security Threat*. London: Pan Books.

———. (1999). *Alien Base: The Evidence for Extraterrestrial Colonization of Earth*. New York: HarperPerennial.

Goran, Morris. (1978). *The Modern Myth: Ancient Astronauts and UFOs*. New York: A. S. Barnes.

Gordon, Andrew. (1995). "*Star Wars*: A Myth for Our Time." In *Screening the Sacred: Religion, Myth, and Ideology in Popular American Film*, edited by Joel W. Martin and Conrad E. Ostwalt Jr., 73–82. Boulder, Colo.: Westview.

Goswami, Amit, Richard E. Reed, and Maggie Goswami. (1993). *The Self-Aware Universe: How Consciousness Creates the Material World*. New York: Jeremy P. Tarcher.

Graham, Elaine B. (2002). *Representations of the Post/Human: Monsters, Aliens and Others in Popular Culture*. New Brunswick, N.J.: Rutgers University Press.

Grau, Christopher, ed. (2005). *Philosophers Explore "The Matrix."* Oxford: Oxford University Press.

Gravett, Sharon L. (1998). "The Sacred and the Profane: Examining the Religious Subtext of Ridley Scott's *Blade Runner*." *Literature/Film Quarterly* 26 (1): 38–45.

Gray, Christy. (2005). "Originals and Copies: The Fans of Philip K. Dick, *Blade Runner*, and K. W. Jeter." In Brooker, *The "Blade Runner" Experience*, 142–56.

Gray, Jonathan. (2005). "Scanning the Replicant Text." In Brooker, *The "Blade Runner" Experience*, 111–23.

Greene, Eric. (1996). *"Planet of the Apes" as American Myth: Race, Politics, and Popular Culture*. Jefferson, N.C.: McFarland.

Gribben, Crawford. (2009). *Writing the Rapture: Prophecy Fiction in Evangelical America*. Oxford: Oxford University Press.

Grimes, Caleb. (2007). *Star Wars™ Jesus: A Spiritual Commentary on the Reality of the Force*. Eumclaw, Wash.: Winepress.

Grof, Stanislav. (1985). *Beyond the Brain: Birth, Death, and Transcendence in Psychotherapy*. Albany: State University of New York Press.

————. (1988). *The Adventure of Self-Discovery: Dimensions of Consciousness and New Perspectives in Psychotherapy and Inner Exploration*. Albany: State University of New York Press.

Grof, Stanislav, and Hal Zina Bennett. (1993). *The Holotropic Mind: The Three Levels of Consciousness and How They Shape Our Lives*. New York: HarperSanFrancisco.

Guinness Book of World Records. (1999). Stamford, Conn.: Guinness.

Guthrie, Stewart. (1993). *Faces in the Clouds: A New Theory of Religion*. Oxford: Oxford University Press.

Haldane, J. B. S. (1928). *Possible Worlds and Other Papers*. New York: Harper & Brothers.

Hamid, Idris Samawi. (2005). "The Cosmological Journey of Neo: An Islamic Matrix." In Irwin, *More "Matrix" and Philosophy*, 136–53.

Hancock, Graham. (1995). *Fingerprints of the Gods*. New York: Three Rivers.

Hancock, Graham, and Robert Bauval. (1996). *The Message of the Sphinx: A Quest for the Hidden Legacy of Mankind*. New York: Three Rivers.

Hancock, Graham, and Santha Faiia. (1998). *Heaven's Mirror: Quest for the Lost Civilization*. New York: Three Rivers.

Hanegraaff, Wouter J. (1996). *New Age Religion and Western Culture: Esotericism in the Mirror of Secular Thought*. Leiden: E. J. Brill.

Hankiss, Elemér. (2001). *Fear and Symbols: An Introduction to the Study of Western Civilization*. Budapest, Hungary: Central European University Press.

Hansen, Gretchen. (2008). "HAL." "50 Most Vile Movie Villains: Part 2." Available online at http://www.ew.com/ew/gallery/0,,20186434_9,00 .html.

Hanson, Michael J., and Max S. Kay. (2002). *"Star Wars": The New Myth*. Philadelphia: Xlibris.

Harrold, Francis B., and Raymond A. Eve, eds. (1995). *Cult Archeology and Creationism: Understanding Pseudoscientific Beliefs about the Past*. Exp. ed. Iowa City: University of Iowa Press.

Hatch, Richard, ed. (2006). *So Say We All: An Unauthorized Collection of Thoughts and Opinions on "Battlestar Galactica."* Dallas, Tex.: BenBella Books.

Hawking, Stephen W. (1988). *A Brief History of Time: From the Big Bang to Black Holes*. New York: Bantam.

Heelas, Paul. (1996). *The New Age Movement: The Celebration of the Self and the Sacralization of Modernity*. Oxford: Blackwell.

Heinlein, Robert A. ([1940] 1953). "If this goes on . . . ." In *Revolt in 2100*. New York: Signet.

Helland, Christopher. (2003). "From Extraterrestrials to Ultraterrestrials: The Evolution of the Concept of Ashtar." In Partridge, *UFO Religions*, 162–78.

Hendershot, Cyndy. (2001). *I Was A Cold War Monster: Horror Films, Eroticism, and the Cold War Imagination*. Bowling Green, Ohio: Bowling Green State University Popular Press.

Henderson, Mary S. (1997). *Star Wars™: The Magic of Myth*. New York: Bantam Spectra.

Herbert, Frank. (1965). *Dune*. Radnor, Pa.: Chilton.

Herzfeld, Noreen. (2002a). "Creating in Our Own Image: Artificial Intelligence and the Image of God." *Zygon* 37 (2): 303–16.

———. (2002b). *In Our Image: Artificial Intelligence and the Human Spirit*. Minneapolis: Augsburg Fortress.

Holden, Stephen. (1997). "Which Route Upward, On a Wing or a Prayer?" *The New York Times* (July 11): C3.

Holland, Owen. (2001). "From the Imitation of Life to Machine Consciousness." In Gomi, *Evolutionary Robotics*, 1–37.

Hon-ming, Chen. (1997). *God's Descending in Clouds (Flying Saucers) on Earth to Save People*. Garland, Tex.: Self-published.

Hopkins, Budd. (1981). *Missing Time: A Documented Study of UFO Abductions*. New York: R. Marek.

———. (1987). *Intruders: The Incredible Visitations at Copley Woods*. New York: Ballantine.

Hopkins, Budd, and Carol Rainey. (2003). *Sight Unseen: Science, UFO Invisibility, and Transgenic Beings*. New York: Pocket.

Hopkins, Patrick. (2005). "Transcending the Animal: How Transhumanism and Religion Are and Are Not Alike." *Journal of Evolution and Technology* 14 (2): 13–28.

Hunt, Dave. (1990). *Global Peace and the Rise of Antichrist*. Eugene, Ore.: Harvest House.

Hynek, J. Allen. (1972). *The UFO Experience: A Scientific Inquiry*. Chicago: Regnery.

Inness, Sherrie A. (2004). *Action Chicks: New Images of Tough Women in Popular Culture*. New York: Palgrave Macmillan.

Irwin, William, ed. (2002). *"The Matrix" and Philosophy: Welcome to the Desert of the Real*. Peru, Ill.: Open Court.

———. (2005). *More "Matrix" and Philosophy: "Revolutions" and "Reloaded" Decoded*. Peru, Ill.: Open Court.

Jacobs, David M. (1992). *Secret Life: Firsthand, Documented Accounts of UFO Abductions*. New York: Fireside.

———. (1998). *The Threat: Revealing the Secret Alien Agenda*. New York: Fireside.

———, ed. (2000). *UFO Abductions: Challenging the Borders of Knowledge*. Lawrence: University Press of Kansas.

James, William. ([1902] 1999). *The Varieties of Religious Experience*. New York: Modern Library.

Jancovich, Marc. (1996). *Rational Fears: American Horror in the 1950s*. Manchester: Manchester University Press.

Jenkins, Henry. (2006). *Fans, Bloggers, and Gamers: Exploring Participatory Culture*. New York: New York University Press.

———. (2008). *Convergence Culture: Where Old and New Media Collide*. Rev. ed. New York: New York University Press.

Jermyn, Deborah. (2005). "The Rachel Papers: In Search of *Blade Runner*'s Femme Fatale." In Brooker, *The "Blade Runner" Experience*, 159–72.

Johansen, Laurie. (1997). "God, Graves, and Graham: A Personal Odyssey Through Rural American Religions." *Skeptic* 5 (2): 76–80.

Johnson, David Kyle. (2008). "A Story that is Told Again, and Again, and Again." In Eberl, *"Battlestar Galactica" and Philosophy*, 181–91.

Johnson, Malcolm. (1977). "Spielberg's 'Encounters' Gripping, Spectacular." *Hartford Courant* (November 13): 1G.

Johnson-Lewis, Erika. (2008). "Torture, Terrorism, and Other Aspects of Human Nature." In Potter and Marshall, *Cylons in America*, 27–39.

Jones, Eric M. (1985). "'Where is Everybody?' An Account of Fermi's Question." Los Alamos, N.M.: Los Alamos National Laboratory.

Jones, Timothy Paul. (2005). *Finding God in a Galaxy Far, Far Away: A Spiritual Exploration of the "Star Wars" Saga*. Sisters, Ore.: Multnomah.

Kapell, Matthew. (1999). "The Americanization of the Holocaust in 'Star Trek: Deep Space Nine.'" *Michigan Academician* 31 (2): 136.

Kapell, Matthew, and William G. Doty, eds. (2004). *Jacking in to "The Matrix" Franchise: Cultural Reception and Interpretation*. New York: Continuum.

Katz, Steven T. (1978). "Language, Epistemology, and Mysticism." In *Mysticism and Philosophical Analysis*, edited by Steven T. Katz, 22–74. New York: Oxford University Press.

Kazantzakis, Nikos. (1960). *The Last Temptation of Christ*. Translated by P. A. Bien. New York: Simon & Schuster.

Keefer, Kyle. (2005). "Knowledge and Mortality in *Blade Runner* and Genesis 2–3." *Journal of Religion and Film* 9 (2). Available online at http://www.unomaha.edu/jrf/Vol9No2/KeeferKnowMortal.htm.

Keith, Jim. (2004). *Saucers of the Illuminati*. Kempton, Ill.: Adventures Unlimited.

Kenyon, J. Douglas, ed. (2005). *Forbidden History: Prehistoric Technologies, Extraterrestrial Intervention, and the Suppressed Origins of Civilization*. Rochester, Vt.: Bear.

Kerman, Judith B. (2005). "Post-Millennium *Blade Runner*." In Brooker, *The "Blade Runner" Experience*, 31–39.

———, ed. (1997). *Retrofitting "Blade Runner": Issues in Ridley Scott's "Blade Runner" and Philip K. Dick's "Do Androids Dream of Electric Sheep?"* 2nd ed. Madison: University of Wisconsin Press.

Kind, Amy. (2008). "You Can't Rape a Machine." In Steiff and Tamplin, *"Battlestar Galactica" and Philosophy*, 117–28.

King, Jon. (1998). *Cosmic Top Secret: The Unseen Agenda*. London: Hodder & Stoughton.

Klass, Philip J. (1983). *UFOs: The Public Deceived*. Amherst, N.Y.: Prometheus.

———. (1988). *UFO-Abductions: A Dangerous Game*. Amherst, N.Y.: Prometheus.

Koch, Howard. (1970). *The Panic Broadcast*. New York: Avon.

Kozlovic, Anton Karl. (2004). "The Structural Characteristics of the Cinematic Christ-Figure." *Journal of Religion and Popular Culture* 8. Available online at http://www.usask.ca/relst/jrpc/art8-cinematicchrist.html.

Kracher, Alfred. (2006). "Meta-Humans and *Metanoia*: The Moral Dimensions of Extraterrestrials." *Zygon* 41 (2): 329–46.

Kukkonen, Taneli. (2008). "God Against the Gods: Faith and the Exodus of the Twelve Colonies." In Eberl, *"Battlestar Galactica" and Philosophy*, 169–80.

Kungl, Carla. (2008). "'Long Live Stardoe!': Can a Female Starbuck Survive?" In Potter and Marshall, *Cylons in America*, 198–209.

Kurzweil, Ray. (2005). *The Singularity Is Near: When Humans Transcend Biology*. New York: Penguin.

Kyer, Melanie Manzer, and Jeffrey A. Kyer. (2004). "Reading *Stargate*/Playing *Stargate*: Role-Playing Games and the *Stargate* Franchise." In Beeler and Dickson, *Reading "Stargate SG-1,"* 184–99.

Kyrou, Adonis. (1963). *Le surréalisme au cinéma*. Paris: Le terrain vague.

LaHaye, Tim, and Jerry B. Jenkins. (1995). *Left Behind: A Novel of the Earth's Last Days*. Nashville: Thomas Nelson.

Lancaster, Kurt. (2001). *Interacting with "Babylon 5": Fan Performance in a Media Universe*. Austin: University of Texas Press.

Landsberg, Alison. (2004). "Prosthetic Memory: *Total Recall* and *Blade Runner*." In *Liquid Metal: The Science Fiction Film Reader*, edited by Sean Redmond, 239–48. London: Wallflower.

Lännström, Anna. (2005). "*The Matrix* and Vedanta: Journeying from the Unreal to the Real." In Irwin, *More "Matrix" and Philosophy*, 125–34.

Larson, Bob. (1989). *Larson's New Book of Cults*. Rev. ed. Wheaton, Ill.: Tyndale House.

———. (1997). *UFOs and the Alien Agenda*. Nashville: Thomas Nelson.

Lawrence, Matt. (2004). *Like a Splinter in Your Mind: The Philosophy Behind "The Matrix" Trilogy*. Oxford: Blackwell.

Leggett, Paul. (2002). *Terence Fisher: Horror, Myth and Religion*. Jefferson, N.C.: McFarland.

Lehner, Mark. (1997). *The Complete Pyramids: Solving the Ancient Mysteries*. London: Thames & Hudson.

Lewis, C. S. (1938). *Out of the Silent Planet*. London: Bodley Head.

———. (1943). *Perelandra*. London: Bodley Head.

———. (1945). *That Hideous Strength*. London: Bodley Head.

———. (1950). *The Lion, the Witch and the Wardrobe*. London: Geoffrey Bles.

———. (1955). *The Magician's Nephew*. London: Geoffrey Bles.

Lewis, James R., ed. (2003). *Encyclopedic Sourcebook of UFO Religions*. Amherst, N.Y.: Prometheus.

Linford, Peter. (1999). "Deeds of Power: Respect for Religion in *Star Trek: Deep Space Nine*." In Porter and McLaren, *"Star Trek" and Sacred Ground*, 77–100.

London, Michael. (1982). "Closer Encounters with 'E.T.'" *Los Angeles Times* (June 27): N1, N26–28.

Luckmann, Thomas. (1990). "Shrinking Transcendence, Expanding Religion?" *Sociological Analysis* 50 (2): 127–38.

Lyons, Linda. (2005). "Paranormal Beliefs Come (Super)Naturally to Some." *Gallup Poll*. Available online at http://www.gallup.com/poll/19558/Paranormal-Beliefs-Come-SuperNaturally-Some.aspx.

Mack, John E. (1994). *Abduction: Human Encounters with Aliens*. New York: Charles Scribner's Sons.

———. (2000). *Passport to the Cosmos: Human Transformation and Alien Encounters*. New York: Three Rivers.

Malone, Peter. (1997). "Jesus on Our Screens." In *New Image of Religious Film*, edited by John R. May, 57–71. Kansas City, Mo.: Sheed & Ward.

Marrs, Texe. (1997a). "Space Invaders: Mysterious Aliens and the UFO Endtime Plot." *Intelligence Examiner* (March): 6.

———. (1997b). "UFOs and the Mark of the Beast." *Intelligence Examiner* (May): 6.

Marsden, George M. (1991). *Understanding Fundamentalism and Evangelicalism*. Grand Rapids: Eerdmans.

———. (2006). *Fundamentalism and American Culture*. Rev. ed. Oxford: Oxford University Press.

Marshall, C. W., and Matthew Wheeland. (2008). "The Cylons, the Singularity, and God." In Potter and Marshall, *Cylons in America*, 91–104.

Martin, Joel W. (2000). "Anti-feminism in Recent Apocalyptic Film." *Journal of Religion and Film* 4 (1). Available online at http://www.unomaha.edu/-jrf/antifem.htm.

Mason, Marilynne S. (1993). "Today's Problems Tomorrow." *Christian Science Monitor* (March 2): 12.

"Matrixism." (n.d.) "Matrixism: The Path of the One." http://www.geocities.com/matrixism.

May, Rollo. ([1972] 1998). *Power and Innocence: A Search for the Sources of Violence*. New York: W. W. Norton.

McCarthy, Todd. (1997). "Zemeckis connects with 'Contact.'" *Variety* (July 14–20): 43.

McConnell, Frank D. (1975). *The Spoken Seen: Film and the Romantic Imagination*. Baltimore, Md.: Johns Hopkins University Press.

McCoy, Alfred W. (2006). *A Question of Torture: CIA Interrogation, from the Cold War to the War on Terror*. New York: Owl Books.

McCreary, Bear. (2008). "BG4: He That Believeth . . . ." Bear's *Battlestar Galactica* Blog (April 5). http://www.bearmccreary.com/blog/?p=241.

McDowell, John C. (2007). *The Gospel According to "Star Wars": Faith, Hope, and the Force*. Louisville, Ky.: Westminster John Knox.

McGrath-Kerr, Rachel. (2004). "Sam I Am: Female Fans' Interaction with Samantha Carter through Fan Fiction and Online Discussion." In Beeler and Dickson, *Reading "Stargate SG-1,"* 200–217.

McHenry, Bryan. (2008). "Weapons of Mass Salvation." In Steiff and Tamplin, *"Battlestar Galactica" and Philosophy*, 221–31.

McKee, Gabriel. (2007). *The Gospel According to Science Fiction: From the Twilight Zone to the Final Frontier*. Louisville, Ky.: Westminster John Knox.

———. (2009). "*Battlestar Galactica* finale: Mysteries solved; Mystery contemplated." SF Gospel (March 21). Available online at http://sfgospel.typepad.com.

McRae, James. (2008). "Zen and the Art of Cylon Maintenance." In Eberl, *"Battlestar Galactica" and Philosophy*, 205–17.

Menzel, Donald H., and Ernest H. Taves. (1977). *The UFO Enigma: The Definitive Explanation of the UFO Phenomenon*. Garden City, N.Y.: Doubleday.

Miller, Walter M. (1959). *A Canticle for Leibowitz*. Philadelphia: Lippincott.

Minsky, Marvin. (1986). *The Society of Mind*. New York: Simon & Schuster.

———. (2006). *The Emotion Machine: Commonsense Thinking, Artificial Intelligence, and the Future of the Human Mind*. New York: Simon & Schuster.

Missler, Chuck, and Mark Eastman. (1997). *Alien Encounters: The Secret Behind the UFO Phenomenon*. Coeur d'Alene, Idaho: Koinonia House.

Mollica, Richard F., and Yael Caspi-Yavin. (1991). "Measuring Torture and Torture-Related Symptoms." *Psychological Assessment* 3 (4): 581–87.

Montenegro, Marcia. (2002). "*Star Wars* Movie, *Episode II: Attack of the Clones*." *Christian Answers for the New Age* (May). Available online at http://www.christiananswersforthenewage.org/.

Moore, Ronald D. (2005). "The Souls of Cylons." Interview by Ellen Leventry. *Beliefnet*. Available online at http://www.beliefnet.com/Entertainment/Movies/2005/05/The-Souls-Of-Cylons.aspx.

Moravec, Hans P. (1988). *Mind Children: The Future of Robot and Human Intelligence*. Cambridge, Mass.: Harvard University Press.

————. (1999). *Robot: Mere Machine to Transcendent Mind*. Oxford: Oxford University Press.

More, Max. (1993). "Principles of Extropy, Version 3.11." http://www.extropy .org/principles.htm.

Morehead, John. (Forthcoming). "Matrixism." In *The Handbook of Hyper-Real Religion*, edited by Adam Possamai. Leiden: E. J. Brill.

Morton, Andrew. (2008). *Tom Cruise: An Unauthorized Biography*. New York: St. Martin's.

Naremore, James. (2003). "The Man Who Caused the Mars Panic." *Humanities* 24 (4): 38–39.

Norman, Ruth E. (1997). "Einstein Speaks from Planet Eros." *Unarius Light Journal* 79: 32–35. Originally channeled in 1988.

Nygard, Roger, dir. (1999). *Trekkies* [Motion Picture]. Hollywood, Calif.: Paramount Pictures.

O'Meara, Thomas F. (1999). "Christian Theology and Extraterrestrial Life." *Theological Studies* 60 (1): 3–30.

Ott, Brian L. (2008). "(Re)Framing Fear: Equipment for Living in a Post-9/11 World." In Potter and Marshall, *Cylons in America*, 13–26.

Otto, Rudolf. ([1923] 1950). *The Idea of the Holy*. Translated by John W. Harvey. Oxford: Oxford University Press.

Palmer, Susan J. (2004). *Aliens Adored: Raël's UFO Religion*. New Brunswick, N.J.: Rutgers University Press.

Palmer, Susan, and Chris Helland. (2003). "UFO Religions Online: Prophetic Failures and the Narrative Techniques of the Ground Crew." In Lewis, *Encyclopedic Sourcebook*, 331–46.

Pandian, Jacob. (2001). "The Dangerous Quest for Cooperation Between Science and Religion." *Skeptical Inquirer* 25 (5): 28–33.

Pareles, Jon. (1996). "When Aliens Start To Look a Lot Like Us." *The New York Times* (May 29): H26.

Partridge, Christopher, ed. (2003). *UFO Religions*. New York: Routledge.

————. (2004). "Alien Demonology: The Christian Roots of the Malevolent Extraterrestrial in UFO Religions and Abduction Spiritualities." *Religion* 34: 163–89.

Patton, Phil. (1998). *Dreamland: Travels Inside the Secret World of Roswell and Area 51*. New York: Villard.

Payne, Marshall. (2005). "The Case for Advanced Technology in the Great Pyramid." In Kenyon, *Forbidden History*, 270–74.

Pearson, Anne Mackenzie. (1999). "From Thwarted Gods to Reclaimed Mystery? An Overview of the Depiction of Religion in *Star Trek*." In Porter and McLaren, *"Star Trek" and Sacred Ground*, 13–32.

Peters, Shawn Francis. (2008). *When Prayer Fails: Faith Healing, Children, and the Law*. Oxford: Oxford University Press.

Peters, Ted. (n.d.) "AstroTheology: Religious Reflections on Extraterrestrial Life Forms." http://www.counterbalance.net/.

———. (1977). *UFOs—God's Chariots? Flying Saucers in Politics, Science, and Religion*. Atlanta, Ga.: John Knox.

Peterson, Gregory. (1999). "Religion and Science in *Star Trek: The Next Generation*: God, Q, and Evolutionary Eschatology on the Final Frontier." In Porter and McLaren, *"Star Trek" and Sacred Ground*, 61–76.

Pew Forum on Religion & Public Life. (2009). "The Religious Dimensions of the Torture Debate." *Pew Research Center* (April 29). http://pewforum.org/docs/?DocID=156.

Picard, Rosalind W. (1997). "Does HAL Cry Digital Tears? Emotions and Computers." In *HAL's Legacy: 2001's Computer as Dream and Reality*, edited by David G. Stork, 279–303. Cambridge, Mass.: MIT Press.

Plotinsky, Benjamin A. (2009). "How Science Fiction Found Religion." *City Journal* (Winter). Available online at http://www.city-journal.org/.

Pohl, Frederik. (1996). "Science Fiction and Scientific Possibilities." *Skeptical Inquirer* 20 (5): 26.

———. (2009). "Me and the Biz." The Way the Future Blogs (February 15). http://www.thewaythefutureblogs.com/2009/02/me-and-the-biz.

Polan, Dana B. (1996). "Eros and Syphilization: The Contemporary Horror Film." In *Planks of Reason: Essays on the Horror Film*, edited by Barry Keith Grant, 201–11. Lanham, Md.: Scarecrow.

Porter, Jennifer E. (2007). "All I Ever Wanted to Be, I Learned from Playing Klingon: Sex, Honor, and Cultural Critique in *Star Trek* Fandom." In *Alien Worlds: Social and Religious Dimensions of Extraterrestrial Contact*, edited by Diana G. Tumminia, 217–36. Syracuse, N.Y.: Syracuse University Press.

Porter, Jennifer E., and Darcee L. McLaren, eds. (1999). *"Star Trek" and Sacred Ground: Explorations of "Star Trek," Religion, and American Culture*. Albany: State University of New York Press.

Porter, John M. (2003). *The Tao of "Star Wars."* Lake Worth, Fla.: Humanics.

Porter, Lynnette, David Lavery, and Hillary Robson, eds. (2008). *Finding "Battlestar Galactica": An Unauthorized Guide*. Naperville, Ill.: Sourcebooks.

Potter, Tiffany, and C. W. Marshall, eds. (2008). *Cylons in America: Critical Studies in "Battlestar Galactica."* New York: Continuum.

Prather, Charles Houston. (1999). "God's Salvation Church: Past, Present and Future." *Marburg Journal of Religion* 4 (1). Available online at http://web.uni-marburg.de/religionswissenschaft/journal/mjr/prather.html.

Price, David H. (2007a). "Buying a Piece of Anthropology: Part 1: Human Ecology and Unwitting Anthropological Research for the CIA." *Anthropology Today* 23 (3): 8–13.

———. (2007b). "Buying a Piece of Anthropology: Part 2: The CIA and Our Tortured Past." *Anthropology Today* 23 (5): 17–22.

Prothero, Stephen. (2007). *Religious Literacy: What Every American Needs to Know—and Doesn't.* New York: HarperCollins.

Raël. (1986). *Let's Welcome Our Fathers From Space: They Created Humanity In Their Laboratories.* Tokyo: AOM Corporation.

———. (1998). *The Final Message.* London: Tagman.

Randle, Kevin D. (1989). *The UFO Casebook.* New York: Warner.

———. (2001). *Invasion Washington: UFOs Over the Capitol.* New York: HarperCollins.

Randle, Kevin D., and Donald Schmitt. (1991). *UFO Crash at Roswell.* New York: Avon.

Redmond, Sean. (2005). "Purge! Class Pathology in *Blade Runner*." In Brooker, *The "Blade Runner" Experience*, 173–89.

Reeves, Byron, and Clifford Nass. (1996). *The Media Equation: How People Treat Computers, Television, and News Media Like Real People and Places.* Cambridge: Cambridge University Press.

Reich, K. Helmut. (1998). "Cog and God: A Response to Anne Foerst." *Zygon* 33 (2): 255–62.

Rhodes, Ron. (1992). *Christ Before the Manger: The Life and Times of the Preincarnate Christ.* Grand Rapids: Baker.

———. (1998). *Alien Obsession.* Eugene, Ore.: Harvest House.

Robertson, Pat. (2001). Interview with Jerry Falwell. *The 700 Club* (September 13). Transcript available online at http://www.commondreams.org/news2001/0917-03.htm.

Rolufs, Heather. (2008). "Eve, Lilith, and the Cylon Connection." In Steiff and Tamplin, *"Battlestar Galactica" and Philosophy*, 349–58.

Rossano, Matt J. (2001). "Artificial Intelligence, Religion, and Community Concern." *Zygon* 36 (1): 57–75.

Rothstein, Mikael. (2003). "Institutionalized Anticipation: Architecture and Religious Symbolism in the Raelian Religion." In Lewis, *Encyclopedic Sourcebook*, 281–98.

Rowley, Stephen. (2005). "False LA: *Blade Runner* and the Nightmare City." In Brooker, *The "Blade Runner" Experience*, 203–12.

Rowling, J. K. (1997). *Harry Potter and the Philosopher's Stone.* Vancouver, Canada: Raincoast Books.

Russo, Christopher. (2004). "Centauri." *Encyclopedia Xenobiologica.* http://infinicorp.com/VEX/aliens/centauri.htm.

Russo, Joe, and Larry Landsman. (2001). *"Planet of the Apes" Revisited: The Behind-the-Scenes Story of the Classic Science Fiction Saga.* New York: Thomas Dunne.

Sagan, Carl. (1985). *Contact.* New York: Pocket.

————. (1994). *Pale Blue Dot: A Vision of the Human Future in Space*. New York: Random House.

————. (1996). *The Demon-Haunted World: Science as a Candle in the Dark*. New York: Ballantine.

————. (2006). *The Varieties of Scientific Experience: A Personal View of the Search for God*. Edited by Ann Druyan. New York: Penguin.

Said, Edward W. (1978). *Orientalism*. New York: Vintage.

Saliba, John A. (2003). "UFOs and Religion: A Case Study of the Unarius Academy of Science." In Lewis, *Encyclopedic Sourcebook*, 191–208.

Sammon, Paul M. (1996). *Future Noir: The Making of "Blade Runner."* New York: HarperPrism.

Schnoebelen, William J. (2003). *Space Invaders*. Philadelphia: Xlibris.

Schuchardt, Read Mercer. (2002). "What is *The Matrix*?" In Yeffeth, *Taking the Red Pill*, 5–21.

Scribner, Scott, and Gregory Wheeler. (2003). "Cosmic Intelligences and Their Terrestrial Channel: A Field Report on the Aetherius Society." In Lewis, *Encyclopedic Sourcebook*, 157–72.

Sharp, Robert. (2008). "When Machines Get Souls: Nietzsche on the Cylon Uprising." In Eberl, *"Battlestar Galactica" and Philosophy*, 15–28.

Shuck, Glenn. (2005). *Marks of the Beast: The "Left Behind" Novels and the Struggle for Evangelical Identity*. New York: New York University Press.

Silvio, Carl, and Elizabeth Johnston. (2008). "Alienation and the Limits of the Utopian Impulse." In Potter and Marshall, *Cylons in America*, 40–51.

Silvio, Carl, and Tony M. Vinci, eds. (2007). *Culture, Identities, and Technology in the "Star Wars" Films: Essays on the Two Trilogies*. Jefferson, N.C.: McFarland.

Sison, Antonio D. (2005). "Epiphany of the Throne-Chariot: Merkabah Mysticism and the Film *Contact*." *Journal of Religion and Film* 9 (1). Available online at http://www.unomaha.edu/jrf/Vol9No1/SisonMerkabah.htm.

Sitchin, Zecharia. (1976). *The 12th Planet: Book I of the Earth Chronicles*. New York: Avon.

————. (1980). *The Stairway to Heaven: Book II of the Earth Chronicles*. New York: Avon.

————. (1985). *The Wars of Gods and Men: Book III of the Earth Chronicles*. New York: Avon.

————. (2007). *Journeys to the Mythical Past*. Rochester, Vt.: Bear.

Skal, David J. (1998). *Screams of Reason: Mad Science and Modern Culture*. New York: W. W. Norton.

Smith, Jonathan Z. (1982). *Imagining Religion: From Babylon to Jonestown*. Chicago: University of Chicago Press.

Sobottka, Stanley. (2009). *A Course in Consciousness*. Available online at http://faculty.virginia.edu/consciousness.

Spradley, Joseph L. (1998). "Religion and the Search for Extraterrestrial Intelligence." *Perspectives on Science & Christian Faith* 50: 194–203.

Stark, Rodney. (1996). *The Rise of Christianity: A Sociologist Reconsiders History*. Princeton: Princeton University Press.

Staub, Dick. (2005). *Christian Wisdom of the Jedi Masters*. San Francisco, Calif.: Jossey-Bass.

Steiff, Josef, and Tristran D. Tamplin, eds. (2008). *"Battlestar Galactica" and Philosophy: Mission Accomplished or Mission Frakked Up?* Chicago: Open Court.

Stenger, Victor J. (1997). "Quantum Quackery." *Skeptical Inquirer* 21 (1). Available online at http://www.csicop.org/si/9701/quantum-quackery.html.

Sterritt, David. (1977). "UFO Saga—Astonishing, Thrilling, Moving." *Christian Science Monitor* (November 17): 32.

Stevenson, Ian. (1966). *Twenty Cases Suggestive of Reincarnation*. New York: American Society for Psychical Research.

———. (1974). *Xenoglossy: A Review and Report of a Case*. Charlottesville: University Press of Virginia.

———. (1975). *Cases of the Reincarnation Type*. 3 vols. Charlottesville: University Press of Virginia.

———. (1984). *Unlearned Language: New Studies in Xenoglossy*. Charlottesville: University Press of Virginia.

Stewart, Eugene R. (1996). "Shades of Meaning: Science Fiction as a New Metric." *Skeptical Inquirer* 20 (5): 19–24.

Stone, Bryan P. (1998). "Religious Faith and Science in *Contact*." *Journal of Religion and Film* 2 (2). Available online at http://www.unomaha.edu/jrf/stonear2.htm.

Storm, Jo. (2005). *Approaching the Possible: The World of "Stargate SG-1."* Toronto: ECW Press.

Strieber, Whitley. (1987). *Communion: A True Story*. New York: Beech Tree.

———. (1988). *Transformation: The Breakthrough*. New York: Beech Tree.

———. (1998). *Confirmation: The Hard Evidence of Aliens Among Us*. New York: St. Martin's.

Stucky, Mark D. (2005). "He is the One: *The Matrix* Trilogy's Postmodern Movie Messiah." *Journal of Religion and Film* 9 (2). Available online at http://www.unomaha.edu/jrf/Vol9No2/StuckyMatrixMessiah.htm.

Tabron, Judith. (2004). "Selling the Stargate: The Economics of a Pop Culture Phenomenon." In Beeler and Dickson, *Reading "Stargate SG-1,"* 167–83.

Talbot, Michael. (1991). *The Holographic Universe*. New York: HarperCollins.

Tarter, Jill. (2000). "SETI and the Religions of Extraterrestrials." *Free Inquiry* 20 (3): 34–35.

Telotte, J. P. (1995). *Replications: A Robotic History of the Science Fiction Film.* Urbana: University of Illinois Press.

Temple, Robert. (1998). *The Sirius Mystery: New Scientific Evidence for Alien Contact 5,000 Years Ago.* London: Arrow.

Thomas, Paul Brian. (2007). "Interstellar Ishtar: UFO Mythologies as Myths of Origin." Paper presented at the annual meeting of the American Academy of Religion, San Diego, California.

Tonne, Herbert. (1996). "It Is Hard to Believe." *Free Inquiry* 16 (3): 40.

Torry, Robert. (1991). "Apocalypse Then: Benefits of the Bomb in Fifities Science Fiction Films." *Cinema Journal* 31 (2): 7–21.

Tsutsui, William. (2004). *Godzilla on My Mind: Fifty Years of the King of Monsters.* New York: Palgrave Macmillan.

Tudor, Andrew. (1989). *Monsters and Mad Scientists: A Cultural History of the Horror Movie.* Oxford: Blackwell.

Tumminia, Diana G. (2005). *When Prophecy Never Fails: Myth and Reality in a Flying-Saucer Group.* Oxford: Oxford University Press.

Turing, A. M. (1950). "Computing Machinery and Intelligence." *Mind* 59 (236): 433–60.

Turner, Victor. (1969). *The Ritual Process: Structure and Anti-Structure.* Ithaca, N.Y.: Cornell University Press.

Unarius Academy of Science. (2001). "Starship Emblem Pin." Advertising Flyer. El Cajon, Calif.: Unarius Academy of Science.

Vallee, Jacques. (1975). *The Invisible College: What a Group of Scientists Has Discovered About UFO Influences on the Human Race.* New York: E. P. Dutton.

———. (1988). *Dimensions: A Casebook of Alien Contact.* New York: Ballantine.

———. (1990). *Confrontations: A Scientist's Search for Alien Contact.* New York: Ballantine.

———. (1991). *Revelations: Alien Contact and Human Deception.* New York: Ballantine.

———. (1992). *Forbidden Science: Journals, 1957–1969.* New York: Marlowe.

van Gennep, Arnold. ([1908] 1960). *The Rites of Passage.* Translated by Monika B. Vizedom and Gabrielle L. Caffee. Chicago: University of Chicago Press.

Verne, Jules. ([1865] 1967). *From the Earth to the Moon.* New York: Airmont.

von Däniken, Erich. (1968). *Chariots of the Gods? Unsolved Mysteries of the Past.* Translated by Michael Heron. London: Corgi.

———. ([1968] 1999). *Chariots of the Gods.* New York: Berkeley.

———. (1970). *Gods from Outer Space: Evidence for the Impossible.* Translated by Michael Heron. New York: Bantam.

———. (1974). *Miracles of the Gods: A New Look at the Supernatural.* Translated by Michael Heron. New York: Delacorte.

————. (2001). *The Gods Were Astronauts: Evidence of the True Identities of the Old "Gods."* Translated by Astrid Mick. London: Vega.

Wagner, Jon, and Jan Lundeen. (1998). *Deep Space and Sacred Time: "Star Trek" in the American Mythos.* Westport, Conn.: Praeger.

Walker, James K. (1999). *"Star Wars:* Beware of the Force." *Watchman Expositor* 16 (2). Available online at http://www.watchman.org/na/starwarsbeware .htm.

Wallace, Anthony F. C. (1956). "Revitalization Movements." *American Anthropologist* 58 (2): 264–81.

Wallis, Roy. (1982). "The Social Construction of Charisma." *Social Compass* 29 (1): 25–39.

Walvoord, John F. (1976). *Armageddon, Oil, and the Middle East Crisis.* Grand Rapids: Zondervan.

————. (1991). *Armageddon, Oil, and the Middle East Crisis: What the Bible Says About the Future of the Middle East and the End of Western Civilization.* Grand Rapids: Zondervan.

Warner, Rebecca. (1997). "A Silver-Paper Unicorn." In Kerman, *Retrofitting "Blade Runner,"* 178–84.

Warren, Bill. (1982). *Keep Watching the Skies! American Science Fiction Movies of the Fifties, Volume I: 1950–1957.* Jefferson, N.C.: McFarland.

————. (1986). *Keep Watching the Skies! American Science Fiction Movies of the Fifties, Volume II: 1958–1962.* Jefferson, N.C.: McFarland.

Watson, Justin. (1997). *The Christian Coalition: Dreams of Restoration, Demands for Recognition.* New York: St. Martin's.

Watzman, Anne. (2003). "Carnegie Mellon Inducts Four Robots Into Newly Established Robot Hall of Fame." *Carnegie Mellon Today* (November 7). Available online at http://cmu.edu/cmnews/extra/031107_robot.html.

Weber, Max. (1968). *On Charisma and Institution Building.* Edited by S. N. Eisenstadt. Chicago: University of Chicago Press.

Weinraub, Bernard. (1997). "Using a Big Budget to Ask Big Questions." *The New York Times* (July 6): H9, H18.

Weldon, John, and Zola Leavitt. (1976). *UFOs: What on Earth is Happening?* New York: Bantam.

Wells, H. G. ([1898] 2005). *The War of the Worlds.* Edited by Patrick Parrinder. New York: Penguin.

————. (1901). *The First Men in the Moon.* London: Collins.

————. ([1933] 2005). *The Shape of Things to Come.* Edited by Patrick Parrinder. New York: Penguin.

Wessinger, Catherine. (2000a). *How the Millennium Comes Violently: From Jonestown to Heaven's Gate.* New York: Seven Bridges.

————. (2000b). "The Interacting Dynamics of Millennial Beliefs, Persecution, and Violence." In *Millennialism, Persecution, and Violence: Historical*

Cases, edited by Catherine Wessinger, 3–41. Syracuse, N.Y.: Syracuse University Press.

Wesson, Paul S. (1990). "Cosmology, Extraterrestrial Intelligence, and a Resolution of the Fermi-Hart Paradox." *Quarterly Journal of the Royal Astronomical Society* 31: 161–70.

Wetmore, Kevin J., Jr. (2005). *The Empire Triumphant: Race, Religion, and Rebellion in the "Star Wars" Films.* Jefferson, N.C.: McFarland.

Wilkinson, David. (1997). *Alone in the Universe? Aliens, "The X-Files," and God.* Downers Grove, Ill.: InterVarsity.

———. (2000). *The Power of the Force: The Spirituality of the "Star Wars" Films.* Oxford: Lion.

Willems, Brian. (2008). "When the Non-Human Knows Its Own Death." In Eberl, *"Battlestar Galactica" and Philosophy*, 87–98.

Williams, Christian. (1982). "E.T. Is Here, and He's Mankind's Best Friend." *Washington Post* (June 21): C1.

Wilson, Clifford. (1972). *Crash Go the Chariots: An Alternative to "Chariots of the Gods?"* New York: Lancer.

———. (1974). *UFOs and Their Impossible Mission.* New York: Signet.

Wimbish, David. (1990). *Something's Going On Out There.* Old Tappan, N.J.: Fleming H. Revell.

Wolf, Fred Alan. (1988). *Parallel Universes: The Search for Other Worlds.* New York: Touchstone.

Wolfe, Ivan. (2008). "Why Your Mormon Neighbor Knows More about This Show Than You Do." In Steiff and Tamplin, *"Battlestar Galactica" and Philosophy*, 303–16.

Wuthnow, Robert. (1988). *The Restructuring of American Religion.* Princeton: Princeton University Press.

———. (1998). *After Heaven: Spirituality in America Since the 1950s.* Berkeley: University of California Press.

Yeffeth, Glenn, ed. (2003). *Taking the Red Pill: Science, Philosophy, and Religion in "The Matrix."* Dallas, Tex.: BenBella Books.

Young, Lawrence A. (1997). *Rational Choice Theory and Religion.* New York: Routledge.

Young, Michael W. (2004). "*Stargate SG-1* and *Atlantis*: The Gods of Technology versus the Wizards of Justice." In Beeler and Dickson, *Reading "Stargate SG-1,"* 95–110.

Young, Simon. (2006). *Designer Evolution: A Transhumanist Manifesto.* Amherst, N.Y.: Prometheus.

Zacky, Brent, dir. (2001). *The Omen Legacy.* Written by Naomi Pfefferman and Brent Zacky. Hollywood, Calif.: Prometheus Entertainment and Fox Television Network.

Zeller, Benjamin Ethan. (2006). "Scaling Heaven's Gate: Individualism and Salvation in a New Religious Movement." *Nova Religio* 10 (2): 75–102.

Zoglin, Richard, and Dan Cray. (1994). "Trekking Onward." *Time* (November 28).

Zukav, Gary. (1979). *The Dancing Wu Li Masters: An Overview of the New Physics*. New York: William Morrow.

INDEX